British Nationalised Shipping

1947 - 1968

W. PAUL CLEGG

and

JOHN S. STYRING

DAVID & CHARLES : NEWTON ABBOT

7513 4315 7

Printed in Great Britain by
Bristol Typesetting Company Limited
for David & Charles (Publishers) Limited
South Devon House Railway Station Newton Abbot

Contents

ABBREVIATIONS

ACCS	Anglo Continental Container Services Ltd
AHL	Associated Humber Lines Ltd
ASN	Atlantic Steam Navigation Co Ltd
BRB	British Railways Board
BRH	British Rail Hovercraft Ltd
BRFS	British Road Ferry Services Ltd
BRS	British Road Services Ltd
BTC	British Transport Commission
CSP	The Caledonian Steam Packet Co Ltd
CSP (Irish)	Caledonian Steam Packet Co (Irish Services) Ltd
F & R	Fishguard & Rosslare Railways & Harbours Co
GWR	Great Western Railway
LMS	London Midland & Scottish Railway
LNER	London & North Eastern Railway
RDS	River Dart Steamboat Co Ltd
SNCF	French Railways (Société National de Chemin de Fer Français)
SR	Southern Railway
TFS	Transport Ferry Service

PREFACE

In the summer of 1946 railway-operated cross-channel services generally were back to normal after the worst debacle on record. The war which caused the loss of many ships also had its long-term effects, by creating a change in public attitudes which led to curtailment or withdrawal of services. The 'good old days' had gone, and in their place developed the postwar way of life known widely as the 'rat race'. Political dogma also had its effect on some of our best-loved shipping services, when on 1 January 1948 our railway companies were nationalised, partly for economic reasons and partly, no doubt, to satisfy the demands of doctrinaire Socialism.

Now, just over twenty-one years later, we can look back and enquire if shipping services have developed satisfactorily since the war, and are providing us, the public, with what we want and need. As far as shipping is concerned the answer, in our view, is probably in the affirmative, but the reader can judge for himself by reading the pages which follow.

The railway and shipping services in 1948 were divided into six regions based broadly on the areas previously covered by the four main companies, with the splitting of the former LNER east coast territory into Eastern and North Eastern Regions, and the combination of the Scottish activities of both the LMS and LNER to form the Scottish Region. The ships became the property of the Railway Executive.

In this book we have attempted to describe the services and the ships which have served on them since 1948, with an occasional glimpse into the past for purposes of comparison, or because of especially interesting features. We do not claim the record to be a complete one in every respect, but we hope it will prove interesting. The statistical information is self-explanatory, the dimensions including the draught of the ship unless otherwise stated, routes being those operative from 1948.

One final comment; we have tried hard to avoid making mistakes, but if any are found we crave our readers' indulgence. We are aware that many of the illustrations have appeared in print before in books and in magazines, but in many cases it has not been possible to trace suitable alternatives. Much of the information too has been published before, this applies particularly to the Clyde section, which in the past has been thoroughly described, but we have tried to introduce new material wherever there seems to be a gap in established knowledge. Within this sphere may be mentioned the attention paid to detailed movements in certain areas (notably the Humber), and also to conversions carried out on various ships.

John S. Styring
Chadwell Lodge
Ware
Hertfordshire

W. Paul Clegg
5 Saffron Close
Lower Parrock Road
Barrowford
Nelson Lancs

ACKNOWLEDGMENTS

Throughout the writing of this book a constant stream of correspondence has been maintained with friends and acquaintances who have knowingly and willingly provided us with information for this book. We can but list their names in gratitude, and if we have omitted anybody, we apologise. They are as follows:

D. S. M. Barrie (BR York and now general manager Eastern Region); R. Blood and G. Barley (Associated Humber Lines Ltd); Bernard Cox; John Edginton (BR Euston); W. S. Evans, manager (Barrow Docks); J. Mayson and R. P. Breakspear (Embassy staff); W. Eccles, managing director and R. A. Wilton, fleet manager (J. Fisher & Sons Ltd); George Goodhew, managing director (Orwell & Harwich Navigation Company Ltd); Captain A. T. Harris (Weymouth); Eric Harrison; F. W. Hawks; John Hendy; L. L. Hobbs, managing director (The River Dart Steamboat Co Ltd); T. H. Hunter, manager (Goole Docks); the records' staff (Harland & Wolff Ltd, Belfast); the office staff (Isle of Man Steam Packet Co Ltd); G. E. Langmuir; Capt R. A. H. Lord (Holyhead); Capt H. H. McGibney; W. H. Mitchell; Stanley Miller; Richard Pryde (World Ship Society—Central Record); Henry Rea; E. C. Robinson, administration assistant (Dover Harbour Board); M. B. Sellars, harbour master (Newhaven); Arthur Streatfield and Staff (BR Waterloo); M. B. Thomas and Staff (BR Liverpool St and Harwich); John Albert, publicity manager and Frank Napoleon assistant traffic manager (Transport Ferry Service); M. V. Van Moole; J. Van der Klooster (Hook Pilot); H. J. Knott, architect and G. Simpson, public relations (Vickers Ltd—Palmers Hebburn Yard); Marshall Walker; C. Wilson Barnes.

We have made use of information provided in a number of existing books on the subject, including C. Grasemann & G. W. P. McLachlan's *English Channel Packet Boats,* (Syren & Shipping Ltd, 1939), and C. L. D. Duckworth & G. E. Langmuir's *Railway & Other Steamers,* (Shipping Histories Ltd, Glasgow 1948), though unlike the latter we use the term 'steamer' only in its literal sense. We have not, however, always relied on these authorities, but have also closely examined back numbers of a number of journals including *Shipbuilding and Shipping Record* (from 1918), the *LNER House Magazine* (from 1932), *Lloyd's Register, The Journal of Commerce & Shipping Telegraph,* and so forth. Thanks to the authorities concerned, we have been allowed access to old records in some shipping offices.

Lastly we would like to thank Jean Clegg, for undertaking much of the typing from, at times, almost illegible script.

We are also grateful to all photographers. Many photographs are credited to 'Author's collection'—in many cases this is because the source is unknown.

ILLUSTRATIONS

Due acknowledgment is given here to those photographers who have generously permitted samples of their work to be included in this book. The remaining illustrations are taken from Paul Clegg's private collection. Associated Humber Lines Ltd: 252, 255, 256 ; Atlantic Steam Navigation Co Ltd: 272, 273, 276, 278 ; P. F. Bowles: 124 ; BR, Eastern Region: 18, 22, 30, 32, 33, 34, 36, 37 ; BR, London-Midland Region: 143, 164 ; BR, Scottish Region: 179 ; BR, Southern Region: 49, 51, 55, 77 (top), 88 (top), 107, 110, 161, 279, 281, 282 ; C. T. Collard: 128 ; Bernard Cox: 87, 88 (bottom), 92, 94, 117 ; B. T. Dixon: 251 ; M. E. Drewry: 257, 259, 261 ; A. Duncan: 17, 20, 24, 39, 238 ; Laurence Dunn: 144 ; J. N. L. Eastland: frontispiece, 100, 102 ; J. Fisher & Sons Ltd: 288 ; the late Rev Wm C. Galbraith: 191 ; F. W. Hawks: 25, 27, 28, 62, 90, 97, 98, 101, 118, 195, 211, 231, 285 ; J. F. Hendy: 42, 54, 57, 59, 64, 65, 66, 67, 70, 71, 84, 99, 120 ; C. A. Hill: 241, 244 ; *Hull Daily Mail*: 236 ; Imperial War Museum: 197 ; I. G. Ireland: 174 ; G. E. Langmuir: 184, 186, 188, 189, 190, 192, 198, 202, 203, 204, 206, 209, 212, 218, 219, 221, 222, 225, 227 ; F. Lewin: 41 ; W. H. Mitchell: 68, 82 (bottom), 109 ; J. P. Mullett: 196 ; Orweel & Harwich Nav Co Ltd: 15 ; H. M. Rea: 138, 146, 148 (top), 150, 152, 154, 157, 160, 173, 176, 177, 289 ; B. Richardson: 144 ; R. H. Tunstall: 80 (top), 82 (top), 213 ; Vickers Ltd: 60 ; B. K. Wakeham: 210.

In addition, the following were specially commissioned for this book, as suitable prints could not be found elsewhere: The Studio Jon, Fishguard: 134, 137, 151 ; *Grimsby Evening Telegraph*: 253.

Frontispiece: MV *Southsea* entering Portsmouth Harbour, 13 July 1967

9

TRANSPORT ACTS

Transport Act 1947

This provided for the nationalisation of Britain's railway companies and the grouping of the same into six regions. Ships were taken over by the Railway Executive. Shipping companies previously controlled by the separate railway companies, eg The Caledonian Steam Packet Co Ltd controlled by the LMS, and the Hull & Netherlands Steamship Co Ltd controlled by the LNER, became subsidiaries of BR. Similarly, the shares held by the LMS in David MacBrayne Ltd, and in the Fishguard & Rosslare Railways & Harbours Co by the GWR, also passed to BR. These changes were effective from 1 January 1948. The British Transport Commission was born.

Transport Act 1962

The Transport Holding Co was formed to take over various branches of British Transport Commission business. The British Transport Commission itself was dissolved and the British Railways Board set up in its place.

Part I, Section 29 of the Act stated that the Transport Holding Co was to be run as a normal company engaged in commercial enterprise. The British Transport Commission shares in Associated Humber Lines Ltd, Atlantic Steam Navigation Co Ltd, and David MacBrayne Ltd passed to the Transport Holding Co. The British Transport Commission shares in The Caledonian Steam Packet Co Ltd, Caledonian Steam Packet Co (Irish Services) Ltd, and the Fishguard & Rosslare Railways & Harbours Co, passed to the Railways Board. These further changes came into effect from 1 January 1963.

The last-named and David MacBrayne Ltd are jointly owned with Coras Iompair Eireann and Coast Lines Ltd, respectively, while Ellerman's Wilson Line Ltd holds 9 per cent of Associated Humber Lines Ltd.

British Railways Act 1967 (Part VI, Section 47)

This enabled the Railways Board to operate shipping services on routes other than those already permitted by previous Acts, by wholesale amendment of those Acts. An almost immediate result was the opening in October 1967 of a new route between Harwich and Dunkirk. It is possible that another result may be a new service between Holyhead and Belfast.

Of the various Acts, this one of 1967 is undoubtedly the most interesting and potentially the most far-reaching.

Transport Act 1968

Effective from 1 January 1969. Many of its measures are being severely attacked, but those affecting shipping will probably not be altered. It is intended that Associated Humber Lines Ltd and Atlantic Steam Navigation Co Ltd will pass from the Transport Holding Co to National Freight Corporation control, and that a new Scottish Transport Group will take over the Transport Holding Co share in David MacBrayne Ltd, and the Railways Board control of The Caledonian Steam Packet Co Ltd. Control of the Stranraer–Larne service is to remain with the Railways Board through The Caledonian Steam Packet Co Ltd.

All regional shipping services came under the aegis of the new BR Shipping & International Services Division on 1 January 1968.

Some very interesting developments and changes can be expected to materialise in the coming years.

THE EASTERN REGION

When the British Transport Commission took over from the LNER only Harwich was being used as a cross-channel port, and thus this region in terms of port facilities can be regarded as the smallest. Services were being run to Antwerp and the Hook of Holland for passengers, to Rotterdam for cargo only and to Zeebrugge for rail-borne cargo.

In more recent prewar days the LNER also operated a passenger-cargo service between Grimsby and Hamburg (under Associated Humber Lines management) and the Zeeland Steamship Co a similar service between Flushing and Harwich. Neither was restored after the war, all passenger connections to Hamburg by AHL being run from Hull and the Zeeland Steamship Co's terminal being transferred to the Hook of Holland. The United Steamship Co's Esbjerg–Harwich passenger-cargo service was restored after the war on a reduced frequency.

Within the Eastern Region's present control is the Tilbury–Gravesend ferry service, though in 1948 and for a time afterwards it was the responsibility of the London Midland Region. Management of the region's New Holland–Hull service was transferred to AHL in 1959.

1 : HARWICH

Of all packet ports, Harwich probably suffered more than any other from the effects of war upon its shipping. No fewer than five ships, *Train Ferry No 2, Train Ferry No 3, Archangel, Bruges* and *Amsterdam,* were lost. A further four, *St Denis, Antwerp, Malines* and *Vienna* were, for one reason or another, including trooping, when they still used Harwich, not returned to civilian service. The services with which the LNER had to deal were those from Parkeston Quay to the Hook of Holland and Antwerp (passenger), Zeebrugge (train ferry) and Rotterdam (cargo). There was no thought of reviving the prewar cruises operated by *Vienna* or the summer-only Zeebrugge excursions operated by *St Denis* (ex- *Munich*) and *Archangel* (ex- *St Petersburg*). Between 1930 and 1939 there had been a surfeit of ships and the railway had been hard put at times to find employment for them. Now, in 1945, the situation was reversed, though happily the Rotterdam cargo service could continue as *Sheringham* survived the war as did *Felixstowe,* but the latter rarely served from Harwich afterwards. *Train Ferry No 1,* modernised and renamed *Essex Ferry* reopened the Zeebrugge train ferry service in July 1946.

The problem really lay in providing sufficient suitable tonnage for the all-important Harwich–Hook of Holland service. *Prague* was the only survivor, and she reopened this link on 14 November 1945, her running mate, for a time, being the Zeeland Steamship Co's *Oranje Nassau,* since the Flushing service, on which she had been previously engaged, was not restored. Thus a nightly service was possible throughout 1946. In the meantime a new ship had been ordered and *Arnhem* entered service in May 1947. At the beginning of 1948 *Prague* returned to John Brown & Co (Clydebank) Ltd, her builders, for a good refit, but again misfortune struck the station, for she caught fire and was rendered completely useless. In April therefore *St Andrew* from Fishguard was transferred to serve the Hook for nearly two months until *Duke of York,* transferred permanently from Heysham in May, had settled down. From June onwards *Arnhem* and *Duke of York* ran opposite each other for most of the time until May 1950, when the station's second new postwar ship *Amsterdam* was delivered. The future regularity of the Hook of Holland passenger service was now assured. From mid-1950 *Arnhem* and *Amsterdam* maintained the nightly service, with *Duke of York* as relief and extra ship.

In 1963 *Duke of York* was withdrawn, and the railway's superb new *Avalon* replaced her. Following the advent of this ship, fully air-conditioned and sumptuously fitted out, came the reinstatement of cruises from Harwich in 1964. Some of these cruises followed a similar pattern to those operated by *Vienna* in prewar days, namely the weekend trips to Amsterdam during the flower season in April and May, but others were introduced on a much more ambitious scale. During 1964 *Avalon* sailed to Copenhagen via the Kiel Canal, on two occasions, and also to Hamburg, while in 1965 one Copenhagen cruise was extended to include Oslo and Gothenburg. The 1966 cruises were even more extensive, taking her to

13

Bordeaux, Lisbon, Helsinki and Tangier, *inter alia,* and in fact she made no weekend trips to Holland that year.

The other service requiring passenger tonnage after the war was that to Antwerp. With *Prague* earmarked for the Hook of Holland route there was no ship available at Harwich, so the LNER had to look elsewhere. Fortunately, of the four ships associated with the Grimsby station in prewar years, three had survived the war and it was decided that one of these should be based on Hull, and two, *Accrington* and *Dewsbury,* should serve the Harwich–Antwerp route. Accordingly both ships, after refit, entered this service during the second half of 1946, *Accrington* reopening the service on 28 July and *Dewsbury* starting the following month. Both ships continued to serve Antwerp, but the demand for passenger berths declined to such an extent that before 1949 ended, it was decided to withdraw the passenger service. Following the departure of *Dewsbury* from Antwerp on 3 February 1950, it was closed to passengers for several months, but a certain amount of public agitation caused its reinstatement and *Dewsbury,* from July, sailed twice weekly in each direction with considerably improved passenger accommodation for twelve passengers. From then on there remained only *Dewsbury* and *Sheringham* to serve Antwerp and Rotterdam respectively. In view of their age replacement became a vital necessity and two small motor vessels with engines aft and no passenger accommodation, but designed to carry unit loads, were ordered. In October 1958 *Isle of Ely* replaced *Sheringham* and four months later *Colchester* replaced *Dewsbury.* The last named had by then served consistently in war and peace for nearly forty-eight years and was the last survivor of the old Great Central Railway Co fleet. The new ships have continued to serve Rotterdam and Antwerp. In 1961 there were four sailings per week to Rotterdam and two to Antwerp, though these tended to vary in frequency. In 1963 there were five to Rotterdam and three to Antwerp, while latterly there have been four to Rotterdam and three to Antwerp. The Antwerp service was withdrawn at the end of May 1968.

As to the Zeebrugge service, we have seen that *Essex Ferry* reopened this in 1946. Further ships were also required here before long to provide a regular nightly service. *Sussex Ferry,* ordered by the LNER after the war, joined *Essex Ferry* in 1947 and in 1951 the BTC introduced a third ship, *Norfolk Ferry,* to the run. This particular service has, since its inception in 1924, been of great importance, handling large quantities of through rail-freight waggons, and no hesitation has been experienced in the provision of new additional ships. In 1957 a new *Essex Ferry* appeared to replace the forty-year-old pioneer rail ferry, and at the beginning of 1964 yet another, named *Cambridge Ferry,* entered service. Thus there are now four modern ships, all with oil engines, available to operate a regular and frequent train-ferry service between the two ports.

Also operated by the LNER and subsequently the BTC Eastern Region in postwar years, was the local ferry service to Felixstowe. (The Shotley route was not restored after the war.) Four small wooden motor vessels were available in 1948 for continuation of the ferry service. These were *Pin Mill* 11 tons, built 1910, which originally opened the service in 1912 ; *Epping* and *Hainault* about 21 tons, built 1914, and *Brightlingsea,* 51 tons, built by Rowhedge Ironworks in 1925. *Pin Mill* was rarely used after 1948. Towards the end of 1959 the BTC announced its intention of withdrawing the service altogether, but a two-year reprieve was granted in deference to public wish. On 31 December 1961 the service was terminated. *Pin Mill* was retained as a work boat at Parkeston Quay, still with its original engine, but the other three vessels were sold. *Hainault* was converted to a private cruiser based at Maldon, and *Epping* was towed to Dover and offered for sale again, but her ultimate fate is not known. At about the time the service was withdrawn a new private company named Orwell & Harwich Navigation Co Ltd, was formed, for the purpose of reopening the service. This concern bought *Brightlingsea,* modernised her, with her reopened the Harwich–Felixstowe ferry service on 1 May 1962, and subsequently used her for quite extensive cruises in the Stour area. This vessel, having been re-engined about 1960, is in excellent condition and has only recently passed her survey with flying colours. She can

Brightlingsea reopens the Felixstowe ferry service on 1 May 1962

15

carry up to 221 passengers. Under private enterprise the Felixstowe ferry service has proved financially successful, though there is no intention of reviving the Shotley service at present.

A new train ferry route from Harwich to Dunkirk, daily in each direction, was opened on 10 October 1967, by *Norfolk Ferry*. For this service a new ship, *La Seyne,* was ordered, by French Railways from Constructions Navales et Industrielles de la Méditerranée. Of about 2,215 tons gross, she will be able to carry lorries, trailers and containers, and up to thirty-six passengers, and is expected to enter service in January 1969.

From 16 August 1968 a new combined day and night Harwich–Hook service was operated by the new *St George* and *Koningin Juliana.*

TSS ESSEX FERRY

BUILT	1919 by Armstrong Whitworth & Co Ltd, Newcastle
GROSS TONS	2,755
DIMENSIONS	350 ft 8 in x 58 ft 9 in x 12 ft
MACHINERY	6-cyl triple-expansion by Wallsend Slipway Co Ltd
	Oil-fired boilers
SPEED	12 knots
ROUTE	Harwich-Zeebrugge

This vessel, of extraordinary appearance, was one of three sisters built for the government's first world war personnel and equipment service between Richborough in Kent and Dunkirk. She was originally named *Train Ferry No 1,* her sisters being numbers *2* and *3* accordingly.

When the war was over they lay idle until 1924, when they inaugurated the first UK–Continental train-ferry services between Harwich and Zeebrugge in the ownership of the Great Eastern Train Ferry Co Ltd. Ten years later they were taken over outright by the LNER and continued on the same route until after the outbreak of the second war.

All three were requisitioned for active service, but only *No 1* survived. She was converted in 1941 for use as an LSS (landing ship, stern chute) and was named HMS *Princess Iris* (*No 2* was named HMS *Daffodil* and served in the same capacity). She could carry 105 troops and either 13 mechanised landing craft Mk 1 or 9 Landing Craft, Mechanised Mk 2 in three rows on the train deck, which were launched through the chute in the centre of the stern. She carried the pennant number F90 and, like HMS *Daffodil* was a member of Force U.

Released late in 1945 she was refitted the following year by John Brown & Co (Clydebank) Ltd, alterations including the extension of deckhouse (her two funnels athwartships had already been replaced by one on the centre line), thus increasing her tonnage from 2,683. In July 1946 she was renamed *Essex Ferry* and reopened the Zeebrugge com-

16

mercial service. As time went on she became more and more dilapidated, and in 1956 a replacement for her was ordered. The suffix *II* was added to free her name for her successor, after whose appearance in 1957 she was sold for breaking up by T. W. Ward Ltd at Grays, Esssex.

TSS *Essex Ferry* lying off Harwich near the end of her career

TSS ANTWERP

BUILT	1919 by John Brown & Co (Clydebank) Ltd
GROSS TONS	2,957
DIMENSIONS	321 ft 8 in x 43 ft 1 in x 14 ft
MACHINERY	Four turbines by John Brown, SR geared
	Coal or oil-fired boilers
SPEED	21 knots

Antwerp, her sister *Bruges* and similar *Malines* were completed in 1920 and 1921 for the Great Eastern Railway's Harwich–Antwerp passenger service which they maintained, with the usual short breaks for overhaul, up to the war. *Antwerp* had accommodation for 438 first-class and 1,245 second-class passengers and sixty crew. The alternative means of fuelling the boilers was an interesting feature, each ship being capable of carrying nearly 200 tons of coal and 96 tons of oil.

By early 1940 the entire Harwich passenger fleet, with the exception of *Malines* and *St Denis,* was sent to Southampton for trooping duties. The two remaining did some special Rotterdam sailings, after which *Malines* appeared at Dunkirk, served in the Mediterranean and was torpedoed near Port Said in July 1942, being later raised and taken over by the MOWT.

Bruges was sunk at the Dunkirk evacuation. *Antwerp* also appeared at Dunkirk and undertook other duties until she appeared in Operation Husky (invasion of Sicily) in July 1943 as HQ Ship for Admiral Ramsay of the Eastern Naval Task Force, by now named HMS *Antwerp*. With *Malines* she served most of the war in the Mediterranean and they were the only ships officially classed as 'Convoy Escorts'. In 1944 she served for a period as a fighter direction ship in Force U (Mediterranean), with the pennant number 4.209, equipped with two 12-pounder AA guns.

Antwerp was returned to the LNER in 1945 and fitted out as a leave ship. As such she served for BAOR leave parties between Harwich and the Hook of Holland until being withdrawn in 1950. In 1951 she was sold for breaking up by T. W. Ward Ltd at Milford Haven without having made a postwar civilian commercial crossing. *Malines* was never returned to the railways, but was managed by the General Steam Navigation Co Ltd in trooping on the Harwich station, finally going to Clayton & Davie Ltd, Dunston-on-Tyne, for breaking up in April 1948.

After the second war, *Antwerp* had changed little since new. Noticeable features included the addition of a deckhouse beneath a new foremast, enlargement of bridge structure, and extension aft of the boat deck. New lifeboats and davits were fitted, and radar installed.

Antwerp at Harwich when new

SS FELIXSTOWE

BUILT	1918 by Hawthorn & Co Ltd, Leith
GROSS TONS	905
DIMENSIONS	215 ft 1 in x 33 ft 2 in x 14 ft
MACHINERY	3-cyl triple-expansion by Hawthorn & Co
	Coal-fired boilers
SPEED	12 knots
ROUTE	Various

Following the closure of the Harwich–Rotterdam passenger service in 1904, only cargo ships were required and *Felixstowe,* with no accommodation for passengers, entered the trade early in 1919 and thus helped to meet the demand for cargo space which still existed. She was a single ship, and served Rotterdam fairly consistently in peacetime for the Great Eastern Railway up to 1922 and after that for the LNER. She did occasionally serve Antwerp, notably from December 1939 for about four months.

In the second war she operated principally in coastal general cargo convoys, being named *Colchester* from 1942 until 10 September 1946, when she reverted to her original name.

In postwar years she never served regularly from Harwich, being diverted to other routes wherever need was greatest. During most of 1947, early 1948 and early 1949 she was operated by AHL in its colours

Felixstowe at Weymouth 1 August 1948

19

between Goole and Antwerp, Amsterdam, Rotterdam and occasionally Hamburg, and once only, in December 1947, between Hull and Rotterdam. For some months in 1948 she ran between Weymouth and the Channel Islands for BR Western Region, her funnel being repainted buff with a black top, though the raised letters 'AHL' were still visible (see illustration). At some time during 1948 or 1949, more probably the latter, she is believed to have served between Loch Ryan and Larne. By the end of 1949 she was withdrawn, she was sold to the Limerick Steamship Co Ltd in 1950 and renamed *Kylemore* in 1951. Seven years later she was disposed of for breaking by N.V. Holland of Hendrik-Ido-Ambacht.

SS SHERINGHAM

BUILT	1926 by Earle's Shipbuilding & Engineering Co Ltd, Hull
GROSS TONS	1,088
DIMENSIONS	256 ft x 36 ft 1 in x 15 ft
MACHINERY	3-cyl triple-expansion by Earle's
	Coal-fired boilers
SPEED	14 knots
ROUTE	Harwich-Antwerp/Rotterdam

With 51,000 cubic feet of cargo space, *Sheringham* was built for the Rotterdam cargo service of the LNER, joining the eight-year-old *Felixstowe*. She did occasionally run to Antwerp, but was engaged primarily on the Rotterdam service right up to the war.

On the outbreak of war in 1939 she was temporarily laid up, but in

Sheringham after the war

20

December again took up the service until about mid-April 1940 when the Germans overran the Low Countries. During the war she was used in coastal convoys and general duties, being allocated to Wm. Sloan & Co for a time for their Glasgow–Bristol Channel run.

After the war she returned to the Rotterdam run, and remained on it fairly consistently until *Accrington* was withdrawn in 1950, after which she replaced that ship on the Antwerp service. Thereafter she served either Rotterdam or Antwerp as occasion demanded until being replaced by MV *Isle of Ely* late in 1958. She was then withdrawn and sold to the Brussels Scrapping Co for breaking up. Her last sailing, which was on the Rotterdam route, took place on 24 October 1958.

TSS PRAGUE

BUILT	1930 by John Brown & Co (Clydebank) Ltd
GROSS TONS	4,220
DIMENSIONS	350 ft 9 in x 50 ft x 15 ft 3 in
MACHINERY	4 turbines by John Brown, SR geared
	Coal-fired boilers
SPEED	19 knots
ROUTE	Harwich-Hook of Holland

Prague was the second of a series of three new sister ships ordered from John Brown by the LNER for its Harwich–Hook of Holland service. Of the others, *Amsterdam*, the last of the three, during heroic war service as a hospital ship, struck a mine on 7 August 1944 off the Normandy coast and sank with heavy loss of life among crew and patients. *Vienna*, the first of the three, was particularly interesting in that she undertook weekend cruises in addition to her normal services, and had her last one cancelled owing to busy traffic on the Hook of Holland service. These cruises were run June-September each year from 1932 to 1939 inclusive, taking in Antwerp, Amsterdam, Ghent, Flushing, Zeebrugge, Hook of Holland and Rotterdam. To give her more covered accommodation, particularly for cruise passengers, her boat deck was extended and more lounge accommodation installed early in 1936. She served in the war in a variety of ways, and was acquired by the MOWT in 1941 and used on the Harwich–Hook of Holland military leave service from 1945 to July 1960 when she was withdrawn. In September she was sold to Van Heyghen Frères for breaking up, arriving at Ghent on 4 September 1960 in tow of the tug *Merchantman*.

Prague was delivered in February 1930, serving the Hook of Holland without any incident of note until the outbreak of war. She had a total capacity of 1,500 passengers, with berths for 444 first-class and 104 second-class passengers.

In 1939 she was requisitioned for trooping and similar services, and had

21

left for Southampton with most of the Harwich fleet by January 1940. At the Dunkirk evacuation she made at least three trips, the final one being on 1 June, when, with over 2,000 French troops aboard, she was holed aft by an enemy bomb and had one engine put out of action. Captain Baxter successfully beached her near Deal. The D Day landings saw her in service as a hospital carrier operating for the American forces.

Almost as soon as the war was over she was returned to the LNER and she reopened the civilian Hook of Holland service on 14 November 1945 sailing three times a week from each port, her running mate until nearly the end of 1946 being the Zeeland Steamship Co's *Oranje-Nassau*. From May 1947 she was joined by the new *Arnhem*. Eary in 1948 she went back to Clydebank for a major refit because, due to the serious lack of available ships at Harwich owing to war losses, she was intended to continue in service. Unhappily she caught fire on 14 March, was burnt right out and sank. Too badly damaged to be economically repaired, she was sold for breaking up at Barrow and arrived there under tow on 14 September. Her place at Harwich was taken by the Heysham steamer *Duke of York*.

Prague made her last sailing between Harwich and Hook of Holland on 25 December 1947. She was broken up by T. W. Ward Ltd.

Prague as she appeared on delivery

SS ACCRINGTON
SS DEWSBURY

BUILT	1910 by Earle's Shipbuilding & Engineering Co Ltd, Hull
GROSS TONS	1,680/1,686
DIMENSIONS	265 ft/276 ft 3 in x 36 ft x 17 ft 11 in
MACHINERY	3-cyl triple-expansion by Earle's
	Coal-fired boilers
SPEED	12 knots
ROUTE	Harwich-Antwerp

Accrington and *Dewsbury* were two of a group of four ships built for the Great Central Railway Co's Grimsby–Hamburg service (see also under *Bury*). *Accrington* was launched on 7 June 1910 and *Dewsbury* was delivered in the same month. At first they could carry about 400 passengers, in three classes, in cabins on the main and poop decks, and in cabins and dormitories on the fore and aft 'tweendecks. Public rooms were on the main deck, the first-class general lounge extending the full width of the ship. By 1915 only two classes were carried ie 106 first- and some 500 third-class passengers. During the first war *Accrington* served as a POW accommodation ship, then ran munitions to France, and later was based at Portsmouth for 'special service'. The war over, she was used to repatriate German prisoners and after being returned to Grimsby took up the Hamburg run again on which she remained virtually until 1935, after which she was managed by AHL. From this time she seems to have been used primarily as a reserve ship mainly on the Grimsby–Hamburg run, but also appeared frequently between Hull and Hamburg in 1938 and 1939, and between Hull and Rotterdam in late 1937, early 1938 and late 1939.

Dewsbury, on the other hand, spent most of the first war maintaining some semblance of commercial service, and when it was over reopened the regular Hamburg run. She remained thereon for most of each year until January 1936, when she was taken off and improved in speed and accommodation, including the installation of more first-class accommodation. From 1 April 1936 until war broke out again she spent her time on the Hull–Rotterdam service opposite *Melrose Abbey*, with short breaks for overhaul and stand-by in and around November and February each winter. She made her last prewar round trip on this run between 2 and 7 September 1939. In late 1939 and early 1940 she made a number of trips to Zeebrugge. During 1940 she was used mainly on the coal trade between Bristol Channel ports and the Clyde ports of Troon and Ayr, while much of the following year was spent on longer coastal voyages carrying general cargo to large and small ports in convoy with other ships. From late 1941 she was engaged in convoy rescue work, as was *Accrington*, though the latter did not take up this work until February 1942. Both ships remained on these duties until being released in mid-1945 and were then returned to their owner, the LNER.

Shortage of suitable ships for the Harwich station, following extensive

23

war losses, meant that both ships took up the Harwich–Antwerp link in 1946, with accommodation for only seventy-seven passengers. *Accrington* made her first sailing from Harwich on 28 July, while *Dewsbury* made hers on 29 August. Thus they continued to serve even though they were now thirty-six years old.

In 1949 plans were announced to close the passenger link between the two ports, and *Dewsbury* made the intended final passenger sailing from Antwerp on 3 February 1950. *Accrington* continued in service as a cargo ship, and, having made her last crossing on 6 January 1951, was laid up at Harwich, and finally sold for about £19,000 to Clayton & Davie Ltd, for breaking up. She arrived at their yard on 2 May 1951. Meantime, *Dewsbury* was not yet finished, and on 7 June 1950 left Hull for a round trip to Rotterdam, the only one she made after 1939. There was consistent public concern over the permanent closure of the Antwerp passenger link, and the authorities responded by bringing back *Dewsbury* later in the year. She now could carry only twelve passengers, but the berth accommodation was really first-class. She continued, mainly on a weekly basis, until her last sailing from Antwerp on 31 January 1959. Discharge of cargo was completed on 2 February and she was then withdrawn and placed on the sale list. She was now the only survivor of the Great Central quartet, was no less than forty-nine years old, and had been in permanent commission. She arrived at Antwerp on 10 March 1959 for breaking up by the Brussels Scrapping Co.

Dewsbury on her postwar Antwerp run

TSS ARNHEM
TSS AMSTERDAM

BUILT	1947/1950 by John Brown & Co (Clydebank) Ltd
GROSS TONS	5,008/5,092
DIMENSIONS	377 ft 1 in x 54 ft 5 in x 15 ft 3 in
MACHINERY	4 turbines by John Brown, SR geared
	Oil-fired boilers
SPEED	21 knots
ROUTE	Harwich-Hook of Holland

Arnhem, the LNER's first postwar cross-channel ship, was launched on 7 November 1946 and delivered in May 1947, being that company's first ship fitted out exclusively for oil burning. She made her maiden voyage on 22 April 1947. Her passenger accommodation at this time consisted of 4 cabins-de-luxe and 319 single-berth cabins of which 95 were fitted with a second 'auxiliary' berth. Originally one-class only, she was altered in 1949 to cater for two classes.

Three years later her consort *Amsterdam* was delivered, having been launched on 19 January. Slightly the larger of the two, the latter has always carried two classes, with berths for 321 first-class and 236 second-class passengers. Between March and May 1954 *Arnhem* had a thorough refit involving some structural alterations, including the layout of windows along the upper deck, which increased her gross tonnage from 4,891 to its present 5,008. Her passenger accommodation now consists of 375 first-class and about 200 second-class berths. Both ships can also carry vehicles (crane-loaded), and large amounts of cargo. The promenade

Arnhem at Harwich 23 July 1966

deck of each ship is devoted to first-class cabins, while the remainder of the first-class and all second-class cabins are on A, B, and C decks.

The two ships are of similar appearance, but the following points are useful in distinguishing them: *Amsterdam* has a deckhouse at the foot of her foremast, *Arnhem* has not; *Arnhem* has a wooden wheelhouse, while that of *Amsterdam* is white-painted steel; *Arnhem* has a much taller radar mast, and, finally, *Arnhem*'s upper deck is plated-in right aft to a point under the after end of the boat deck while *Amsterdam*'s is open abaft the fourth lifeboat.

When off for overhaul in March and November respectively each in turn is replaced by the other or by the station's third ship. From 1948 to 1963 this was *Duke of York,* since then it has been *Avalon. Arnhem* arrived at the Inverkeithing yard of T. W. Ward Ltd for scrapping on 16 August 1968. *Amsterdam* was due to be withdrawn by the end of September 1968.

TSMV SUFFOLK FERRY
TSMV NORFOLK FERRY

BUILT	1947/1951 by John Brown & Co (Clydebank) Ltd
GROSS TONS	3,134/3,157
DIMENSIONS	404 ft 6 in x 61 ft 6 in x 12 ft 1½ in
	399 ft 10 in x 61 ft 4 in x 12 ft 0¾ in
MACHINERY	Two 2-stroke single acting 6-cyl Sulzer diesels by John Brown
SPEED	14/13 knots
ROUTE	Harwich-Zeebrugge
	Norfolk Ferry Harwich-Dunkirk (from October 1967)

The LNER 'went diesel' for the first time when it ordered *Suffolk Ferry,* launched on 7 May 1947. She was delivered in August 1947 and was the first of a series of ferries specially designed for the carriage of railway rolling stock, in particular goods waggons, of which thirty-five can be carried in four rows inside the hull. The stock is shunted in over the stern, where there are two tracks. *Norfolk Ferry,* almost a sister ship, was delivered in July 1951, and in effect both ships replaced the old steam train ferries of 1917, *Train Ferry No 2* and *Train Ferry No 3,* which were lost in the second war. They have little to commend them in appearance though they can provide an interesting channel crossing for twelve passengers.

On 2 October 1967 *Norfolk Ferry* opened a new route for BR from Harwich to Dunkirk. This variation from customary practice was made possible by the passing of the British Railways Act 1967. Section 47 of the Act permits BR to operate on routes other than those originally sanctioned in 1948.

Suffolk Ferry at Harwich 23 July 1966

TSS DUKE OF YORK

BUILT	1935 by Harland & Wolff Ltd, Belfast
GROSS TONS	4,325
DIMENSIONS	357 ft 3 in x 52 ft 3 in x 14 ft 8 in
MACHINERY	4 turbines by Harland & Wolff, SR geared
	Oil-fired boilers
SPEED	21 knots
ROUTE	Harwich-Hook of Holland

Launched on 7 March 1935, *Duke of York* ran trials on 3 June and subsequently entered service, succeeding TSS *Duke of Abercorn* as relief and extra ship on the Heysham–Belfast run.

Although she had ample accommodation for 389 first-class and 1,111 third-class passengers she was introduced with service as a cargo ship in mind, and had special accommodation for livestock and extensive cargo space, her original gross tonnage being 3,743. Hatches were of the roller type. First-class passenger accommodation consisted of 139 berths in single- and double-berth cabins, including two cabins-de-luxe, a 38-seater dining-saloon and lounge on the bridge deck, and a smokeroom with bar at the after end of the promenade deck. All cabins were on the boat and promenade decks. Third-class accommodation was on lower, main and poop decks, and consisted of a public lounge, restaurant, smokeroom,

27

and 78 two- and four- berth cabins for 228 passengers and 10 berths in the ladies' dormitory. She originally had two funnels and a straight stem, but these were subsequently altered, she was the first cross-channel steamer to cater especially for a tourist class, and she was well equipped with up-to-date aids including mechanical stokers, electronic telegraph (an improvement on the old mechanical type), wireless telephone, echo-sounder and tachometer.

It is interesting to recall that in these prewar years there were, on occasion, as many as five ships serving between Heysham and Belfast, while now demand for space is such that two can usually cope quite well.

The *Duke of York* served extensively in the war and took part in the evacuation from Dunkirk. In 1942 she was converted to serve as an infantry landing ship (pennant number 4.400) carrying 250 troops and 10 assault landing craft (LCA's). Renamed HMS *Duke of Wellington*, her first excitement came on the night of the 18 August 1942, when she was involved in the Dieppe raid. When active hostilities ceased in Europe she was based on Harwich for a time, trooping across the Channel, and then returned to Heysham, making her first postwar Belfast sailing on 31 October 1947.

Although she was apparently well settled once again at Heysham, she made her last sailing from there on 14 May 1948. Early in that year the Harwich steamer *Prague* was burned out while refitting, and this station being very short of ships while Heysham had lost none of its fleet during the war, BR decided that *Duke of York* should be brought round to fill the

Duke of York at Hook of Holland 28 June 1959

gap. There were protests by the locals at the loss of their newest ship, but, as odd-man-out of the four, she was the obvious choice, and she left Heysham on 20 May 1948, arriving Harwich on 22 May.

About 25 May 1948 *Duke of York* made her first peacetime sailing from Harwich. By the end of the 1940s she was beginning to look very old-fashioned compared with her modern running mates, and in November 1950 she was sent to Harland & Wolff Ltd Belfast for extensive modernisation including her conversion to oil burning, and the replacement of her original two funnels by one large funnel. Considerable changes were also made in the layout of her passenger accommodation, so that she now had 359 first-class berths in 198 cabins, and 160 second-class berths in 54 cabins. This alteration involved the conversion of the former third-class accommodation amidships on B deck to first-class, the extension of the first-class accommodation into No 2 hold on B and C decks, and the fitting of second-class cabins in place of the former third-class lounge on B deck aft. All rooms were completely refurbished and many minor improvements were carried out. Officers' and crew cabins were also modernised. These changes increased her gross tonnage from 3,743 to 4,190.

She returned to Harwich in mid-May 1951. Just two years later she became involved in an accident which caused further rebuilding to take place. About 4.17 am on 6 May 1953, while approaching Harwich, she was involved in a collision with an American cargo ship *Haiti Victory* (7,607 tons), which sliced into her side just forward of the superstructure. There was some loss of life, and several people were injured. Her passengers were taken off by the *Haiti Victory* and another American ship. *Duke of York* then spent some six months off service under repair at

Fantasia (ex-*Duke of York*) in Chandris' colours

Palmers Hebburn-on-Tyne yard. A new 90 ft forepart, in which was incorporated a splendid modern raked stem was fitted. Her gross tonnage increased to 4,325. She re-entered service in February 1954.

During her career at Harwich, she did occasionally serve elsewhere. From 3 July 1950 she ran twice weekly for a time between Southampton and Cherbourg, and she sailed from Holyhead to Dun Laoghaire in summer 1951.

Her replacement (TSS *Avalon*), having been ordered, *Duke of York* was on the sale list in early summer 1963 and was bought in May by the Chandris (Greek) subsidiary Marivic Navigation Incorporated. On 20 July 1963 she arrived at Harwich, dressed overall, after her last crossing, being delivered to her new owners almost at once. Renamed *York* she was then sent to Smith's Dock Co Ltd for structural alterations to be carried out and left for Piracus in November. On arrival there further modifications were done at Chandris' own yard at Ambelaki, and on 15 March 1964 she started on her maiden cruise, with the new name *Fantasia*. She is still carrying out cruises of from 7 to 13 days' duration in the Aegean area with berths for 381 persons in one- two- three- and four-berth cabins on four decks. As will be seen from the photograph her external appearance has altered little.

TSMV *Essex Ferry* lying off Harwich 4 July 1966

TSMV ESSEX FERRY

BUILT	1957 by John Brown & Co (Clydebank) Ltd
GROSS TONS	3,242
DIMENSIONS	399 ft 4 in x 61 ft 4 in x 12 ft
MACHINERY	Two 2-stroke single acting 6-cyl Sulzer diesels by John Brown
SPEED	13 knots
ROUTE	Harwich-Zeebrugge

Replacing *Essex Ferry II* (ex- *Train Ferry No 1*) this ship is specially designed to carry large rail waggons, accommodating thirty-eight on four tracks on the train deck. Access is by two tracks over the stern. She was launched on 24 October 1956 and made her maiden voyage from Harwich on 15 January 1957. There is good accommodation for twelve first-class passengers.

MV COLCHESTER
MV ISLE OF ELY

BUILT	1959/1958 by Goole Shipbuilding & Repairing Co Ltd
GROSS TONS	866
DIMENSIONS	241 ft 10 in x 37 ft 6 in x 13 ft 2 in
MACHINERY	4-stroke single acting 8-cyl diesel by Ruston & Hornsby Ltd, Lincoln
SPEED	13½ knots
ROUTE	Harwich-Antwerp/Rotterdam

These ships were the first specially-constructed unit-load vessels built for the Eastern Region. *Isle of Ely* made her maiden voyage on 27 October 1958 replacing *Sheringham,* while *Colchester* made hers on 2 February 1959 replacing *Dewsbury.* They can carry forty-two standard containers and have no accommodation for passengers. *Colchester* was the first BR ship to enter service in the new blue livery at the beginning of October 1964. It is interesting to note the revival of the blue five-pointed star on the bows, first worn by prewar passenger vessels. The ships switch routes frequently and it is not possible to associate one or other of them with either service for any length of time.

During May–June 1968 *Isle of Ely* was altered by Redhead's to carry up to 150 containers in cellular holds and on deck. From June 1968 they served Rotterdam, the service to Antwerp being terminated at the end of May. While being altered, *Isle of Ely* was replaced by MV *Derwent Fisher,* on charter. *Colchester* was expected to be transferred to another region in October 1968—possibly Fishguard.

31

Colchester at Harwich 1 October 1964

TSMV CAMBRIDGE FERRY

BUILT 1963 by Hawthorn Leslie (Shipbuilders) Ltd, Hebburn-on-Tyne
GROSS TONS 3,294
DIMENSIONS 403 ft x 61 ft 4 in x 12 ft 1 in
MACHINERY Two 4-stroke single acting 7-cyl diesels by Mirlees-National Ltd, Stockport
SPEED 13½ knots
ROUTE Harwich-Zeebrugge

Launched on 1 November 1963, this train ferry is the fourth to be built since the war for the Eastern Region's Zeebrugge service, and she accommodates up to thirty-five railway freight waggons on four tracks, which are recessed into the main deck so that road vehicles can also be carried. Access to the main deck is by stern ramp and containers are loaded by travelling gantries (10 tons capacity). On the upper deck, above which is the navigating bridge, is one long deckhouse containing officers' and crew cabins and also six double-berth outside cabins for passengers, which were originally intended for vehicle drivers only. Dining-room, galley, etc, are in the same deckhouse, but the master's suite, and radio office, are on bridge level.

She was the first British ship to be fitted with the Flume stabilisation system. This comprises two separate lateral internal tanks, capable of being manipulated independently of each other, in which water can flow from side to side. This flow is controlled by constrictions, thus balancing the roll of the ship. She left Harwich on her maiden voyage on 2 January 1964.

Cambridge Ferry on passage Zeebrugge–Harwich October 1965

TSS AVALON

BUILT	1963 by Alexander Stephen & Sons Ltd, Linthouse
GROSS TONS	6,584
DIMENSIONS	404 ft x 59 ft 8 in x 15 ft 9 in
MACHINERY	2 turbines by A. Stephen & Sons, DR geared
	Oil-fired boilers
SPEED	21½ knots
ROUTE	Harwich-Hook; Continental cruises

The largest ship ever owned by any British railway company until the *St George* appeared, and the first to be completely air-conditioned, *Avalon* was designed to boost the reputation of the Hook of Holland service, replacing *Duke of York,* but she was fitted out with off-season cruising also in mind. Her launch, due 10 April 1963, was postponed because of an electricians' strike, and eventually took place without the usual ceremony on 7 May. She made her maiden commercial voyage from Harwich on 25 July as planned.

She is fitted with twin rudders aft, fin stabilisers, bow rudder and bow transverse thrust unit. There are three continuous decks, main, upper and shelter, with promenade and navigating bridge decks above. The lower deck extends forward and aft of the machinery space. Hull and superstructure are all-welded. She has accommodation for 750 passengers on all decks except bridge and shelter, there being 331 first-class and 287 second-class berths with 132 'un-berthed'. Three holds with 'tweendecks, two forward and one aft, carry cargo and cars. *Public rooms*: Promenade deck, first-class lounge forward; second-class lounge aft. Shelter deck, first-class smokeroom forward; second-class smokeroom aft; first-class restaurant between smokeroom and machinery casing; second-class self-service cafeteria abaft casing on port side.

When occupied in cruising she carries only 300-320 one-class passen-

Avalon at Harwich 16 April 1965

gers. Berths available for cruises: Promenade deck, 6 2-berth cabins-de-luxe; 4 special cabins with private bath. Upper deck, 1-berth cabins outside; 1-berth cabins inside; 2-berth cabins outside; 3-berth cabins. Main deck, 1-berth cabins outside; 1-berth cabins inside; 2-berth cabins outside; 2-berth cabins inside; 3-berth cabins; 4-berth cabins. Lower deck, 2-berth cabins only. She left Harwich for her first cruise on 24 April 1964, bound for Amsterdam for the weekend. She has since made several similar weekend trips, but on 21 May 1964 sailed for her first visit to a Scandinavian port, Copenhagen, on an 8-day cruise. In May 1966 she made her first cruise to Lisbon and Oporto and early in October she visited Tangier.

She is a very successful ship but does not serve any other packet route. She had an interesting diversion on the night of 22 August 1966 when she sailed from Hull to Gothenburg on charter to Ellerman's Wilson Line Ltd whose own new ship, *Spero,* was not ready in time. Her annual overhaul takes place in January. Freed from essential service by the new ships, she reverted to cruising on 6 September 1968, travelling to Lisbon, Tangier and Vigo, *inter alia,* for fourteen days.

TSMV SEA FREIGHTLINER I
TSMV SEA FREIGHTLINER II

BUILT	1968 by John Readhead & Sons Ltd, South Shields (Swan Hunter Group)
GROSS TONS	4,034
DIMENSIONS	388 ft 6 in x 53 ft x 14 ft 6 in
MACHINERY	Two Mirlees diesels 6-cyl K-type
SPEED	13½ knots
ROUTE	Harwich-Zeebrugge/Rotterdam

Sea Freightliner I sailed on her maiden voyage to Zeebrugge on 18 March 1968. Her sister, launched on 15 March followed some months later, and inaugurated the Rotterdam unit service on 18 June 1968.

Sea Freightliner I was the first specially designed cellular-container ship to enter the water from a British yard. All the cargo space consists of sectionalised holds containing cellular compartments to take 148 30-ft, high-capacity containers, or permutations of 20-ft or 40-ft containers. Of these, 110 can be stacked three-high in the cellular holds, and the remaining 38 on the folding steel hatch covers. The provision of controlled temperatures means that refrigerated containers can also be carried.

The superstructure aft has accommodation for a complement of eighteen plus relief crew.

The vessels are each equipped with a bow rudder, bow thrust unit and twin rudders aft. The main engine can be controlled from the bridge, and for periods of up to about twelve hours the engine room can be unmanned. Turn-round in port is only five hours, thanks to modern terminal handling facilities, and the round trip takes about twelve hours.

Sea Freightliner I approaching Parkeston Quay 21 May 1968

TSMV ST GEORGE

BUILT	1968 by Swan Hunter (Shipbuilders) Ltd, Walker on Tyne
GROSS TONS	7,356
DIMENSIONS	420 ft x 65 ft 6 in x 16 ft 6 in
MACHINERY	4 Ruston geared diesels
SPEED	21 knots
ROUTE	Harwich-Hook of Holland

Ordered from the then Associated Shipbuilders Ltd (Swan Hunter yard) in November 1966, *St George* is the largest ship yet built for or owned by the British Railways Board. The board's partner on the service, the Zeeland Steamship Co, ordered a similar ship from Cammell, Laird & Co Ltd, Birkenhead, at about the same time. The latter ship was launched on 2 February, 1968, with the name *Koningin Juliana*. *St George* was launched on 28 February. Both ships are to operate day and night services, and rendered redundant *Arnhem* and *Amsterdam*, as well as the two 1939 Dutch passenger ships *Koningin Emma* and *Prinses Beatrix*.

St George has been designed with both bow and stern doors to permit straight-through driving, and has capacity for 220 cars, or a combination of thirty-four lorries and ninety cars. Accommodation is provided for 1,200 passengers on the daylight run, but for 700 only on the night run, with cabins for about 550 in berths. The ship is fitted with twin controllable-pitch propellers, twin stern rudders and a bow thrust unit.

She left Harwich on her maiden crossing on 17 July 1968.

St George near Harwich July 1968

2. THE THAMES

The Atlantic Steam Navigation Company Ltd, a wholly owned subsidiary of the BTC from 1954 to 1962, has operated ships from Tilbury since 1946. Details of these services appear on page 264.

The Tilbury–Gravesend ferry service is the responsibility of the Eastern Region. In 1948 there were three passenger ferries and two drive-on car ferries, all reciprocating steamers, in service. The car-ferry service was closed on 31 December 1964. A reprieve was urged by some local authorities and the RAC, but BR maintained that the service had been uneconomical after the Dartford–Purfleet tunnel was opened a few months earlier. *Tessa* and *Mimie* were subsequently withdrawn and sold for breaking up.

The passenger-only service is still maintained. In the winter of 1960-1 the three original vessels, *Catherine, Edith* and *Rose,* were replaced by new motor ships with the same names. Excursions and cruises from Gravesend and Tilbury to Greenwich and Tower Bridge have been run normally by *Edith* during the summer months, usually from June to September, each year from 1963 to 1966. On 27 June 1965 the Gravesend terminal was transferred from Town Pier to West Pier.

When the BTC came into being it inherited control of Grand Union (Shipping) Ltd, which in 1948 operated five cargo ships on services to Antwerp and Rotterdam. In July 1948 control was disposed of to Messrs Tom and Spratt.

TSS ROSE
TSS CATHERINE
TSS EDITH

BUILT	1901/1903/1911 by A. W. Robertson & Co Ltd, London
GROSS TONS	259/259/283
DIMENSIONS	129 ft x 32 ft 6 in x 5 ft *Edith* 136 ft x 37 ft x 5 ft 3 in
MACHINERY	4-cyl compound by A. W. Robertson
	Coal-fired boilers
SPEED	9 knots
ROUTE	Tilbury-Gravesend passenger ferry

All three ships, built for the above service operated by the London Tilbury & Southend Railway Co, were taken over by the Midland Railway Co in 1912 (retaining the all-black funnels of the LT&S). In 1923 they were taken over by the LMS and given the latter company's yellow funnels with black tops. The length between perpendiculars is in each case some 4 ft 6 in less than the overall length, the difference being accounted for by the quite severe counter of the stern. They retained canvas dodgers on the bridge and oil lighting in the saloons throughout, and it is said that it took a full five hours to raise the necessary head of steam.

Originally there was a fourth member of the series named *Gertrude,* which was sold in 1932 to the new Medway Steam Packet Co Ltd by whom she was renamed *Rochester Queen.* In the following year she was resold to M. H. Bland & Co Ltd, Gibraltar, for use as a tender, being named at first *Caid,* later *Gibel Derif.* She was finally broken up in 1962 at Bland's own yard.

The other three, who remained in service right up to BTC days, lasted a surprisingly long time, and could carry 655, 648 and 850 passengers respectively. The suffix *II* was added to their names in 1960 when replace-

Catherine crossing the Thames

ments were ordered. *Catherine II* was withdrawn in late 1960 and sold for breaking up in Belgium in December of that year. The other two remained in service until 28 February 1961, the month in which the new MVS *Catherine* and *Edith* appeared. Three months later they, too, were sold for breaking in Belgium. *Catherine II* arrived at Boom for breaking by van den Bossche on 7 April 1961 ; *Edith II* and *Rose II* arrived there on 13 May.

TSS TESSA
TSS MIMIE

Tessa

BUILT	1924 by Lytham Shipbuilding & Engineering Co Ltd
GROSS TONS	368
DIMENSIONS	141 ft x 39 ft 4 in x 6 ft 3 in
MACHINERY	4-cyl compound by Lytham Shipbuilding & Engineering Co
	Coal-fired boilers
SPEED	9 knots
ROUTE	Tilbury-Gravesend car ferry

Mimie

BUILT	1927 by Ferguson Bros (Port Glasgow) Ltd
GROSS TONS	463
DIMENSIONS	151 ft x 40 ft 6 in x 6 ft 6 in
MACHINERY	4-cyl compound by Ferguson Bros (Port Glasgow) Ltd
	Coal-fired boilers
SPEED	9 knots
ROUTE	Tilbury-Gravesend car ferry

The LMS ordered these similar ships for the Tilbury–Gravesend car ferry service, and what a remarkable pair they were in their simplicity. Surely few more functional vessels have ever been launched. They had a bow and stern, the counter of which extended some 6 ft beyond the water line, but little else. They could accommodate some twenty to thirty cars on clear deck space fore and aft the superstructure. *Mimie* could take 300 passengers and *Tessa* 250. Loading was at the sides of the ship over ramps through sliding doors, of which there were two on each side. No mast was carried, the necessary lights being carried on the front of the funnels, which originally had cowls. They were not easy to tell apart, the most significant feature being the position of the lifeboat; on *Tessa* it hung over the starboard bow, on *Mimie* it was over the stern.

The opening in 1964 of the Purfleet Tunnel, a few miles to the west of the ferry crossing, providing a through road to Dartford, sounded the death knell of the ferries. They continued to be patronised to some extent but there was not sufficient trade to keep the service going. The last crossing was made by *Mimie* on 31 December 1964 when the service was closed, and both ships were subsequently offered for sale. Breakers bought them and they both arrived in Bruges on 11 May 1965.

Mimie—showing main deck 'through-way' for passengers

MV CATHERINE
MV EDITH
MV ROSE

BUILT	1960/1960/1961 by J. S. White & Co Ltd, Cowes
GROSS TONS	213
DIMENSIONS	110 ft x 27 ft x 4 ft 6 in
MACHINERY	6-cyl uni-directional Lister & Blackstone oil engine, Voith-Schneider propeller
SPEED	9 knots
ROUTE	Tilbury-Gravesend

Built to replace the ancient steamers with the same names, these ferries can carry a maximum of 475 passengers, no cars being accommodated. There is fixed seating for 209 passengers ; 71 in the heated after lounge, 72 in the forward heated lounge, and 66 on the open deck above. A crew of four is carried. *Catherine* was the first of the three, being launched on 4 November 1960. *Rose* came last, launched on 19 January 1961. *Catherine* and *Edith* made their maiden voyages at the end of February 1961. The ships are equipped with VHF radio telephone, and the engine can be controlled direct from the bridge. There are three hydraulically operated gangways on each side providing for speedy embarkation and disembarkation. Since 1963, cruises up river to Greenwich and Tower Pier have been run each summer, from about Whit-weekend to near the end of September. These were started by *Catherine* on Whit-Sunday 1963 and she made a few more that year, but the remainder were made by *Edith* which also operated them throughout 1964, 1965 and 1966 as she was the only one fitted with a loud-speaker system and equipped for catering.

Rose arriving at Tilbury 31 July 1965

Towards the end of 1966 The Caledonian Steam Packet Co Ltd was looking for a replacement for the paddler *Talisman,* to operate mainly on the Largs–Millport service. In the event, *Rose* was selected and she changed hands on 11 April 1967. She left Tilbury for the Clyde via the East Coast on 24 April, with windows boarded up and fuel drums lashed on deck. In May she was renamed *Keppel* (qv).

THE SOUTHERN REGION

The services taken over by the Southern Region on 1 January 1948 were those previously operated by the SR from Dover, Folkestone, Newhaven and Southampton, and the ferry services to the Isle of Wight. The Weymouth station, originally part of the Western Region, was transferred to the Southern on 1 November 1948. Thus all south coast cross-channel services now came under the control of the Southern Region.

3 : DOVER AND FOLKESTONE

Like Harwich these two packet ports lost a number of ship during the war. The SR passenger ships *Maid of Orleans* and *Maid of Kent,* and three cargo ships, *Tonbridge, Minster* and *Fratton,* were all sunk, while *Biarritz* was retained in postwar years on trooping services. In addition *Côte d'Azur* and *Côte d'Argent,* owned by the Société Anonyme de Gérance et d'Armement, were also sunk. These losses presented the authorities with problems, but there was another factor to be taken into account, namely, the condition of the harbours at Calais and Boulogne which had suffered considerable devastation particularly during the closing stages of the war. Thus, even though some ships were available, it was not possible to reinstate regular comfortable services until much time and money had been spent on virtually rebuilding the quays and facilities on the French side of the Channel. Cargo services were not really affected since four ships survived the war (*Hythe, Whitstable, Maidstone* and *Deal*) ; ample to provide regular and frequent sailings. Since cargo ships do not need the complicated terminal facilities necessary to passenger services, the cargo services were the first to be reopened ; to Calais in August 1945 and to Boulogne in March 1946, *Hythe* being used on both occasions.

Although in prewar years both Dover and Folkestone had been the starting points for cargo services to Calais and Boulogne, in postwar years the importance of Folkestone in this connection grew, so that after about 1953 there were rarely any cargo-only ships sailing from Dover. The frequency of general cargo services changed little over the years. So long as there were at least two ships available, there were usually five or six sailings per week in each direction between Folkestone and Boulogne. From November 1958 only *Deal* remained, and the service was therefore reduced to run three times per week in each direction. After *Deal*'s withdrawal in February 1963 the service limped along with a chartered coaster, *Dorset Coast,* and a decision had to be reached on the future of the service. In the event a special unit-load-only service was planned to operate as from 31 May 1965, offering a 24-hour through-delivery to Boulogne from the Bricklayers Arms depot in London, where HM Customs would clear all goods. Containers were to be loaded onto railway flat waggons during the afternoon, travel by train to Folkestone overnight and connect with the 11.0 am sailing for Boulogne, arriving at the latter port two hours later. Import traffic was also to be cleared in London, but at the Hither Green depot. At first the service was fairly successful, but it never attained economic importance and was finally withdrawn at the end of November 1966. There are now no cross-channel cargo ships based at Dover or Folkestone.

The train-ferry service between Dover and Dunkirk, inaugurated on 14 October 1936, came out of the war best of all as far as available ships were concerned. Of the three original ferries none was lost and the service was restored soon afterwards by *Shepperton Ferry* and *Hampton*

45

Ferry, owned by the SR, and *Twickenham Ferry,* built for the SR but owned by the Angleterre-Lorraine-Alsace, Société Anonyme de Navigation. Generally there have been two sailings per day in each direction, one in daylight for goods and one at night for passengers, ie the 'Night Ferry'. In 1951 a fourth ship, *Saint Germain,* joined the service. She is a modern twin-screw motor vessel of 3,094 gross tons, and is owned by the French Railways (Société National de Chemin de Fer Français). From 1953 to 1961 inclusive, *Hampton Ferry* served between Stranraer and Larne during the summer months but the regularity of the Dover–Dunkirk service was not affected.

In recent years there have been, in summer, as many as eight sailings from Dover each twenty-four hours and, on occasion, one or more of the ships has been pressed into service on the Boulogne route. The reason for this was the vast increase in space demanded by private motorists crossing the channel. Moves to boost commercial traffic on the service have also been made, including drastic cuts in rates, up to 45 per cent, free berths for lorry drivers from October 1965, and the installation of unit-load facilities at Dover operative from May 1966. These facilities include a gantry crane with a safe working load of 25 tons to handle the 20 ton containers, and a fleet of trailers and tractors for loading the units on board. A maximum of six such containers (measuring 20 ft x 8 ft x 8 ft) can be carried. No doubt increasing competition from other channel operators—notably Townsend Bros Ferries Ltd—has been partly responsible for the improvements on the Dunkirk run. A new train/car ferry has been ordered by BRB from Swan Hunters.

The principal passenger service operating in the area in prewar years was that between Dover and Calais. The 'Golden Arrow' was the most famous of them all, and was maintained by *Canterbury.* She survived the war and reopened the service on 16 April 1946, being replaced by her successor, *Invicta,* the following October. *Invicta* has operated it with considerable reliability. In recent years there have been constant rumours of her withdrawal and of the termination of the sailing, but fortunately no moves have so far been made. However, the ship is now twenty-eight years old and clearly she will not be permitted to continue in service much longer.

Following the loss of *Côte d'Azur* and *Côte d'Argent,* which before the war had operated a secondary passenger service between Dover and Calais, the SNCF at first showed no interest in providing new-built or any other ships for this route. In fact nothing of theirs appeared until 1958 when TSMV *Compiègne* (3,473 gross tons), a drive-on stern-loading car ferry, entered the stakes. In 1966 she was joined by TSMV *Chantilly* which made her official maiden commercial voyage on 2 July, although she had already made several trips between the two terminals. Townsend Bros Ferries Ltd is in direct competition with SNCF on this route.

Calais now has two car-ferry berths. The first, opened in 1951, can handle loads of up to twelve tons from stern loaders only, while the second, opened in May 1965, can accommodate both bow and stern loaders and weights up to thirty-five tons. The Dover-Calais car-ferry service is strictly the preserve of SNCF and BR ships do not operate thereon except under abnormal circumstances.

Although the SR had the car ferry *Autocarrier* in service between Dover and Calais as early as 1931, and also had *Dinard* suitably altered in winter 1946-7, cars were in all cases crane-loaded until 1953 when the present Dover–Boulogne drive-through service was begun. The terminal at Boulogne was opened on 16 June 1952, but that at Dover not until 30 June 1953, when Mr. A. T. Lennox-Boyd, then Minister of Transport, performed the opening ceremony. *Dinard* inaugurated the Dover–Boulogne crane-loaded car-ferry service in June 1947, vehicles being loaded at No 1 Berth, Admiralty Pier. In postwar years *Autocarrier* did not remain on any one route for any great length of time, though she was mainly based on Folkestone.

The new through drive-on service was inaugurated by *Dinard* and *Lord Warden. Dinard,* at the age of thirty-four, was withdrawn near the end of 1958, and her place was taken early the following year by the new *Maid of Kent.* Subsequently two more drive-on ships have taken up the service, *Normannia* (converted like *Dinard*) in 1964, and *Dover* in 1965. With this increase in the number of ships and therefore the number of sailings, additional terminal facilities were required at Dover, which by now already had two berths, and at Bolougne. Boulogne's second berth was opened on 13 June 1965, and Dover's third in June 1966. Only BR ships serve on this route as a rule, although the services to both Calais and Boulogne are jointly advertised by such slogans as 'Drive the BIG FLEET Way to the Continent'. In high summer there are as many as sixteen sailings to Boulogne and eight to Calais during a 24-hour period.

The increase in train-ferry sailings on the Dunkirk route in recent years has been partly responsible for the gradual withdrawal of cargo-ship services across the Straits. Until October 1965 the Boulogne car ferries were reserved solely for the use of motorists and their cars, but in that month they were opened for use by commercial vehicles and drivers. This development was taken a step further when it was announced that drivers of export loads could travel free of charge. This move, and the opening of the Newhaven vehicle service (qv), sealed the doom of independent cargo-ship services in the area.

For decades Folkestone has been the poor sister of Dover. In SR days, Dover always had first claim on ships to fill emergencies and for relief duties. A similar situation has also existed in postwar years, so that by now Folkestone is very quiet and it seems that the time is not far distant when sailings will cease altogether. It has been shown how cargo sailings have gradually been withdrawn.

Before the war the SNCF took no part in Folkestone–Calais sailings, but afterwards, having lost both Calais–Dover ships, they reached agreement with the SR on the operation of an all-year-round service between Calais and Folkestone. As France had no available ship, it was left to the SR to open the service with *Canterbury* late in 1946 though this ship had in

47

fact sailed on the route early in 1945 on trooping duties. About February 1947 *Isle of Thanet* entered the service and from then on the afore-mentioned ships and *Autocarrier* maintained the service between them. In 1951 TSS *Côte d'Azur*, 4,037 tons, owned by SNCF, took over the run regularly and up to the present time has remained on it for most of the year. For about three months each winter BR provide a ship and normally *Maid of Orleans* is used.

In the immediate prewar years the Folkestone–Boulogne service was maintained by *Biarritz, Maid of Orleans* and *Maid of Kent* (1925). As none of these ships was available afterwards, it was arranged that the three which were, *Canterbury, Isle of Thanet* and *Autocarrier,* should be allocated to the Folkestone station for both the Calais and Boulogne routes. It was in 1947 that the Boulogne service first became summer-only. In June 1949 the new *Maid of Orleans* took up regular principal sailings to Boulogne. As time passed the lifting of various restrictions enabled cheap-day no-passport excursions to be run, and *Isle of Thanet* became mainly responsible for these, with *Canterbury* helping out when required. After the *Isle of Thanet* was withdrawn in 1963, the burden of these excursions during the 1964 season fell upon *Canterbury*, after which she was withdrawn. To replace her, *St Patrick,* late of Weymouth and Southampton, joined the station for the 1965 season. She is still there, operating also to Calais on occasion, in winter frequently relieving *Côte d'Azur*.

During winter 1967–8 passenger facilities at Folkestone were given a long overdue £94,000 face-lift.

TSS BIARRITZ

BUILT	1915 by Wm. Denny & Bros Ltd, Dumbarton
GROSS TONS	2,495
DIMENSIONS	341 ft 3 in x 42 ft x 12 ft 7½ in
MACHINERY	4 turbines by Denny, SR geared
	Oil-fired boilers
SPEED	24 knots

In spite of thirty-five years' active life, this ship served the travelling public for only eighteen of them, and that between the wars. She was launched on 7 December 1914, and on nearing completion in March 1915 for the Straits of Dover service of the South Eastern and Chatham Railway Companies was taken over by the Admiralty and converted for use as a minelayer. She subsequently served in a variety of capacities, and took part in the destruction of the German warship *Breslau* in the Aegean Sea on 20 January 1918. After spending the closing months of the war and some time afterwards on cross-channel trooping duties, she went to Vickers Armstrongs (Shipbuilders) Ltd, Barrow in 1921 for a complete refit. From then until 1925 she served principally between Dover and Calais.

Her winter 1925-6 overhaul on the Clyde saw her conversion from coal burning. Other alterations carried out at this time included the glassing-in with sliding windows of the first-class promenade deck amidships, the enlargement of both first- and second-class entrance foyers on the boatdeck, the redesigning of the private cabins forward, and the transfer of the dining saloon from the promenade deck to the main deck, and of the smokeroom from the same deck to a position abaft the new dining saloon, now seating seventy-six, on the starboard side. She could now carry about 1,400 passengers in two classes. After this refit she returned to service in late March 1926 and served mainly between Folkestone and Boulogne until the second war, though she did return to Dover on occasion for relief and extra duties. During a further refit in the early 1930s she was given larger funnels.

After the 1939-45 war broke out, about 20 May 1940, she was, like so many other cross-channel ships, placed at the disposal of the Dover Admiralty, and became involved in some trooping. On 21 May she made what is believed to have been the last visit to Boulogne by a SR ship under relatively normal conditions, before the Dunkirk evacuation began. During the Dunkirk crisis she made about twenty trips across the channel but on her last crossing she was extensively damaged and had to undergo a lengthy refit. Next, she was trooping for a time between Stranraer and Larne before tendering on the Clyde. Later she was in use as a Fleet

Biarritz arriving at Dover under tow for breaking-up 30 November 1949

Air Arm target ship. In preparation for D Day she was converted to an assault craft, given the pennant number 4.96 and was placed in the Exbury Assault Group J1.

After VE Day she was used as a leave ship. In the immediate postwar years she had several overhauls, but was not returned to regular civilian service. In her wartime grey livery she continued to carry out her trooping duties, alternating between the Harwich–Hook of Holland and Dover–Calais routes. Her condition was rapidly deteriorating and, as time went on, it was clearly not economical to refit her to civilian standards. She was laid up at Southampton from August 1948, and eventually taken to Dover for breaking by Dover Metal Industries Ltd.

TSS DEAL
TSS HYTHE
TSS WHITSTABLE

BUILT	1928/1925/1925 by D. & W. Henderson & Co Ltd, Glasgow
GROSS TONS	829/700/865
DIMENSIONS	229 ft 6 in x 35 ft 9 in x 12 ft 9¼ in
MACHINERY	6-cyl triple-expansion by D. & W. Henderson Coal-fired boilers
SPEED	15 knots
ROUTE	Dover/Folkestone-Calais/Boulogne

Hythe was launched on 24 May 1925, *Whitstable* on 23 June 1925, and *Deal,* the last of the series, on 10 February 1928. In prewar days all served mainly from Dover and Folkestone, *Hythe* and *Whitstable* each with accommodation for about five passengers, *Deal* with no such accommodation

When war came all served in one capacity or another ; *Deal* from 1940 to 1943 as a barrage balloon vessel, being based at Sheerness and returned to the railway in the latter year ; *Hythe* as a transport in which capacity she served Dunkirk at least twice, lifting some 674 men on 31 May 1940. During part of the war, *Whitstable* was on the Stranraer–Larne run, and she re-entered the Boulogne service about the middle of 1946.

Hythe, which (with *Maidstone* qv) had reopened the Dover–Calais cargo service in August 1945, reopened the Boulogne service on 4 March 1946. She apparently carried twelve passengers at this time. After sorties elsewhere she remained on this service from July 1947 until being withdrawn and broken up in 1956 by Dover Metal Industries Ltd.

Late in 1958 *Whitstable* was transferred to the Weymouth–Channel Islands service for a few months and was sold in 1959 for breaking up by de Koophandel, Nieuw Lekkerkerk, where she arrived on 28 April in tow of tug *Nestor*.

Deal served Folkestone–Boulogne fairly consistently from mid-1947, being on her own after 1958, operating three days a week in each direction. She was finally withdrawn at the end of February 1963, laid up at Dover and put on the sale list. Van Heyghen Frères took her for scrap, and she arrived at Ghent on 22 May 1963. There was no railway-owned ship available to replace her, and so Coast Lines' MV *Dorset Coast* was taken on charter.

Hythe entering Dover Harbour about 1938

TSS ISLE OF THANET

BUILT	1925 by Wm. Denny & Bros Ltd, Dumbarton
GROSS TONS	2,789
DIMENSIONS	342 ft x 48 ft 6 in x 12 ft 10 in
MACHINERY	4 turbines by Denny, SR geared
	Oil-fired boilers
SPEED	22 knots
ROUTE	Folkestone-Boulogne

Isle of Thanet was rightly a famous and well-loved ship, serving reliably in peacetime and with distinction in wartime. She made her inaugural voyage on the Dover–Calais run on 24 July 1925, but thereafter was mostly associated with the Folkestone station, serving either Boulogne or Calais, as the season or requirements demanded. Originally she carried over 1,400 passengers and had a gross tonnage of 2,701, but

51

both were subsequently altered. She was primarily a day ship, so cabin accommodation was very limited, there being only twenty-four cabins of varying quality including two de-luxe state-rooms on the boat deck. Public room accommodation was distributed mainly between the boat deck and main deck, the dining saloons for both classes being on the latter. She was a big improvement on her predecessors mainly because of increased covered space and extra seats for about 250 passengers.

During the war she served in various capacities beginning on 1 September 1939 when she sailed from Southampton to Le Havre with a party of the First RAF Wing on board. She was later converted to a hospital ship at Southampton and as such, based on Dover, helped in the Dunkirk evacuation. Later, based on Preston, she was used as a Fleet Air Arm target ship, and early in 1943 was fitted out as a landing ship infantry (hand hoist) with pennant number 4.262, becoming part of the Exbury Assault Group J1. She was HQ ship of this group, and carried out lengthy manoeuvres and took part in mock landings between Calais and Boulogne. In the late summer of 1944 she was on the refugee run between Southampton and Ostend, and Newhaven and Dieppe.

In 1945 she was returned to the SR and, after a refit, entered the Newhaven–Dieppe service on which she remained fairly consistently until the end of 1946. From February 1947 she served on the Folkestone–Calais run until she reopened the postwar civilian Dover–Boulogne service on 1 July 1947. She maintained this until reverting to the Folkestone–Calais route in May 1948. In the following month she took up the Folkestone–

Isle of Thanet towards the end of her career

Boulogne service and from then onwards alternated between these two Folkestone runs for most of her remaining life. In addition she was occasionally relief ship on the Dover–Calais 'Golden Arrow' route (the last time being early in 1962) and sometimes appeared elsewhere, eg on the extra Friday-night Southampton–Channel Islands summer sailing from 1951 to 1957. In the summer of 1951 she was sent to Holyhead to serve Dun Laoghaire, but was not used there. Since 1958 particularly, she has been associated with the summer day excursions from Folkestone to Calais and Boulogne. She was usually laid up at Dover during the winter months. 1963 was her last year in service, and she made her final crossing from Boulogne to Folkestone on Sunday 15 September, and was then sent to Dover to be laid up. Early in 1964 she was sold to Hughes Bolckow & Co Ltd, Blyth, for breaking up, and left Dover on 10 June in tow of Hull tug *Headman*.

TSS CANTERBURY

BUILT	1929 by Wm. Denny & Bros Ltd, Dumbarton
GROSS TONS	3,071
DIMENSIONS	341 ft 6 in x 50 ft 6 in x 12 ft 10 in
MACHINERY	4 turbines by Denny, SR geared
	Oil-fired boilers
SPEED	22 knots
ROUTE	Folkestone-Boulogne

Canterbury was a single ship launched on 13 December 1928 and was specially provided for the Channel connection between Dover and Calais of the London–Paris 'Golden Arrow' express service, arranged jointly by British and French Railways. She originally had a gross tonnage of 2,912, and arrived at Dover amid wide acclamation on 29 April 1929, making her maiden voyage and inaugurating the new service on 15 May. She was the last word in luxury for her 400 first-class passengers, having a number of private cabins, a palm court and a garden lounge among her amenities. All was not well, however, for in her early days she had recurring mechanical trouble of one sort or another, and in winter 1931-2 she was taken in hand for an extensive refit. At the same time she was con-verted into a two-class ship, and these alterations caused an increase in gross tonnage. Thereafter she continued on the 'Golden Arrow' run until the outbreak of war.

From September 1939 she was in use as a transport based at Southamp-ton and during May 1940 she served a variety of routes, eg Rotterdam–Harwich, Cherbourg–Weymouth, Boulogne–Dover, carrying refugees, being then available at Dover for the Dunkirk evacuation. She made five trips, lifting some 3,000 personnel in all. She was then used successively as a Fleet Air Arm target ship and as a landing ship infantry with pennant number 4.107 attached to the Exbury Group. In this capacity she attended the Normandy invasion. From early December 1944 she was engaged in trooping between Ostend and Dover, and in January 1945 she inaugurated the military leave service between Calais and Folkestone, on which she remained, also serving Dover, until February 1946 when she went to the Tyne for a refit. This involved rebuilding parts of the ship removed for war service, eg mainmast, some deckhouses and life-boats, and the installation of radar. She was the first channel packet to be so equipped.

On 16 April 1946 she reintroduced the 'Golden Arrow' service and maintained it until being replaced by her successor, *Invicta,* in October. At the beginning of December she reinstated the Calais–Folkestone winter service. She was on the 'Golden Arrow' service from January to June 1947, reverting then to the Folkestone–Calais run which she maintained until May 1948, when she moved to the summer Folkestone–Boulogne route. After that she served this run consistently, occasionally relieving on the 'Golden Arrow' and Folkestone–Calais services. In later years, particularly since 1960, she was responsible for the cheap day excursions to Boulogne.

She made her last sailing from Boulogne to Folkestone on Sunday 27 September 1964, and was then laid up at Dover and kept in reserve through the following winter. Sold for breaking up by Brussels Scrapping

Canterbury leaving Dover for the breakers' yard 30 July 1965

54

Co, she left Dover for Antwerp in tow of the Belgian tug *Burgemeester Vandame* on 30 July, having been delayed for two days because of bad weather. Her moveables were stripped at Antwerp, and hull demolished at Willebroek. *St Patrick,* late of Weymouth and Southampton, came to Folkestone to replace her in spring 1965.

TSS AUTOCARRIER

BUILT	1931 by D. & W. Henderson & Co Ltd, Glasgow
GROSS TONS	822
DIMENSIONS	220 ft 3 in x 35 ft 7 in x 11 ft 6 in
MACHINERY	8-cyl triple-expansion engines by D. & W. Henderson Coal-fired boilers
SPEED	15 knots
ROUTES	Various

Autocarrier was to have been another cargo vessel of the *Haslemere* type, but was altered before completion to enable her to carry passengers and cars in reply to Townsend Bros *Forde* already operating a car-carrying service from Dover. She was, therefore, the first specially con-structed UK railway-owned cross-channel car ferry, though she was never provided with drive-on facilities. Cars were always loaded by dock-side crane or the ship's own two 5-ton derricks. She was launched on 5 February 1931, ran trials on 23 March and entered service between Dover and Calais on 31 March. She could carry 120 passengers (reduced to 100 postwar) and about 30 cars. Accommodation: Boat deck, Saloon/buffet

Autocarrier approaching Folkestone 14 July 1950

forward. Main deck, Gent's saloon forward on starboard side; Ladies' saloon forward on port side; about 16 vehicles or containers amidships; bar aft on the centre line. Lower deck, about 8 cars forward of machinery space; about 5 cars aft of machinery space.

During the war she appeared at Dunkirk, lifting some 712 men on 3 June, and subsequently served as a recreation ship for the Royal Navy. Afterwards, up to about August 1946, she ran cargo services from Southampton, and then generally ran cargo-only from Dover or Folkestone, though she did carry cars and passengers from time to time. Latterly she served Folkestone–Boulogne fairly consistently. In 1948 a stump mainmast was fitted. She was finally withdrawn and laid up early in 1954. Van Heyghen Frères of Ghent bought her for breaking up, and she left Dover under tow on 6 August 1954.

TSS HAMPTON FERRY
TSS SHEPPERTON FERRY

BUILT	1934/35 by Swan Hunter and Wigham Richardson Ltd
GROSS TONS	2,989/2,996
DIMENSIONS	360 ft x 63 ft 2 in/62 ft 10 in x 12 ft 6 in
MACHINERY	4 turbines by Parsons Marine Steam Turbine Co Ltd, SR geared
	Oil-fired boilers
SPEED	16 knots
ROUTE	Dover-Dunkirk

Early in the 1930s a joint plan was conceived by French and English railway authorities to operate a steamer service, on which railway waggons and passenger coaches could be accommodated, between the two countries. Dover and Dunkirk were the terminals selected, and the SR ordered three special stern-loading ships. *Twickenham Ferry* was delivered first in July 1934, *Hampton* followed in November, and *Shepperton* came last in March 1935. Difficulties of one kind or another arose, and the service did not, in fact, start until October 1936. It was a tremendous success. Passengers now boarded the special train 'Night Ferry' at Victoria, remained on the coaches overnight, and arrived in Paris the following morning. The ships have altered little and can accommodate twelve sleeping cars or forty loaded goods waggons, a garage for twenty-five cars is built above the train deck at the stern, and coaches and road vehicles can also be carried on the train deck aft. Whitbread tankers carrying beer are regular users of the service. From time to time internal alterations have taken place, and in postwar years some 500 one-class passengers are being carried, with berth accommodation in single and

56

double cabins, and open 'rug and pillow' berths in the ladies' and gentlemen's saloons.

Twickenham was transferred to a French concern, Angleterre-Lorraine-Alsace, Société Anonyme de Navigation late in 1936. The others, retained by the SR, were requisitioned late in 1939 and converted for use as mine-layers carrying 270 mines. As HMS *Hampton* and HMS *Shepperton,* and

Shepperton Ferry leaving Dover 29 July 1965

generally keeping in each other's company, they began minelaying on 11 September outside Dover, continued outside Folkestone and later in the Thames estuary. From July 1940 both were engaged in transport duties between Stranraer and Larne.

The war over, both ships were converted from coal to oil burning (they could carry 130 tons of coal) in 1947 and the following year the gantry cranes were removed from aft. The 'Night Ferry' continued as before with little change to affect the ships until 1953. On 31 January of that year the car ferry *Princess Victoria,* serving between Stranraer and Larne sank in storm conditions and it was necessary for another ship to replace her, particularly during the busy summer months. *Hampton Ferry* was selected, and each summer from 1953 until 1961 (from about June to September) she served on that route. As the new *Caledonian Princess* was due to appear at Stranraer late in 1961, *Hampton* made her last Stranraer–Larne crossing on 2 October 1961 and left for Dover the following day. She has not returned to Stranraer though *Shepperton* has relieved *Caledonian Princess* during her annual overhaul (February to March) from 1963 to 1965.

The life of these ships is not exciting but occasionally something new turns up. *Shepperton* was chartered by the War Office to run light to Flushing from Dunkirk on 23 and 24 June 1965, then to take on army personnel and vehicles for transport to Dover. In recent years these ships have been advertised along with the other car ferries and their use

57

encouraged. Rumours of replacement have been circulating recently but to date no definite news has materialised.

When the ships were given the new BR livery in 1965 the upper strake was painted white right up to the bows, as seen in this picture. This is how they looked when they first appeared in 1936. However, on return from their spring 1966 overhaul, their paintwork had reverted to the more recent BR pattern with the white 'stepped-up' beneath the bridge.

There is passenger accommodation on only two decks. On the upper deck forward are ladies' and gent's saloons, while immediately abaft them are single- and double-berth cabins. Amidships are dining saloon, smoke-room and bar, and further aft more private cabins. Forward on the lower deck are saloons with settee berths.

Early in July 1968 *Hampton Ferry*, with stern altered to fit the Zeebrugge link span, opened a new service between that port and Dover.

TSS INVICTA

BUILT	1940 by Wm. Denny & Bros Ltd, Dumbarton
GROSS TONS	4,191
DIMENSIONS	348 ft 3 in x 52 ft 3 in x 12 ft 9 in
MACHINERY	4 Parsons turbines, SR geared by Denny
	Oil-fired boilers
SPEED	22 knots
ROUTE	Dover-Calais

Designed to replace Canterbury on the 'Golden Arrow' service between Dover and Calais, *Invicta* was caught up in the war and, after completion, spent a year laid up in the Clyde near Clynder. She was then taken over by the Admiralty and served as a transport (HMS *Invicta*), appearing at the Dieppe raid, and was also used as an assault craft during the Normandy invasion. She was fitted out to carry 250 troops and 6 LCA's and was part of Assault Group J1 based on Exbury. Originally coal-fired, she was fitted with mechanical stokers.

The war over, her extensive refit of 1946 included conversion to oil burning, and she replaced *Canterbury* on the 'Golden Arrow' run on 15 October 1946. She has two continuous decks (main and upper) and her promenade deck almost stretches the length of the ship; she has a bow rudder and was fitted with Denny-Brown stabilisers in 1947. She carries 1,400 passengers, the first-class accommodation being mainly forward and the second-class aft; her upper restaurant seats eighty-four. Her accommodation was modernised at Southampton towards the end of 1962.

On 26 April 1963 she officially reopened the Western Entrance to Dover Harbour, following the removal of the blockships sunk in 1940 to keep out the enemy. She has very rarely deviated from her regular route, but odd weekends in and since 1964 have seen her sailing to Boulogne and, on very rare occasions, she has crossed from Folkestone. She is in good condition but as she is twenty-eight years old her days are surely numbered. During the winter it has been her practice to lay off for several months from about early November during which time her annual overhaul is carried out, and she has been replaced by *Maid of Orleans* from Folkestone for much of the time although *Isle of Thanet, St Patrick* and *Canterbury* have substituted for her on occasion.

Principal Accommodation: Upper (B) deck, first-class tea-lounge forward; 2 state rooms amidships, 10 cabins amidships (30 berths approx). Main (C) deck, first-class smokeroom/bar forward; first-class general lounge amidships; first-class ladies' room amidships; first-class restaurant aft. Lower (D) deck first-class saloon forward; second-class restaurant aft; second-class lounges aft; second-class bar aft. (E) deck, first-class ladies' saloon forward; second-class ladies' saloon aft.

Invicta leaving Dover 16 July 1966

TSS DINARD

BUILT	1924 by Wm. Denny & Bros Ltd, Dumbarton
GROSS TONS	1,769
DIMENSIONS	325 ft x 43 ft 9 in x 12 ft 6 in
MACHINERY	4 turbines by Denny, SR geared
	Oil-fired boilers
SPEED	19½ knots
ROUTE	Dover-Boulogne

Launched on 9 May 1924, *Dinard* took up the Southampton–St Malo service the same year. She had an original gross tonnage of 2,294 and had accommodation for 1,300 passengers with berths for 354. She was, in fact, a conventional passenger ship. Little of spectacular interest marked her career until she was called up for active service in the war as a hospital ship. She went to Dunkirk in this capacity on several occasions and on 29 May 1940, when she had 271 stretcher cases on board, she was heavily attacked by torpedo and machine-gun fire, but she escaped unharmed. She subsequently appeared at Scapa, then in the Mediterranean during the invasion of Sicily, returning to Europe for D Day operations. In May 1945 she was refitted for transport duties (though she was fitted with armaments at some stage) and then operated as a troop ship and prisoner-of-war carrier between Newhaven and Dieppe and Dover and Calais.

In the autumn of 1946 she was sent to Palmers of Hebburn-on-Tyne for conversion to enable her to act as a car ferry carrying numerous cars.

At Palmers a tremendous amount of work was done on her, and it is worth recording it in some detail because this was the first major alteration of its kind ever done in this country. Before any changes could be started, all wartime remnants such as admiralty stores, armaments and fittings and de-gaussing equipment had to be removed, and repairs to the hull had to be carried out because mine damage had caused it to be slightly hogged and twisted.

Dinard on trials after conversion 25 June 1947

Alterations
New steering gear forward and aft
Bow rudder fitted
New teak wheelhouse fitted and, attached thereto, a new steel deck-house

Foremast shortened and moved about 30 ft towards the stern

Boat deck abreast smokeroom plated in and sliding windows fitted

Existing dining room converted to new smokeroom and bar

Two de-luxe cabins fitted in after end of forward deckhouse on boat deck

Deckhouse between funnels removed

New funnels fitted

Main mast shortened and refitted

Boat deck extended aft and steel underside fitted

New dining saloon (100 seats) installed on promenade deck

Reception area, lounge and lavatories installed abaft dining saloon

Deck in all car spaces refitted with bare steel

Space cleared abaft reception area for twenty-two cars

Poop deckhouse removed and steel deck installed joining promenade deck with poop deck

Opening cut in promenade deck at stern to allow loading of cars

Main deck abaft bow steering gear completely stripped for carriage of cars.

A 16 ft turntable fitted at forward end

A recent photograph of *Viking* (ex-*Dinard*) showing that the front of the boat deck has been enclosed

61

Dinard showing how the promenade deck was cut away at the stern

She emerged from this treatment in June 1947, with a reduced gross tonnage of 1,769, accommodation for 361 passengers and 70 cars, and, above all, a completely new look. She ran trials on 25 June and arrived in Dover the day after. Amid celebrations, she opened the Dover–Boulogne lift-on car-ferry service on 1 July. Subsequently she also served on occasion between Folkestone and Boulogne but was at Silley Cox yard at Falmouth during February and March 1952 to have hinged stern doors inserted in the stern plating at the after end of the main deck to enable cars to be driven on over the stern. On 30 June 1953 she inaugurated the through drive-on service between Dover and Boulogne and thereafter remained on that route, with odd breaks for overhauls, etc until being withdrawn in October 1958 and put on the sale list.

Early in 1959 she was bought by Rederi A/B Vikinlinjen, Finland, renamed *Viking,* and sent to the Danish firm of Aalborg Vaerft where her car capacity was increased slightly and she was otherwise modified for new services in the Baltic. Since then she has been in regular, though usually seasonal, service between ports in Finland, Sweden and Mariehamn in the Aland Islands. She did not alter structurally again until about the end of 1965 when the forward end of the boat deck was plated over. About the same time she was sold to Rederi A/B Solstad, Finland.

TSS MAID OF ORLEANS

BUILT	1949 by Wm. Denny & Bros Ltd, Dumbarton
GROSS TONS	3,777
DIMENSIONS	341 ft 6 in x 52 ft 3 in x 12 ft 5½ in
MACHINERY	4 turbines by Denny, SR geared
	Oil-fired boilers
SPEED	22 knots
ROUTE	Folkestone-Boulogne/Calais

Ordered by the SR to replace *Biarritz, Maid of Orleans* was launched on 17 September 1948 and made her maiden voyage from Folkestone to Boulogne on 23 June 1949. She was the first Straits vessel built with stabilisers, following the success of these on the Southampton ship *Falaise.* She also has a bow rudder. When new she was fitted with a conventional funnel, but during a refit at Southampton in the winter of 1958-9 it was altered to its present shape in an effort to keep exhaust clear of the first-class restaurant. Towards the end of 1962 a further refit was carried out and second-class accommodation was improved by the provision of additional seating and enlarged buffet services. At Immingham yet more seating was fitted in March 1966.

Accommodation: Boat A deck, first-class lounge forward; two state-rooms forward. Upper B deck, first-class smokeroom forward; entrance hall amidships; restaurant aft. Main C deck, sixteen 2-berth cabins (eight each side, formerly twelve each side) forward; second-class ladies' saloon (nine settees) aft; second-class gent's saloon (ten settees) aft; second-class lounge/bar aft; second-class smokeroom/buffet aft. Lower D deck, first-class ladies' saloon (eight settees) forward; first-class gent's saloon (eight settees) forward.

During the 1962 and 1966 refits it was on C Deck aft that most of the alterations were made. She carries some 1,400 passengers, and 30 cars (winter only) crane-loaded into the aft hold.

In late autumn and winter each year she relieves in turn *Côte d'Azur* on the Folkestone–Calais run, and *Invicta* on the Dover–Calais run. In October 1965 it was announced that she was to be converted to a side-loading car ferry for the Fishguard station, but within a month these plans were cancelled.

Maid of Orleans arriving at Folkestone 21 September 1965

TSS LORD WARDEN

BUILT	1952 by Wm. Denny & Bros Ltd, Dumbarton
GROSS TONS	3,333
DIMENSIONS	362 ft 1 in x 60 ft 8 in x 12 ft 11 in
MACHINERY	2 turbines by Denny, DR geared
	Oil-fired boilers
SPEED	20 knots
ROUTE	Dover-Boulogne

Launched on 14 December 1951, *Lord Warden* is the first drive-on drive-off car ferry built for the BTC and she entered service on the Dover–Boulogne route on 17 June 1952. Like *Maid of Orleans* she originally had a conventional funnel, but had the 'fireman's helmet' fitted at Southampton early in 1957. Although designed with stabilisers, those made for her were actually put into the Royal Yacht *Britannia* and she did not get hers until a year later. She can carry 700 one-class passengers and 120 cars. As her car deck at the stern has no cover she is able to carry high loads such as double-decker buses when required. She has rarely served elsewhere, but on 29 July 1963 she took over the BR Folkestone to Boulogne excursion for the damaged *Isle of Thanet*. At Dover, in early October 1964 she became the first Straits ship to receive the new BR livery. She was, in a sense, the guinea pig for the new livery, for when she was first done the authorities from London were invited to view her. They made no changes save that the black top section of the funnel had to be made deeper.

On the boat deck her accommodation consists of a smokeroom forward. On the promenade deck she has a buffet and extensive lounge seating forward and a restaurant aft. Amidships on this deck are seven outside two-berth passenger cabins with private facilities, four on the port side,

Lord Warden arriving at Dover 22 July 1966

three on the starboard side. In the centre part of the 'midships section are a ladies' room and passport and ticket office, etc.

On the main (car) deck there is a 16 ft-diameter turntable at the forward end and, further aft, are four fireproof curtains.

Early in 1967 her restaurant was converted to a self-service cafeteria.

TSS MAID OF KENT

BUILT	1959 by Wm. Denny & Bros Ltd, Dumbarton
GROSS TONS	3,920
DIMENSIONS	373 ft x 60 ft 3 in x 13 ft
MACHINERY	2 turbines by Denny, DR geared
	Oil-fired boilers
SPEED	20 knots
ROUTE	Dover-Boulogne

A drive-on, drive-off stern-loading vehicle ferry, *Maid of Kent* is a splendid ship and probably the best looking of all railway-owned ships of this type. Launched on 27 November 1958, she was heralded as 'The Pocket Liner', and when she entered service on 28 May 1959 she fully merited this compliment. Basically, she consists of two continuous decks, main and upper, with mezzanine between the two, and boat and bridge deck. 190 cars can be stowed on the main and mezzanine decks, the latter being reached by ramps from the main deck. The turntable aft is power-

Maid of Kent arriving at Dover 22 July 1966

66

operated. For passengers' comfort there is a smokeroom/bar forward on the boat deck (126 seats), self-service cafeteria and lounge below it (184 seats), restaurant aft on the upper deck (168 seats) and a ladies' room. The self-service cafeteria was the first to be built into a new Southern Region ship. She can carry 1,000 one-class passengers. Her restaurant was converted to a self-service cafeteria in 1966.

Navigational aids include radar, direction finder and radio-telephone, while other features are lateral bow-thrust unit, bow rudder, Denny-Brown stabilisers, fibre-glass lifeboats and twenty-six inflatable life-rafts. She is the only Dover or Folkestone vessel registered in Dover, all the rest being registered in London except for *Normannia* which is registered at Southampton. Closed circuit television was installed in 1966. She has never served on any other route to date.

Normannia leaving Dover 22 May 1965

TSS NORMANNIA

BUILT	1952 by Wm. Denny & Bros Ltd, Dumbarton
GROSS TONS	2,217
DIMENSIONS	309 ft 2 in x 49 ft 8 in x 12 ft 6½ in
MACHINERY	2 turbines by Denny, DR geared
	Oil-fired boilers
SPEED	19 knots
ROUTE	Southampton-Le Havre (to 1963)
	Dover-Boulogne (from 1964)

Normannia, ordered by the BTC for the Southampton station was a close copy of *Falaise,* and was delivered in January 1952 to replace the old *Hantonia* on the Le Havre service. This was an all-year-round service, and she was relieved during her winter overhaul by *Falaise*. In her Le Havre days she carried some 1,400 passengers in two classes and 12 cars, the latter crane-loaded. Her first-class berth accommodation consisted of two-berth cabins-de-luxe, one- two- and three-berth cabins and berths in the ladies' rooms. Her second-class accommodation was one- and two-berth cabins and berths in the ladies' and gent's lounges. During these years she also appeared occasionally at Weymouth on the Channel Islands service (eg in March 1963 while *Caesarea* had a new compass fitted). In spring 1951 she took two weekend cruises to Amsterdam and Ostend from Folkestone.

She made her final sailing from Le Havre on 3 December 1963, and, being replaced by *St Patrick,* she set off for Hawthorn Leslie Ltd, Hebburn-on-Tyne, to be converted to a stern-loading drive-on car ferry. Cabins and public rooms were removed from the main and upper decks to provide room for 111 cars (68 on the main deck, 43 on the upper deck, reached by hydraulically operated folding ramp). The promenade deck was stripped except for the smokeroom which was enlarged to seat 86 passengers. A passport office, self-service cafeteria (114 seats), lounge buffet (112 seats), ticket office and *bureau-de change* were installed. She now takes 500 passengers. At the forward end of each car deck a hand-operated 16 ft turntable was fitted. The stern door, hydraulically operated, is 17 ft wide. Gross tonnage was reduced from 3,543 to 2,217 but her dimensions remained the same.

Normannia as a conventional passenger ship in Southampton

She emerged from this marathon refit on 1 April 1964 and made her first public sailing from Dover to Boulogne on 21 April. Since then she has also appeared on the Newhaven–Dieppe service on several occasions and on 9 July she inaugurated the Holyhead–Dun Laoghaire service because the new ship *Holyhead Ferry I* was not ready in time. She continued on this run until *Holyhead Ferry I* entered service on the morning of 19 July and she was sent back to Dover that same evening. She is fitted with stabilisers and closed circuit television, and is altogether a more attractive ship than *Falaise*. In spring 1967 her restaurant was converted to a self-service buffet.

TSS ST PATRICK

BUILT	1948 by Cammell Laird & Co Ltd, Birkenhead
GROSS TONS	3,482
DIMENSIONS	321 ft 4 in x 50 ft 5 in x 13 ft 3 in
MACHINERY	4 turbines by Cammell Laird, SR geared
	Oil-fired boilers
SPEED	20 knots
ROUTE	Weymouth-Channel Islands (1948-63)
	Southampton/Weymouth-Le Havre/St Malo (1963-4)
	Folkestone-Boulogne/Calais (from 1965)

Launched on 20 May 1947, *St Patrick* ran trials on 23 January 1948 and took up service on the Channel Islands route as 'third ship', for relief and extra sailings, in February. She was owned by the Fishguard & Rosslare Railways & Harbours Co, being technically chartered to BR for the Channel Islands service until being transferred to Southern Region proper in 1959. In 1950 and 1951 she served for a short time between Holyhead and Dun Laoghaire.

A sister to *St David,* she had similar accommodation for two classes until she was given an extensive refit at Mountstuart Dry Dock, near Cardiff, to improve her amenities and to enable her to take her place alongside the new ships on the Weymouth station. She was nearly four months at Mountstuart from December 1960, and alterations included the removal of much of the original sleeping accommodation, modernising all rooms to enable her to be used as a one-class-only ship, and the fitting up of new cabins (including two-berth cabins-de-luxe), berths in ladies' and gent's saloons and reclining seats in the shelterdeck lounge.

She retained the GWR coat of arms (removed only recently), on her bow, and her tonnage increased from 3,352 to 3,482. A plan to fit stabilisers fell through, apparently because of lack of space.

During her years at Weymouth she ran several day-trips each season from Weymouth and Torquay to Guernsey, and from the Channel Islands to St Malo, *inter alia*; but 1963 was her last full season there.

She was required at Southampton following the withdrawal of *Falaise* and *Normannia* and made her last regular crossings to the Channel Islands on 10 October 1963.

Immediately afterwards she was given a quick overhaul at Southampton and on 4 December replaced *Normannia* on the Le Havre service, which she officially closed on 10 May 1964. On the following day she opened the seasonal St Malo service replacing *Falaise*. During the ensuing summer she varied the service a bit, usually making two runs per week from Southampton and one from Weymouth. She finally closed the St Malo–Weymouth link on 23 September and the St Malo–Southampton link on 27 September. Neither has been revived.

Early the following month, at Newhaven, she was the first Southern Region ship to be given the new livery *in toto*. In December she took up sailings between Dover and Calais, at first supplementary to the

St Patrick on passage Boulogne–Folkestone 19 May 1965

'Golden Arrow'. Not long afterwards she was put on the Folkestone–Calais route and at the beginning of the 1965 season she was switched to the Folkestone–Boulogne service. By now she had reverted to the two-class accommodation system, though it was hardly worth while. First-class passengers have for their sole use only a bar/lounge, rest room and some cabins, while second-class passengers are free to use the rest of the ship, including all available deck space. There are eight berths for first-class passengers.

In spite of her frequent changes of duty she has been singularly free from accidents. The worst known so far happened on 1 February 1964 when she damaged her bows against the dock wall at Southampton, inward bound from Le Havre. Repairs at Mountstuart took six weeks and she was replaced by *Winchester* (twelve passengers) on a reduced frequency. She ran between Weymouth and the Channel Islands at the end of August 1968 vice the damaged *Caesarea*. Her place at Folkestone was taken by the Dover car-ferry *Lord Warden* ; an unusual move.

TSS DOVER

BUILT	1965 by Swan Hunter & Wigham Richardson Ltd, Tyneside
GROSS TONS	3,602
DIMENSIONS	369 ft x 57 ft 2 in x 12 ft 9 in
MACHINERY	Two sets Pametrada turbines by Wallsend Slipway and Engineering Co Ltd
	Oil-fired boilers
SPEED	20 knots
ROUTE	Dover-Boulogne

Dover, the most recent addition to the Dover–Boulogne drive-on car ferry fleet owned by the Southern Region, was launched on 17 March 1965. She may well be the last in view of the decision to build a channel tunnel. Her name was the result of a nationwide competition among members of the public, won by a Dover man. She made her press voyage from Dover in thick fog on 13 June 1965, and on arrival at Boulogne formally opened the new terminal there. On 17 and 18 June she was 'on show' to the public in the Pool of London, being the first BR cross-channel ship to appear there. She entered service proper on 24 June, but had been in service only four days when her troubles started, culminating in shortage of power, decreasing speed and intense vibration. The faults were rectified and she took up service again on 5 July, since when she has missed few sailings, though she has had her share of close contact with quay walls.

205 cars can be carried on two decks, main and mezzanine, and to assist handling there is a turntable at the forward end of the main deck. The usual practice is for cars to drive on the stern at the port side, move

Dover leaving Dover for refit on the Tyne 24 April 1966

71

forward up this side, round the front of the deck, and back along the starboard side so that they are ready for immediate disembarkation. Clearly *Dover* was BR's answer to the drive-through ships operated by competitors. 850 one-class passengers are provided for, the principal facilities consisting of two restaurants (self-service and waiter-service), lounge-tea bar (196 seats) and veranda bar aft on the boat deck, a novelty on BR ships. On occasion she carries up to 1,000 passengers. Her restaurant was made self-service in spring 1967. She is fitted with fin stabilisers, bow rudder, twin stern rudders and bow transverse propulsion unit. So far she has not served any other route except that early in 1967 and again in 1968 she sailed for a short time between Newhaven and Dieppe. On 9 February 1967, she carried out ramp tests at the Central Electricity Generating Board ramp at Folkestone, but results were inconclusive because the state of the tide caused her car deck to be some 4 ft below the top of the quay.

---

4 : NEWHAVEN

The Newhaven–Dieppe cross-channel service is the only one truly jointly owned and operated. This dates from 1867, when the necessary agreement was drawn up between the Western Railway of France and the London Brighton & South Coast Railway Co, the former having the larger interest. Today the co-operators are SNCF and the BRB. This crossing is geographically the most direct between London and Paris, but, although popular, never really attained the importance attached to the Dover–Calais passenger service. Because of the long sea passage and the need to attract trade from other routes, the Dieppe ships have, until recently, usually been very fast with speeds in excess of 25 knots being frequently maintained.

Although all cargo ships on the Dieppe service have been French built and operated, it used to be the practice for the French and British railways to operate the same number of ships each for passenger traffic. In 1939 there were three French passenger ships *Newhaven* (1911), *Rouen* (1912) and *Versailles* (1921), and three British ships *Paris* (1913), *Worthing* (1928) and *Brighton* (1933). There were also three cargo ships, *Bordeaux* (1912), *Rennes* (1925) and *Brest* (1900). In 1939 the French authorities placed orders for two passenger ships and two cargo ships designed to replace their existing fleet in its entirety. The war which interfered with this building programme also caused a number of losses. *Brest, Rennes, Paris* and *Brighton* were sunk. Replacements were on order for the three French passenger ships, which all survived, therefore they were not renovated for service after the war. Thus there remained only *Bordeaux* and *Worthing* to take up the peacetime cargo and passenger services respectively.

The majority of channel ports had been severely damaged and rendered almost useless by the bitter last-minute fighting of the Germans, but not so Dieppe. For some reason it was not so heavily defended as the others and was captured almost intact by Canadian forces in September 1944. Thus it was in early use by forces supply ships, which switched to more central ports like Calais and Dunkirk when these had been cleared. Dieppe was therefore the first channel port on the French side to reopen for civilian passenger services, which, as before, were operated from Newhaven. As *Worthing* was the only survivor it was necessary to borrow tonnage from other sources, and it fell to *Isle of Guernsey* to open the service. She served for a few months, then others, notably *Isle of Thanet* and *Dinard,* helped out for a time. In April 1947, *Londres,* the first of the pair of French twin-screw turbine steamers ordered in 1939, entered service, followed a few months later by her near sister *Arromanches.* Both ships were built at Le Havre, and known as *Dieppe* and *Newhaven* respectively when building started. Late in 1940 the names were altered to *Londres* and *Vichy,* the latter being eventually launched as *Arromanches* in March 1946. Their gross tonnages were 2,434 and 2,600 respectively.

Although the service was operated all the year round as before, it was agreed that each partner would need only two ships. As the French now had two new vessels, and the Southern Region only one old one, *Worthing,* the latter ordered a new fast ship in 1947. *Brighton* took up the run in 1950 and the balance of the fleets was thus restored. By now the service was running normally, there being both day and night sailings in each direction all the year round, though in winter some sailings were curtailed. In 1953 the SNCF brought out another new twin-screw turbine steamer named *Lisieux.* She also came from Le Havre and had a gross tonnage of 2,943. *Worthing* was subsequently withdrawn in 1954 and *Londres* thereupon transferred to the British flag. Again there were two British ships (*Brighton* and *Londres*) and two French ships (*Lisieux* and *Arromanches*), maintaining the service.

In the meantime *Bordeaux* carried on the cargo run alone until the new TSMV *Nantes,* ordered in 1939, appeared in 1946. Two years later her sister *Rennes* entered service and *Bordeaux* was no longer required. The new ships with a gross tonnage of just over 1,000 were built by Forges et Chantiers de la Méditerranée, Penhoct. In 1950 a third similar ship named *Brest,* appeared. The speed of this trio was about 14 knots. Besides cargo they could carry up to sixty average-sized cars, and it became the practice for them to carry the vehicles of passengers who intended to travel by passenger ship, leaving port first so that their arrival at the destination more or less coincided with the arrival of the passenger ship. When these ships were in service there was at least one sailing per day (except Sunday) in each direction, frequently more.

In common with other services on which only conventional passenger ships served, patronage dropped during the 1950s on the Dieppe run, and it was decided that the winter service should be withdrawn after

October 1958. The summer (March to October) service in ensuing years was reasonably well patronised while the cheap-day no-passport excursions, usually operated by *Brighton,* were particularly successful. However, there seemed a very real danger of services from Newhaven being terminated altogether, until it was announced that BR was considering, in June 1963, modifying the quay installations to take vehicular ferries and converting two passenger ships to stern loading. MOT permission to spend the necessary £800,000 was finally obtained in September 1963.

In October 1963 work began on building a ramp and other facilities for the new Dieppe drive-on service, and in January 1964 *Falaise* (from Southampton) went to the Tyne for the necessary conversion. This ship officially inaugurated the new service on 1 June 1964. To make way for her under the British flag, *Londres* was withdrawn near the end of 1963 and subsequently sold for further service in the Mediterranean. In the meantime two new ships designed specially for this service were ordered from French yards. TSMV *Villandry* was launched at Nantes (Dubigeon–Normandie yard) on 20 November 1964, and TSMV *Valencay* was launched at St Nazaire (Chantiers de l'Atlantique) on 6 February 1965. Very similar in appearance and general layout, they can carry up to 150 cars on two decks and 1,200 passengers, have a speed of about 21 knots and a gross tonnage of 3,445 and 3,477 respectively. Machinery in each ship consists of two Pielstick diesels. These two ships and *Falaise* were intended to replace the cargo ships and passenger ships then operating, with small cargo being loaded aboard on 1 ton four-wheeled trolleys known as 'brutes' (British Railways Universal Trolleys) and larger loads and containers on 10 ton capacity pallets handled by special pallet trucks.

In anticipation of the appearance of the new car ferries in 1965, *Arromanches* was withdrawn after the summer of 1964, laid up and offered for sale. Bought in February 1965 by Petros Nomikos Ltd for service in Greek and neighbouring waters for about £122,500, she was partially repainted white at Dieppe, renamed *Leto* and left for Piraeus the following month. On arrival there she underwent some alterations and modifications, notably the installation of air-conditioning, the refitting and rebuilding of accommodation and the addition of extra life-saving equipment. In April 1965 she took up a regular service between Piraeus, Tinos and Mykonos, with accommodation for 1,500 passengers in two classes and was one of the very few Greek two-class ships. She finished on this run at the end of October 1965 and in 1966, 1967 and 1968 operated a daily service on similar short routes. Her berth accommodation for first-class passengers consists of 36 in cabins and 100 in dormitories with about 150 in dormitories in the second-class accommodation.

The first of the new French-built vessels, *Villandry,* entered commercial service on 30 May 1965, followed by *Valencay* early in July, though both had already undertaken press trips and ramp tests. Until *Valencay* appeared the cargo ships had continued in service, but after 8 July *Nantes* and *Rennes* were withdrawn, both being offered for sale. They

74

were sold in March 1966 to Lebanese buyers for local cargo work, being named *Lassi II* and *Lassi III* respectively. *Brest* continued to serve three times a week in each direction (from Newhaven on Tuesdays, Thursdays and Saturdays) and was threatened with withdrawal on several occasions until making her final crossing in July 1966, being then laid up pending disposal. She has since served on other cargo routes (eg Folkestone to Boulogne) and early in 1967 was laid up in Dieppe, being sold later in the year to Messrs O. J. Metaxas and renamed *Lassi IV,* joining her sisters under the Lebanese flag. *Lassi IV* has subsequently been resold to Samir Soc. Nav. S.A. (Panama) and renamed *Samir.*

During the first part of the 1965 season *Lisieux* and *Brighton,* the only conventional passenger ships left, were engaged mainly in normal service and in daylight excursions or special sailings respectively, but by June so few passengers were being carried that *Lisieux* was withdrawn, making her last sailing from Newhaven on 26 June. At the end of June the passenger and car-ferry services were combined, though *Brighton* continued to operate on excursions. *Lisieux* was subsequently chartered to the French Line (Compagnie Générale Transatlantique) for channel and local excursions, an unusual and interesting departure from their normal practice. During the ensuing months *Lisieux* was engaged on four main routes:

Torquay–Guernsey (Wednesday ; day excursions) 14 July–29 September.
Weymouth–Guernsey (Friday ; day excursions) 13 August–1 October.
St Malo–Jersey (Monday, Tuesday, Thursday, Saturday, Sunday) 10 July–2 October.
St Malo–Weymouth (from St Malo Thursday ; from Weymouth Friday night) 12 August to 2 October.

At the close of this season of interesting and successful excursions, *Lisieux* was laid up and later offered for sale. In February 1966 she was sold to Greek buyers for about £240,000 and refitted at Le Havre before setting out for Piraeus in April under the name *Apollon.* In the following month she took up her new duties on the Piraeus–Cylra–Paros route owned by Nomikos Lines. Both *Apollon* and *Leto* are still in service for Nomikos Ltd.

With *Lisieux* gone only *Brighton* remained to cater for excursionists. She was fast and popular and on several occasions during 1965 and 1966 carried well over 1,000 passengers. However in August 1966 it was made known that she was to be withdrawn at the end of the season. She made her last trip on 18 September, was laid up and put on the sale list. Here was a ship with good accommodation and only sixteen years old just waiting to be snapped up, and it must have come as a great relief to many people to learn that she was not to 'go Greek' as others had done, but that, under Jersey Lines' flag, she was to make the day trips to the Channel Islands from Torquay and Weymouth *inter alia,* early in the 1967 season.

Thus there are now no conventional passenger ships nor purpose built cargo ships based at Newhaven. Passengers, cars, commercial vehicles

75

and cargo are all handled by the vehicle ferries *Falaise, Villandry* and *Valencay*. Of these only *Falaise* flies the British flag, so that it would seem necessary to redress the balance by BR diverting a ship from elsewhere to serve Newhaven. *Normannia* has served the route in a reserve capacity on a number of occasions so it is possible that she could be used. At the end of April 1966 plans to operate a service, mainly for commercial vehicles, between Newhaven and Le Havre, were being discussed, but nothing has yet materialised.

One further point remains to be mentioned. In time for the 1965 season the majority of ships owned and operated by BR had been given the new livery of blue hull, and red funnel with a black top and white motif. This did not apply to ships based at Newhaven. SNCF would not accept the new colours entirely but ultimately agreed to compromise. Thus *Falaise* and *Brighton* eventually appeared in blue hulls and red funnels without the white motif. All three appeared early in 1968 with a replica of the 'joint service' flag on their funnels.

TSS WORTHING

BUILT	1928 by Wm. Denny & Bros Ltd, Dumbarton
GROSS TONS	2,343
DIMENSIONS	306 ft x 41 ft 6 in x 10 ft 7 in
MACHINERY	6 turbines by Denny, SR geared
	Oil-fired boilers
SPEED	24 knots
ROUTE	Newhaven-Dieppe

Launched on 3 May 1928, *Worthing* was fitted out as a day and night boat and so had to have a careful balance between berth and public room accommodation. She could carry 1,122 passengers. Her maiden voyage took place from Newhaven on 5 September 1928. There were some private cabins and a lounge on the promenade deck, below which was the dining saloon forward and more cabins aft. An interesting feature was the wearing, even up to the war, of the London, Brighton & South Coast Railway house flag although she had been owned throughout by the SR.

She appeared at the Dunkirk evacuation on three occasions in May and June 1940 as a hospital carrier, and survived several attacks by enemy aircraft. In 1941 she changed her role for that of a Fleet Air Arm target ship and in 1942 she was fitted out as a landing ship, infantry (hand hoist) with six landing craft, assault, carried under davits over the side of the ship. With a pennant number 4.249, she carried 180 men and for defence had one 12-pounder and four 20 mm AA guns. As such she formed part of the Assault Group J2 based on Southampton.

After the war she returned to the Newhaven station, and re-entered the

Worthing on 11 November 1949

Dieppe service on 24th March 1945. At the end of the 1954 season she was withdrawn and sold early in 1955 to J. S. Latsis' concern in Greece for pilgrim carrying and for cruise work in the Mediterranean and was given the name *Phryni*. She was replaced in the British Transport Commission share of the Newhaven–Dieppe fleet by TSS *Londres* taken over from the SNCF. Her survey became overdue in June 1960, and she was apparently broken up at about that time.

Phryni (ex-*Worthing*) showing that she was not much altered for her work in the Mediterranean

77

Londres at Newhaven 6 June 1963

TSS LONDRES

BUILT	1943 by Forges et Chantiers de la Méditerranée, Le Havre
GROSS TONS	2,444
DIMENSIONS	308 ft 5 in x 42 ft 4 in x 10 ft 9 in
MACHINERY	6 turbines by Forges et Chantiers de la Méditerranée, SR geared
	Oil-fired boilers
SPEED	24 knots
ROUTE	Newhaven-Dieppe

Known as *Dieppe* before being launched, this steamer was, at first, jointly owned by the SR and the Chemin de Fer de l'Ouest, so was her sister-ship *Arromanches,* which also served Newhaven from 1947 to 1964.

After the surrender of France *Dieppe* was renamed *Londres* and had already been launched when the Germans took over. She was used by the latter as a minesweeper, again being renamed, this time *Lothringen*.

The war over, she was found at Kiel, and, having returned to her builders for renovation, she at last entered the civilian service for which she was intended on 18 April 1947. She continued to be jointly owned until 1955, but in that year the BTC took her over outright and operated her as a replacement in the fleet for its own *Worthing,* withdrawn the previous autumn. She could carry some 1,450 passengers. In anticipation of the appearance of the converted *Falaise* on this route in the summer of 1964, *Londres* was withdrawn at the end of the 1963 season and bought the following December by Typaldos Bros Ltd, of Piraeus, Greece, and renamed *Ionion II* for her journey to Piraeus. She was subsequently renamed *Sofoklis Venizelos*.

With Typaldos Bros Ltd she generally operated 'domestic' sailings of only one or two days' duration from Piraeus to places like Crete.

On 14 April 1966, when she was undergoing a refit in Piraeus, she caught
fire and was beached outside the harbour on the following day.
Subsequently she was written off, and has not sailed since.

Sofoklis Venizelos (ex-*Londres*) showing that some changes were
made in her appearance, particularly at the bows

TSS BRIGHTON

BUILT	1950 by Wm. Denny & Bros Ltd, Dumbarton
GROSS TONS	2,875
DIMENSIONS	311 ft 9 in x 43 ft 5 in x 11 ft 1¾ in
MACHINERY	2 steam turbines by Denny, SR geared
	Oil-fired boilers
SPEED	24 knots
ROUTE	Newhaven-Dieppe

Athough ordered by the SR in October 1947, *Brighton* was a long time
at the builders and was not delivered until April 1950. She carried 1,450
passengers in two classes; sleeping accommodation consisting of two-
berth cabins-de-luxe, two-berth ordinary cabins, and open berths in the
ladies' and gent's saloons. She was credited with being the fastest BR
ship on the South Coast, covering the sixty-four mile crossing with
ease in 3½ hours.

Until Newhaven became a terminal for drive-on drive-off car ferry
sailings in June 1964, *Brighton* was the pride of the Newhaven fleet, but
from then on she was relegated to carrying out no-passport and special
excursions. At this she was successful, and after *Lisieux* (French) was
withdrawn on 26 June 1965 coped with this traffic on her own, the other
French vessel *Arromanches* having been withdrawn in late 1964. She

79

Brighton at Newhaven 10 October 1965

has rarely served on any other route, but as recently as 26 July 1966 she sailed from Folkestone to Boulogne with a party of Lourdes Pilgrims aboard, sailing light from and to Dieppe. By August 1966 it was understood that she would be withdrawn and offered for sale after her excursion of 18 September 1966.

Early in December 1966 Jersey Lines Ltd announced that they had

La Duchesse de Bretagne (ex-*Brighton*) leaving Weymouth for Guernsey in July 1967

bought the ship, and that she would be used during the 1967 season for excursions to the Channel Islands and St Malo from South Coast resorts like Weymouth and Torquay. For this trade she was renamed *La Duchesse de Bretagne*. She left Newhaven on 25 January 1967 for refitting at Antwerp, new features including a Watney 'Olde English' lounge-bar, reclining seats, and drive-on ramps at both sides near the stern. She left Antwerp on 30 April for berthing trials at various ports. She entered service for her new owners from Torquay on 15 May 1967. In 1968 she ran cross-channel excursions from Southampton, Torquay and Plymouth. Her new colours are, dark blue hull, white superstructure and wine-red under black top on the funnel.

TSS FALAISE

BUILT	1947 by Wm. Denny & Bros Ltd, Dumbarton
GROSS TONS	2,416
DIMENSIONS	310 ft 6 in x 49 ft 8 in x 12 ft 6 in
MACHINERY	4 turbines by Denny, SR geared
	Oil-fired boilers
SPEED	20 knots
ROUTE	Southampton-St Malo (to 1963)
	Newhaven-Dieppe (from 1964)

Launched on 25 October 1946 *Falaise* was designed for the SR passenger services from Southampton, but has from time to time served on all routes now operated by the Southern Region with the exception of Folkestone–Boulogne and Weymouth–Channel Islands. She has even appeared at Folkestone on her cruise schedules.

She was originally a conventional passenger steamer and could carry 1,527 passengers (in two classes) and up to thirty-one cars, the latter being loaded into the hold forward by dockside crane. Sleeping accommodation consisted of two cabins-de-luxe, one- two- and three-berth cabins and open berths in the ladies' room for first-class passengers, while for the second-class passengers there were one- and two-berth cabins and open berths in the ladies' and gent's lounges. She is equipped with radar, Denny-Brown stabilisers and radio telephone facilities.

Most of her time up to and including 1963 was spent on the St Malo run in summer and on the Le Havre run for part of the winter, relieving the *Normannia*. In 1947 and 1948 she ran on the Dover–Calais 'Golden Arrow' service for a few weeks in summer. Her cruises, operated each year from 1948 to 1963 during May and early June (before the St Malo run started), were particularly successful and she carried only 216 one-class passengers to give greater comfort. These cruises usually operated

F

Falaise leaving Newhaven 18 July 1965. Note 'Joint Service Flag'

at weekends. They generally started from Southampton and took her to
places like St Malo, Jersey, Le Havre and Rouen. She could fit in up to
seven such cruises each year, the last one she made being from 7 to 10
June 1963 to Rouen and incorporating a day trip to Paris by train. Her
Benelux cruises, organised to coincide with the bulb season, were run
from Folkestone, the first from 5 May, the second from 12 May 1961.

She was withdrawn from the St Malo service at the end of the 1963
season, made the final crossing from St Malo on the weekend of 6
October 1963 and was sent to Palmers Hebburn-on-Tyne yard of Vickers

Falaise before conversion, passing Calshot

Armstrong (Shipbuilders) Ltd, arriving there on 6 January 1964 for conversion to a stern-loading drive-on car ferry. Considerable alterations were carried out to the passenger accommodation and stern doors and hydraulically operated hinged ramp were fitted. The job took several months and she emerged very much lacking her former grace. Her main car deck holds 75 cars (coaches and commercial vehicles can also be carried), and a folding ramp leads to the upper car deck holding 25 cars. Also on this deck is the lounge-tea bar with seating for 137 passengers. The smokeroom-lounge, redecorated and seating 100, is in the same place as originally, on the promenade deck. Cabin accommodation includes two-berth cabins with or without bath and reclining seats. She now carries only 700 passengers in one class.

She made her inaugural trip for the press between Newhaven and Dieppe on 31 May 1964 and next day opened the public service proper. She has continued to operate on this service, though since May and July 1965, when the two new French ships entered service, she has tended to take the less remunerative off-peak sailings. During her refit in May 1965 she was fitted with a waiter-service restaurant.

It was as a car ferry that she operated between Dover and Boulogne (replacing *Normannia*) in April 1965. She has been unfortunate in having a number of collisions with the piers at Newhaven. When this has happened her sailings have, to date, been taken by *Normannia,* or *Valencay,* or cancelled altogether. The conversion to car ferry did not affect her dimensions but reduced her gross tonnage from 3,710 to 2,416.

During her March 1967 overhaul, carried out by Smith's Dock Co Ltd, her cafeteria was reduced in size and her restaurant enlarged.

5: ISLE OF WIGHT

In 1939 there were three routes to the Isle of Wight, Portsmouth–Ryde for passengers only, Portsmouth–Fishbourne and Lymington–Yarmouth for vehicles and passengers. Cargo could be carried on all routes. Now in 1967, the same routes are in operation and handle the same traffic. In addition, of course, there are the hovercraft and hovermarine services (qv).

The Ryde passenger route in the more immediate prewar days was served by seven paddlers of which up to five were generally used on the Portsmouth station and two on the seasonal sailings from Southsea. Although most of the ships were used during the war on duties such as minesweeping and assisting at the Dunkirk evacuation, the Portsmouth route was kept open throughout, served mainly by *Shanklin, Merstone* and her sister *Portsdown*. Until 1944 the Isle of Wight was banned to all save troops and residents, so these three ships were able to handle the traffic. *Portsdown* was, in fact, mined near Southsea in September 1941 and thereafter PS *Solent* from Lymington helped out when required.

Apart from the loss of *Portsdown* and *Southsea* (also in 1941 on active service), the fleet returned to the SR intact after the war. *Ryde* came first and took up sailings early in the 1945 season. By mid-1946 the other two, *Whippingham* and *Sandown,* were back in service and in 1947 things were pretty well back to normal. The fleet, however, was two ships down on 1939 and in 1946 the SR ordered two motor ships to replace *Southsea* and *Portsdown*. The first screw ships to run regularly since the 1870s, they entered service in 1948 and were given the names *Southsea* and *Brading*. They were successful and in 1951 a third similar ship appeared named *Shanklin*. With their increased speed and higher passenger capacity they not only filled the gap left by the lost paddlers, but also caused the withdrawal of two more, *Merstone* and *Shanklin*.

By the mid-1950s the new motor ships were mainly engaged in the service runs, while *Whippingham, Sandown* and *Ryde* were giving

The paddlers *Ryde* and *Sandown* in their winter quarters at New-haven 10 October 1965

excursions from Southsea and Portsmouth and also acting as extra ships at busy weekends on the main service. As the years passed cruises became less popular and less use was made of the conventional ships as more people took their cars to the Island. Consequently the season during which the Southsea piers were used became shorter, fewer cruises were run, and fewer ships were needed, even at peak times. Efforts were made to attract more custom, eg the addition of a late-night sailing from Portsmouth on certain days from 16 January 1961. But the situation continued to deteriorate with the result that the largest and most uneconomical of the paddlers, *Whippingham,* was withdrawn in September 1962.

In 1963 there were, then, three motor ships and two paddlers *Ryde* and *Sandown* in service, the last two serving only in summer on odd excursions and on extra sailings to the Island. In September 1965 *Sandown* was withdrawn, having served one season in the new BR livery. Contrary to expectations, *Ryde* appeared again in 1966 and it seems that BR are genuinely loath to part with her. The 1966 season was the shortest ever on the Southsea service lasting only from 26 June to 4 September, but an interesting innovation was the cruise programme which actually started earlier in June, but finished in late August. On Monday morning only, a ship left Portsmouth, called at both Southsea piers (Clarence and South Parade), crossed to Ryde and then sailed for Yarmouth giving passengers a short time ashore before returning to the piers via Southampton Water.

While the three motor ships can be expected to last some time, *Ryde,* now thirty years old, will not serve much longer.

The conventional passenger ships, diesel and paddler alike, all use the Harbour Pier at Portsmouth which is connected to the Harbour Station by sloping roadway. The drive-on car ferries serving Fishbourne use a ramp situated apart from the station at a point some distance away to the south.

The three ships in service in 1939, *Fishbourne, Wootton* and *Hilsea* all survived the war and the service continued without let or hindrance. The capacity of these ships was only about eighteen vehicles and in 1960 a pair of larger, faster ships carrying thirty-four cars each, was ordered to replace them. It was intended that they should be called *Fishbourne* and *Wootton* but in the event the names *Fishbourne* and *Camber Queen* were chosen. The former entered service in July 1961 and when the latter appeared on 29 August 1961 an hourly service from Portsmouth was introduced for the first time. The crossing time was reduced from 60 minutes to a little over 35 minutes, certainly a big improvement. This new service should in fact have begun on 3 June, but was postponed because of late delivery of ships. The older ships were subsequently withdrawn. A third ship of a similar type was ordered by BR in March 1968, for delivery in spring 1969, and she will have accommodation for 400 passengers and 48 cars. Her builders are Richards' of Lowestoft.

In the late 1930s the Lymington–Yarmouth service combined features of the other Island routes in that it operated by both types of

85

vessels, paddler and drive-on motor vessel.

A service of sorts was maintained throughout the war with two of the ships in service in 1939, namely PS *Solent* and TSMV *Lymington*. PS *Freshwater* was taken over for war service, returning in 1946. In 1948 the modern diesel-electric *Farringford* took up the run, relegated *Freshwater* to spare ship, and made *Solent* (now forty-six years old) redundant. Thus there were now two ugly drive-through vessels operating full time. In 1959 a third drive-through vessel, *Freshwater*, was introduced replacing the paddler of that name.

A Solent cruise brochure issued for 1966, advertising, among others, sailings from Portsmouth to Yarmouth, delighted enthusiasts by showing on the cover a picture of a happy couple on the car ferry *Falaise*!

PS SOLENT

BUILT	1902 by Mordey, Carney Ltd, Southampton
GROSS TONS	161
DIMENSIONS	133 ft 6 in x 20 ft 2 in x 6 ft 4 in
MACHINERY	2-cyl compound-diagonal by Mordey, Carney Ltd
	Coal-fired boilers
SPEED	11 knots
ROUTE	Lymington-Yarmouth

Although ancient by the time she came under the control of BTC Southern Region, *Solent* lacks any particularly interesting history. She was built for the Lymington station of the London & South Western Railway Company, and remained there for most of her life, serving the Isle of Wight fairly widely, though the first war put paid to her trips to Alum Bay and Totland Bay. Until the appearance of *Lymington* in 1938 there was no drive-on ferry serving this route and it was the practice to tow barges, on which vehicles could be carried, behind the service paddler. *Solent* was the last ship to operate this system, and when *Lymington* entered service, the former went into reserve. *Solent* could tow up to four barges.

When war broke out she re-entered regular service and also ran occasionally between Portsmouth and Ryde, notably during November 1944.

The war over she reappeared occasionally, but was rendered completely redundant when the new *Farringford* entered service early in 1948. The rest of the year she spent laid up until being sold in September to H. G. Pounds of Portsmouth for breaking up, being towed there in the same month. She was not broken up completely, but most of her superstructure was stripped and soon after she was beached near Portchester, at the north-east corner of Portsmouth Harbour, where she was converted for use as a café beside the main road.

In postwar years she could carry a maximum of 398 passengers and she made her last regular sailings in 1947, thereby never sailing under the BTC flag.

Bert's Cafe (ex-*Solent*) near Portchester October 1958

PS SHANKLIN

BUILT	1924 by J. I. Thorneycroft and Co Ltd, Southampton
GROSS TONS	399
DIMENSIONS	190 ft x 26 ft 1 in x 6 ft
MACHINERY	2-cyl compound diagonal by D. & W. Henderson & Co Ltd, Glasgow
	Coal-fired boilers
SPEED	12 knots
ROUTE	Portsmouth-Ryde/excursions

Launched on 6 June 1924 for the SR *Shanklin* was similar to, but not the sister of, *Duchess of Norfolk* (1911) which operated on the same service, and was until recently, Cosens' *Embassy*. She carried some 700

87

Shanklin in postwar years

Monarch (ex-*Shanklin*) approaching Bournemouth 9 August 1960

passengers. The first-class cabin occupied most of the main deck aft, with the first-class promenade (boat) deck above it. This extended the full width of the ship as far forward as the mast. Until the war she had an open bridge. The bow rudder was worked by a hand wheel on the foredeck, which was reserved for luggage and mail bags. A prominent feature of the ship was the inner funnel casing which projected above the outer casing as is clearly seen in the illustration.

During the war, she remained on service, painted grey, having a wheelhouse strengthened by a concrete roof, erected as protection against strafing.

After the war the wheelhouse was painted white when she returned to civilian colours. By the end of the 1940s she was becoming too uneconomical and was withdrawn on 30 November 1950 and bought by Cosens & Co Ltd the following year. She was renamed *Monarch* and was used for summer excursion work. At the end of the 1960 season she was withdrawn and offered for sale, subsequently being bought by Haulbowline Industries (Cork) Ltd, for breaking up. She arrived at Cobh on 2 March 1961. She was replaced at Portsmouth by the new MV *Shanklin*.

TSMV FISHBOURNE
TSMV WOOTTON
TSMV HILSEA

BUILT	1927/1928/1930 by Wm. Denny & Bros Ltd, Dumbarton
GROSS TONS	136/149/149
DIMENSIONS	118 ft x 25 ft 1 in x 4 ft 6 in
MACHINERY	2 sets Gardner 2-stroke diesels; heavy oil by L. Gardner & Sons, Manchester
SPEED	8 knots
ROUTE	Portsmouth-Fishbourne

The SR ordered these ships for the new drive-on car-ferry service to Fishbourne. Until then cars had been crane-loaded onto barges, and Ryde pier had been used. The ships could carry 100 passengers and 18 cars, and were fitted with two propellers at each end and four rudders. They appeared to be double-ended, but were not so. The first of the three, appropriately named *Fishbourne,* ran trials on 23 June 1927. *Wootton* and *Hilsea* were, in general, similar to *Fishbourne,* but made more use of electric power. *Fishbourne*'s winches, for example, were manually operated, while those on the other ships were electrically operated. This also applied to capstans and other gear. On the two later ships the public accommodation was improved (including the installation of electric heating equipment) and longer ramps were fitted.

During the war they remained on station, except for appearing at the Dunkirk evacuation, for which they were fitted with concrete 'umbrellas'.

Two replacements, larger and faster, were ordered in 1960, and in 1961 *Wootton* and *Fishbourne* had the suffix *II* added to their names to free them for their successors, though, in the event, the name *Wootton* was not revived.

Fishbourne II was replaced by her namesake on 7 July 1961 and was placed in reserve, only to be brought out again two days later when the new ship was having teething troubles. She was still not finished, for she was in service again the following September, when she ran aground at Fishbourne, causing the service to be cancelled for the rest of the day. Soon after this she was withdrawn for good, and arrived at Southampton for lay-up on 26 January 1962, being later sold for breaking up to H. G. Pounds, Portsmouth. She was however, resold to Doeksen Salvage Co, Holland for operation as a car ferry across the River Shannon (Eire) between Tarbert (Co Kerry) and Killiner (Co Clare).

Wootton II went to Southampton to lay-up on 21 September 1961. She also was bought by Pounds early in 1962, resold for breaking in Holland, and left Portsmouth on 31 May for Maasluis near Rotterdam, in tow of the tug *Hazelgarth*, arriving there three days later. *Hilsea,* sent to Southampton on 5 October 1961, also passed through Pounds' hands but, like *Fishbourne II,* was resold to Holland for conversion to an esturial car ferry. She left for Portsmouth in March 1962, leaving in the same month for Holland in tow of tug *Holland*. The Shannon car-ferry service should have started in June 1963, but so far it has not materialised.

Wootton leaving Portsmouth

Freshwater in the 1950s

PS FRESHWATER

BUILT	1927 by J. S. White & Co Ltd, Cowes
GROSS TONS	264
DIMENSIONS	158 ft 9 in x 42 ft 6 in x 5 ft 8 in
MACHINERY	2-cyl compound diagonal by J. S. White
	Coal-fired boilers
SPEED	12 knots
ROUTE	Lymington-Yarmouth

Launched in May 1927 this little ship took up the Yarmouth run, with accommodation for 500 passengers. Her layout was simple. The first-class accommodation was aft (saloon on the promenade deck, ladies' room on the lower deck); the second-class accommodation was forward (saloon-bar on the lower deck). In her early days an interesting feature was her use of a stay-sail on the mast to assist berthing at Lymington, which is a difficult operation at low water with a cross wind. During her career with the railways she led an uneventful life though she did appear at the Dunkirk evacuation in 1940.

In 1946 and 1947 she was used in summer for short periods only, and was relegated to spare boat when the new *Farringford* appeared in March 1948, though in the summer of that year she had a regular spell of about two weeks on duty when *Farringford* broke down. She remained in reserve, serving as extra boat each summer, up to 1959. On 18 September 1959 she was withdrawn and laid up at Southampton. In June the following year she was bought by Brighton & South Coast Steamers Ltd and renamed *Sussex Queen*. She was not a success and in 1961 operated in the Swanage–Bournemouth–Wight area as *Swanage Queen*. Again she failed to attract public support and was offered for sale in October 1961. She was laid up at Topsham for some time and was bought in February 1962 by a Mr S. M. Townsend who apparently intended to operate her in the Dorset area but necessary repairs proved too costly and in May she was resold to Belgian breakers, arriving at Bruges on 17 May 1962.

Swanage Queen (ex-*Freshwater*) in Swanage Bay 30 July 1961

PS MERSTONE

BUILT	1928 by Caledon Shipbuilding & Engineering Co Ltd, Dundee
GROSS TONS	342
DIMENSIONS	190 ft x 25 ft 1 in x 7 ft 2½ in
MACHINERY	2-cyl compound diagonal by A. & J. Inglis Ltd, Glasgow Coal-fired boilers
SPEED	13½ knots
ROUTE	Portsmouth-Ryde

When new, *Merstone*, built for the SR, was easily spotted by reason of her wheelhouse (earlier vessels were not blessed with this 'Captain's Home Comfort') and large deckhouse amidships. *Merstone* was launched on 26 January 1928 and ran almost entirely between Portsmouth and Ryde, apart from serving for a short time during the war as a naval personnel ferry to ships in preparation for D Day. During the war she was painted grey and had a concrete wheelhouse cover. The re-entry of the newer, larger PS *Ryde* to the run in 1945 relegated her mainly to spare duties and she was finally withdrawn when the British Transport Commission took over in 1948. She could carry a maximum of 723 passengers. She was however not sold for breaking up for some time, being scrapped at Newhaven late in 1952.

Her sister *Portsdown* had the misfortune to strike a mine off Southsea on the early morning mail sailing to the Isle of Wight on 20 September 1941 and she subsequently sank.

Merstone in 1949

PS WHIPPINGHAM

BUILT	1930 by Fairfield Shipbuilding & Engineering Co Ltd, Glasgow
GROSS TONS	825
DIMENSIONS	254 ft x 59 ft x 7 ft 2 in
MACHINERY	2-cyl compound diagonal by Fairfield Coal-fired boilers
SPEED	16 knots
ROUTE	Portsmouth-Ryde/excursions

Launched on 1 May 1930, *Whippingham* was designed principally for long distance excursions, which in those days were frequent and extensive from Portsmouth and other local piers. Her sister, *Southsea,* was mined off the mouth of the Tyne on 16 February 1941, subsequently beached and written off, as not worth repairing. *Whippingham* was the first railway ship to appear on the Portsmouth–Ryde ferry service with the promenade deck carried forward to the bows. Other features included large deckhouses amidships, large first-class cabin on the upper deck aft, and a semi-cruiser stern. In prewar years, besides acting as relief and extra ship on the ferry run, she went far afield in her excursions, including visits to Weymouth and trips round the Isle of Wight.

These outings ceased at the end of the 1939 season, and she was kept

Whippingham off Southsea 18 June 1960

at Portsmouth until appearing at Dunkirk. On 1 June 1940 she is reputed to have lifted some 2,700 men on one visit, and to have sailed with her sponsons only about a foot above the water-line. In 1941 she was requisitioned for duties as a paddle mine-sweeper, with the pennant number J136, and the next year was converted to an AA ship.

She was returned to the SR in April 1945 and shortly afterwards was sent for a refit which included the replacement of a number of windows in the fore and aft saloons by portholes. She reappeared on the Portsmouth–Ryde route in 1946 and, during the ensuing years, carried out numbers of excursions, though these were less adventurous than they had been. 'Viewing the Liners' at Southampton was a particularly popular trip which she ran. As time went on she was seen less on her regular route and more as a reserve ship on peak period sailings until 1962, which was her last full season in service. Her great size, exceeded by only one other BR paddler (1,183 passengers, maximum) and the continuance of coal burning forced her retirement. She made her last voyage on 1 September 1962, was on the sale list by early December, was bought by Belgian breakers and left Portsmouth on 17 May 1963 for Ghent in tow of the tug *Bulldog II*, for scrapping by Van Heyghen Frères.

<hr>

PS SANDOWN
PS RYDE

BUILT	1934/1937 by Wm. Denny & Bros Ltd, Dumbarton
GROSS TONS	684/566
DIMENSIONS	223 ft x 52 ft 6 in x 7 ft 2 in
MACHINERY	3-cyl triple expansion by Denny
	Coal-fired boilers
SPEED	14 knots
ROUTE	Portsmouth-Ryde/excursions

Sandown, the first Portsmouth paddler to be fitted with the above machinery instead of the more usual two-cylinder compound engine, was launched on 1 May 1934 replacing PS *Duchess of Kent*. She was a success and a second ship *Ryde* was ordered from the same plans. *Ryde* was launched on 23 April 1937, replacing PS *Duchess of Norfolk* (1911) which was then sold to Cosens & Co Ltd, and renamed *Embassy*. The accommodation layout was similar on both ships. The third-class passengers had for their use a saloon forward on the upper deck, while for first-class passengers there was a smokeroom on the upper deck and a lounge aft on the same deck, with promenade deck above it. On the foredeck was a hatch through which goods and mail could be loaded, this being carried out by quayside cranes. Until 1950 both ships had

Sandown in the late 1930s—compare with page 84

only a foremast, full length. This was cut down in 1950 and a radar scanner fitted on top. Mainmasts were fitted in 1954.

Both ships were requisitioned in 1939 for mine-sweeping duties, and made up part of No 7 Flotilla based on the Forth. They were altered for this job in many ways. *Ryde* had a section of deckhouse cut away (reducing her gross tonnage from its original 603) to make room on deck for paravanes and other gear. Their pennant numbers were J20 and J132 respectively. They remained there, except for appearances at the Dunkirk evacuation, until 1942, when they were converted to AA ships.

Ryde was the first SR ship to return to civilian service; this she did in February 1945, followed soon afterwards by *Sandown*. Apart from masts, the most obvious alteration which has taken place since the war is the replacement of the large picture windows in the foredeck by portholes. In later years *Ryde* could carry a maximum of 1,011 passengers, *Sandown* 974. The latter ship was distinguishable from the former in two principal ways; she had a continuous line of deckhouses, while *Ryde*'s were separate, and she had fewer ventilators abaft the funnel. 1965 was *Sandown*'s last season in service, she made her last crossing on 19 September and then retired to Newhaven. She was on the sale list in November and was sold early in 1966 for breaking up in Belgium, arriving at Antwerp in tow of the Belgian tug *Temi III* on 17 February. *Ryde* is still in service but clearly her days are numbered. She spent a few days in mid-September 1968 on the Thames on charter to 'Gilbey's Gin'.

TSMV LYMINGTON

BUILT	1938 by Wm. Denny & Bros Ltd, Dumbarton
GROSS TONS	275
DIMENSIONS	148 ft x 36 ft 9 in x 5 ft 8 in
MACHINERY	Two 12-cyl 4-stroke, single acting oil engines each driving a Voith-Schneider propeller by W. H. Allen Sons & Co Ltd, Belfast
SPEED	9 knots
ROUTE	Lymington-Yarmouth

Launched on 7 January 1938, *Lymington* was one of the first ships in the UK to be fitted with a Voith-Schneider propeller, which did give some trouble in the early days. She entered service in spring 1938 and was the first drive-on ship to appear on the route, accommodating 20 cars in two rows of 10 on the main deck and a maximum of 430 passengers. She is truly double-ended, has an electrically-operated gangway at bow and stern, and is fitted with four rudders to assist manoeuvrability.

During the 1939-45 war she was retained on the Yarmouth run, being painted grey and given a concrete cover to protect the bridge from air attack.

Known *ab initio* as 'The Crab' because of her ability to turn in her own length and move bodily sideways, this little ship is still in service and, although the crossing is only thirty minutes or so, is provided with a small snack-bar on the boat (upper) deck. She was built for the SR and has sometimes made novel departures from her normal routine including a number of sailings between Portsmouth and Fishbourne on relief duties. At Portsmouth in April 1968 her twin funnels were painted red with black top, in lieu of grey with black top.

Lymington at Yarmouth 15 August 1966

DEPV FARRINGFORD

BUILT	1947 by Wm. Denny & Bros Ltd, Dumbarton
GROSS TONS	489
DIMENSIONS	178 ft x 49 ft 10 in x 6 ft
MACHINERY	Two 4-stroke single acting 6-cyl diesels by English Electric Co Ltd, Stafford, connected to electric motors
SPEED	10½ knots
ROUTE	Lymington-Yarmouth

Ordered by the SR, this ship was launched on 21 March 1947 and finally delivered in January 1948, entering service on 4 March. Her paddle wheels can be worked independently of each other, and she has four rudders, one at each quarter. She can carry 36 cars and a maximum of 812 passengers. The first-class saloons are on the upper deck which is fully enclosed, the other saloons are below. Both funnels are on the same side. The bridge runs the full width of the ship and she has a ramp at the bow and stern. Her appearance on the route relegated *Freshwater* to spare ship.

Farringford at Yarmouth 15 August 1966

Shanklin arriving at Portsmouth 2 October 1965

TSMV BRADING
TSMV SOUTHSEA
TSMV SHANKLIN

BUILT	1948/1948/1951 by Wm. Denny & Bros Ltd, Dumbarton
GROSS TONS	837/837/833
DIMENSIONS	200 ft 3 in x 47 ft 8 in x 7 ft
MACHINERY	Two 2-stroke single acting 8-cyl Sulzer diesels by Sulzer Bros, Winterthur, *Shanklin*'s by Denny
SPEED	14½ knots
ROUTE	Portsmouth-Ryde

Brading and *Southsea* were ordered by the SR to replace the paddlers lost during the second war. Both were launched on 11 March 1948, entering service in November and December 1948 respectively. They were the first screw vessels to serve regularly between the two ports and are exceptionally broad in relation to length being nearly 4¼ to 1 instead of the more usual 9 or 10 to 1. They can carry 1,331 passengers and were the first Portsmouth–Ryde ships to be fitted with radar.

The almost identical *Shanklin* joined them in 1951 (replacing PS *Shanklin* withdrawn at the end of November 1950). In 1953 *Brading* and *Southsea* carried Admiralty staff in the official procession at the Spithead Review. *Brading* was in trouble on 14 June 1963 when she was the subject of a bomb scare and a paper parcel was found and thrown overboard, and again six days later when a fire was started on board. No doubt the work of the Isle of Wight Republican Army! On 31 May 1964 *Shanklin* visited Yarmouth, possibly her first visit there. She normally runs excursions during the summer months, calling at Southsea, viewing liners at Southampton and making triangular runs in the Solent.

99

In their spring 1967 overhauls all three were given a new look. A new 'spar' deck, on which 170 seats were installed, was built on at the stern on the same level as the bridge deck. New accommodation in the after saloon on the main deck seats nearly 200. The bar and cafeteria were moved from the after saloon to the other end of the deck and were enlarged, new seating for 100 being fitted. *Brading* and *Southsea* emerged with 'stove pipes' projecting from the funnel tops, but during their 1967-8 overhauls the funnels were built up to conceal these pipes, resulting in deeper black tops. These alterations did not alter the ships' gross tonnage nor their certificates.

Shanklin after alterations May 1967

Freshwater at Yarmouth 15 August 1966

TSMV FRESHWATER

BUILT	1959 by Ailsa Shipbuilding Co Ltd, Troon
GROSS TONS	363
DIMENSIONS	164 ft x 42 ft 6 in x 6 ft
MACHINERY	Two 2-stroke single acting 8-cyl diesels by Crossley Bros Ltd, Manchester
SPEED	10½ knots
ROUTE	Lymington-Yarmouth

Making her maiden voyage on 21 September 1959, *Freshwater* took the name of the paddler she replaced. She can carry a maximum of 620 passengers and 26 cars, the latter being driven on over ramps at bow or stern. She is exceptionally manoeuvrable, having a Voith-Schneider propeller at bow and stern. In mid-1962 she ran for a short trial period between Portsmouth and Fishbourne.

The centre portion of the main deck is completely clear for its full length, permitting stowage of vehicles in three lines, although portable cattle stalls can be rigged at each end if required. There are lounges with settee seating on the lower deck, forward and aft, and on the main deck on port side and on starboard side. In addition there are a bar and buffet on the starboard side of the main deck. Permanent seating on deck is provided for 200 persons. The navigating bridge is situated amidships above the boat deck, and extends the full width of the ship.

She is double-ended, and has no need of rudders, because the bow propeller is on the port side and the aft propeller on the other side so that she can turn by manipulating the controls to vary the direction of thrust of the propellers.

Camber Queen arriving Portsmouth 3 August 1967

TSMV FISHBOURNE
TSMV CAMBER QUEEN

BUILT	1961 by Philip & Son Ltd, Dartmouth
GROSS TONS	293
DIMENSIONS	166 ft 3 in x 43 ft x 6 ft
MACHINERY	Two 2-stroke single acting 8-cyl oil engines by Crossley Bros Ltd, Manchester
SPEED	10¼ knots
ROUTE	Portsmouth-Fishbourne

Replacing the three older motor vessels, *Fishbourne, Wootton, Hilsea* on this service, these two new ferries *Fishbourne* and *Camber Queen* have succeeded in reducing the crossing time from one hour to a little more than thirty-five minutes. They were launched on 15 March and 13 April 1961 respectively. *Fishbourne* made her maiden voyage on 7 July but was taken off again a couple of days later with ramp trouble. *Camber Queen,* originally to have been named *Wootton,* made her maiden voyage on 29 August 1966 when the accelerated service officially started. They can carry 168 passengers and 34 cars, loaded by hydraulic ramp at bow and stern, and stored on the main-deck throughway. A Voith-Schneider propeller is fitted at each end. Early in 1962 both ships had an extra mast, taller than the existing one, fitted on top of the wheelhouse for navigational reasons. They rarely serve elsewhere, though *Camber Queen* has operated between Portsmouth and Yarmouth at least twice, namely on 5 September 1961 when *Fishbourne II* grounded on the ramp at Fishbourne and stuck there, and for a few days from 22 January 1963 when Fishbourne was obstructed by floating ice.

6: SOUTHAMPTON

No packet port can have as sorry a tale to tell as Southampton. From the grandeur of the late 1930s, when there were no fewer than nine passenger ships and two cargo ships based there, Southampton's status had fallen to virtual insignificance in 1966, when only two cargo ships served. This deterioration is bewildering, particularly when it is understood that the port was owned directly by the BTC until being transferred to the Docks Board, and that the railways had marine workshops there until they were closed down early in 1964.

The situation in 1939 was almost idyllic. The two cargo steamers *Haslemere* and *Ringwood* were running to various ports, notably the Channel Islands and St Malo. Passenger services were being run on a nightly basis; to Le Havre with *Hantonia* and *Normannia* (both 1911); to St Malo with *Dinard* and *St Briac* (both 1924), and to Guernsey and Jersey with *Isle of Jersey, Isle of Guernsey* (both 1930) and *Isle of Sark* (1932).

There was also *Brittany* (1933), which was Southampton-based, though she served between the Channel Islands and St Malo, Granville, Cherbourg, etc. In addition, a daylight run to St Malo was introduced in 1939, served usually by *Lorina* (1918) or by *St Briac,* which also operated cruises to Rouen or to St Malo, Dinard and the Channel Islands. As the European war developed and the invading forces moved westwards, all services were gradually withdrawn and all ships were 'called up' to serve in a variety of ways. Southampton was perhaps fortunate in that only three of its fleet were lost, *Normannia* and *Lorina* being sunk during the Dunkirk evacuation while *St. Briac* was rammed and sunk in March 1942.

The first passenger service to reopen after the war was that to the Channel Islands on 25 June 1945, run by *Isle of Guernsey,* joined later by *Isle of Jersey* and *Isle of Sark.* This soon gained nightly regularity. Not long afterwards the Le Havre service was reopened by *Hantonia,* but it was not until the new steamer *Falaise* appeared in 1947, that the St Malo service was restored. She took this up on a seasonal (July to September) basis, from 14 July, and at first there were only two sailings per week in each direction, though latterly there were three. This short season enabled the ship to carry out the early season short cruises operated in prewar days by *St Briac.* After the new *Normannia* replaced *Hantonia* on the Le Havre run in 1952, it was usual to operate three sailings each way in summer and two in winter.

In 1947 the cargo sailings to the Channel Islands and St Malo were augmented by *Winchester.*

By 1953 not only were the three original Channel Islands 'Isles' engaged on that run during the season, but *Isle of Thanet* was borrowed from Folkestone for additional weekend runs, from about 1951 to 1957. On this service, at least, business was brisk in the early 1950s. *Normannia* continued to serve Le Havre and *Falaise* served St Malo as well as making her early season cruises. The cargo ships *Haslemere* and *Ringwood* gener-

103

ally served the Channel Islands, and *Winchester* St Malo. It was about this time that first attempts made to close the Le Havre service failed.

In 1959 the first major changes came, when the new cargo motor ships *Elk* and *Moose* replaced the old steamers on the Channel Islands run. These are interesting names, for they revived a type of nomenclature used particularly in the 1880s and 1890s by the GWR, mainly for its Weymouth ships. All sorts of ruminants had appeared, including *Gazelle, Ibex,* and *Roebuck,* but never *Elk* or *Moose.* It is fortunate for old time's sake that these new ships do, on occasions, serve the Weymouth–Channel Islands service. *Winchester* mainly served Le Havre and St Malo until 1964, when she was transferred on a more or less permanent basis to Weymouth.

In 1959, plans were made, amid great protest, to terminate passenger sailings to the Islands from Southampton, and to concentrate on the use of Weymouth with new ships. It was a sensible move in terms of economy, but was none the less much regretted by travellers and local authorities. But, indeed, who are travellers that they complain? They must needs use Weymouth henceforth. 1959 was the last season during which all three 'Isles' served the Islands route. *Isle of Jersey* was withdrawn at the end of that season, and in 1960 the two remaining served alone. *Isle of Sark* was withdrawn in November 1960, leaving *Isle of Guernsey* to continue alone until she formally closed the service on 12 May 1961. She was then transferred to Weymouth.

These moves left only the Le Havre and St Malo services in operation for passengers. These continued to run as before, that to St Malo seasonal only, allowing *Falaise* to operate cruises and to relieve *Normannia* on the all-year-round Le Havre service.

In 1963 it was decided that *Normannia* should be taken away from Southampton and converted to a car ferry for the Dover station, though the MOT took care to state that this would not automatically mean the closure of the Le Havre service. *Normannia* came off in December 1963, and was replaced by *St Patrick,* formerly of Weymouth. It was perhaps inevitable that the ministry would eventually give way to BR pressure for permission to close the service. Permission was given in March 1964, with the promise that the service should continue until the Norwegian-based Thoresen link between Southampton and Cherbourg was inaugurated. Handed over on a plate to one's competitors? Perhaps. There are certain channels of official thought which it is almost impossible to follow. *St Patrick* left Le Havre on the last sailing to Southampton on 9 May 1964. The cargo service was replaced by one operated on a twice weekly basis by the General Steam Navigation Co Ltd, using MV *Oriole.* Apparently it was successful.

Falaise, like *Normannia,* was also taken off the Southampton station for conversion, and *St Patrick* opened the St Malo season on 11 May 1964. During the next few months she made sailings to St Malo from both Southampton (two per week) and Weymouth (one per week). She finished her season on these runs, leaving St Malo for Southampton on

27 September. This proved to be the last BR passenger sailing between the two ports. The withdrawal of the service was approved by the ministry in April 1965, so that it was not reopened that year. The analysis of the 1964 figures makes interesting and astonishing reading. On five sailings there were 100 passengers or fewer ; on fifteen sailings under 200 ; on twenty-two sailings under 300 ; on twenty-nine sailings under 400. On only four occasions were there between 700 and 985 on board, and there were never more than 1,000. Less than 800 tons of cargo were carried throughout the season, which consisted of 45 sailings. No wonder withdrawal was considered necessary. But it was a retrograde step.

None of these passenger services is ever likely to be restored by BR though other companies, first Thoresen, and now Normandie Ferries, are making a success of the Le Havre service with drive-on ships.

With regard to Channel Islands–French ports traffic it is well known that the Jersey–France services and excursions were operated after 1933 by the small neatly-proportioned turbine steamer *Brittany*. The service was usually run all the year round, and, in postwar years, when *Brittany* was withdrawn for winter overhaul, the cargo ship *Winchester* (twelve passengers) would take over. For a few winters it was the practice to withdraw *Brittany* for several months and extend the Weymouth–Channel Islands sailings to include St Malo, but in winter 1961–2 *Brittany* was restored to the service.

1962 was the last year in which *Brittany* operated in the area, making sailings to St Malo, Granville, Cherbourg, Alderney and Sark. She was withdrawn in November, and was replaced during the rest of the winter by *Winchester* until the 1963 season, such as it was, was opened by *St Patrick*. This was the final season of BR-operated inter-island–French ports sailings, *St Patrick* making the last on 30 September 1963.

However, not only have the links been maintained in subsequent years by passenger steamer, but this passenger steamer is a one-time railway steamer, *Sir Richard Grenville*, now *La Duchesse de Normandie*. She has, in fact, expanded the services, having called at quite unusual places like Paimpol in addition to the more usual ports like St Malo and Granville. In 1966 she revived sailings to Cherbourg, and is an improvement on *Brittany* in that she is equipped with a car-lift, and can thus be used as a drive-on ferry at any state of the tide. Twenty-five cars can be carried on deck aft. Her owners, Jersey Lines Ltd, bought the Newhaven steamer *Brighton* from BR near the end of 1966, and in 1967 opened up excursions to the Islands from South Coast ports. So once again another firm is taking over trade abandoned by BR.

TSS HANTONIA

BUILT	1911 by Fairfields Shipbuilding & Engineering Co Ltd, Govan
GROSS TONS	1,595
DIMENSIONS	290 ft 4 in x 36 ft 1 in x 15 ft 3½ in (depth)
MACHINERY	4 Parsons turbines by Fairfield, SR geared Oil-fired boilers
SPEED	18 knots
ROUTE	Southampton-Le Havre

Hantonia goes down in history as the first turbine cross-channel packet equipped with gearing, direct drive having been used hitherto. She was launched on 23 December 1911 as *Louvinia* but renamed *Hantonia* the following month. Designed as a day and a night ship, she could carry about 700 passengers, and was also fitted with two cargo hatches. She took up the Le Havre service for the London & South Western Railway early in 1912, and with her sister *Normannia,* replaced the steamers *Alma* and *Columbia* (1894).

In the second war *Normannia* was sunk off Dunkirk on 30 May 1940. From late 1939 until about January 1940 *Hantonia* ran between Folkestone and Calais on general trooping duties, and then went to serve between the Channel Islands and French ports. From May 1942 she served as an RN accommodation ship until being handed over to the Southern Railway in 1945.

Shortly afterwards she restarted the Le Havre service which she main-

Hantonia at her best in the 1930s

tained until replaced by the new *Normannia* early in 1952. She was subsequently sold to T. W. Ward Ltd for breaking up, arriving at their Grays, Essex, yard in June.

TSS HASLEMERE
TSS RINGWOOD

BUILT   1925/1926 by D. & W. Henderson & Co Ltd, Glasgow
GROSS TONS   832/755
DIMENSIONS   229 ft 6 in x 35 ft 9 in x 12 ft 9¼ in
MACHINERY   6-cyl triple-expansion by D. & W. Henderson
               Coal-fired boilers
SPEED   15 knots
ROUTE   Southampton-Channel Isles/Le Havre/St Malo etc

In the mid-1920s the SR ordered no fewer than nine similar cargo ships for services from Dover, Folkestone and Southampton (there was also to be a tenth, *Autocarrier* qv). It is surprising that they found the cargo to support them, particularly when passenger ships serving the same routes could also carry cargo. At least they had their uses during the war, when three of the group were lost ; *Minster* 8 June 1944, *Tonbridge* 22 August 1941, and *Fratton* 18 August 1944, all in home waters.

Haslemere, Ringwood and *Fratton* were used principally on services

Ringwood leaving St Peter Port, Guernsey July 1947

107

from Southampton to Le Havre, St Malo, Honfleur, Caen, Cherbourg and the Channel Islands, though after the war services to Honfleur and Caen were not revived, and to Cherbourg were run only occasionally. *Haslemere* and *Ringwood* (launched 13 April 1926) had 30,000 cu ft of cargo space and could carry eight passengers in four double-berth cabins.

During the war *Haslemere* served as a barrage balloon vessel for coastal convoys based on Sheerness from 1940 to 1943 ; she was then laid up and returned to the railway in 1945. *Ringwood* was requisitioned for service as an auxiliary net-layer in 1940 and carried the pennant number T245. She also was returned in 1945.

After the war they reverted to the cross-channel service from Southampton, very occasionally serving the Channel Islands from Weymouth. *Ringwood* finished her time on this latter route from February 1958. In 1959 both were replaced by the new motor vessels *Elk* and *Moose*, and were sold for breaking up, *Haslemere* going to Vereenidge Iszerhandel, Utrecht ; *Ringwood* to De Koophandel, Nieuw Lekkerkerk.

TSS ISLE OF JERSEY
TSS ISLE OF GUERNSEY

BUILT	1930 by Wm. Denny & Bros Ltd, Dumbarton
GROSS TONS	2,180/2,189
DIMENSIONS	306 ft x 45 ft x 12 ft 6 in
MACHINERY	4 Parsons turbines by Denny, SR geared Oil-fired boilers
SPEED	19 knots
ROUTE	Southampton-Channel Islands

These ships were the first to be ordered for the Southampton–Channel Islands passenger service by the SR, replacing, among others, the veteran steamer *Alberta* (1900). *Isle of Jersey* was launched in November 1929, followed early in 1930 by her sister ship and both served the Islands consistently until the war.

During hostilities both ships were taken over for service as hospital ships, *Jersey* being sent to northern waters where she remained until she came south for the Normandy landings, making eleven trips to the beaches. *Guernsey* was at Dunkirk and lifted 490 personnel on 30 May 1940, but by the end of this trip she had so much minor damage spread throughout her that the evacuation was over by the time repairs were completed. She was then in use as a Fleet Air Arm target ship, and in 1943 was modified to carry infantry as part of Assault group J2, Southampton, with the pennant number 4.245, and joined her sister at the Normandy landings.

Both ships were returned to the SR in 1945. *Guernsey,* early in the year, ran between Newhaven and Dieppe, and on 25 June reopened the Southampton civilian service to the Channel Islands being joined by *Jersey* in October. The latter ship stayed on this route until the end of the 1959 season. By then the decision had been taken to run down and eventually terminate the passenger sailings to the Channel Islands from Southampton. *Jersey* was the first of the three ships then serving the run to be withdrawn. In March 1960 she was bought by Mohammed Senussi Giabor of Tripoli, towed from Southampton for the Tyne on 21 March by *Masterman,* and fitted out for service as a pilgrim ship by Smith's Dock Co Ltd at North Shields. She left the Tyne for Tripoli as *Libda* on 28 April 1960.

The arrival of *Libda* was eagerly awaited in Tripoli, and she was hailed as the forerunner of the Libyan Mercantile Marine. She entered harbour dressed overall and several receptions were held on board her. Work was started on her by a local yard to make her more suitable for the pilgrim trade, but in the meantime a firm foreign to Libya, possibly Greek, obtained certain 'rights' to the Libyan pilgrim business as this firm already had larger ships on the job. *Libda* was then almost discarded out of hand, and lay for several months in the centre of the harbour, with a little work still being done on her, but by the end of 1960 she was moved to the 'grave-yard' berth just inside the West Mole. There she lay, rapidly deteriorating, until being sold for scrap early in 1963 to La Spezia. She was actually known as *Libya* during this period, and not *Libda.* Unfortunately, strenuous efforts have failed to reveal a photograph of her.

Guernsey, the last of the three to survive, operated a much reduced

Isle of Guernsey arriving Southampton November 1949

service alone over winter 1960-1, spent Easter 1961 serving from Weymouth and reverted to the Southampton service until making the last sailing on 12 May. She was then transferred permanently to Weymouth and remained in service there until making her last trip on 16 June, being then replaced by the new *Sarnia*. Interspersed with her Southampton/ Weymouth–Channel Islands sailings during June, she also carried out a number of cheap day excursions from Weymouth and Torquay to Guernsey. Laid up in reserve until August she was then offered for sale and in November 1961 was bought for breaking by Van Heygen Frères. She arrived at Ghent in tow of the tug *Zeetijger* on 20 November. One of her lifeboats was presented to Guernsey sea scouts. Both ships could carry some 1,400 passengers in two classes, and had a bar-lounge forward, underneath which was a number of private cabins. There were also cargo holds, forward and aft.

TSS ISLE OF SARK

BUILT	1932 by Wm. Denny & Bros Ltd, Dumbarton
GROSS TONS	2,233
DIMENSIONS	306 ft x 45 ft x 12 ft 6 in
MACHINERY	4 turbines by Denny, SR geared
	Oil-fired boilers
SPEED	19½ knots
ROUTE	Southampton-Channel Islands

Following the success of the two earlier 'Isles' of 1929-30, *Isle of Sark* was ordered, and was of very similar lines to the others, though she

Isle of Sark approaching Southampton November 1949

incorporated a number of improvements including the extension further aft of the forecastle bulwarks. An innovation was her maierform stem, but this type has never appeared on any subsequent channel packet. She was launched on 13 November 1931. In 1936 she was the subject of further experiment when the original version of the now well-known Denny-Brown stabiliser, then known as a gyro-stabiliser, was fitted.

She continued on the Channel Islands service right up to 28 June 1940, when she made the last peacetime sailing from the Channel Islands before the Germans arrived. She did not therefore appear at the Dunkirk evacuation. Following the closure of the Channel Islands service, she operated between Fishguard and Rosslare for a time until being adapted for use as a radar training ship based successively at Douglas, the Clyde and the Forth. After that she served as an AA ship.

In postwar years she maintained the Channel Islands service with accommodation for 1,400 passengers in two classes Like the other 'Isles' she had extensive cargo holds fore and aft. She made her last voyage in November 1960, and was offered for sale almost at once. Van Heyghen Frères bought her for scrap in March 1961, and she arrived at Ghent on 7 April.

As far as is known she served elsewhere for only one period, in January 1950, when *St Helier* was undergoing repairs.

TSS BRITTANY

BUILT	1933 by Wm. Denny & Bros Ltd, Dumbarton
GROSS TONS	1,522
DIMENSIONS	260 ft x 41 ft 6 in x 10 ft 6 in
MACHINERY	4 Parsons turbines by Denny, SR geared
	Oil-fired boilers
SPEED	16 knots
ROUTE	Guernsey, Jersey-French ports (St Malo, Cherbourg, Granville, etc)

Brittany was built specially for these routes which were revived and maintained from June 1932 by SS *Vera* (1898). Launched on 12 April 1933, she entered service two months later and was an immediate success. She was a neat little ship, small enough to withstand the frequently uneconomical and poorly-patronised winter runs. She could carry 845 passengers, the accommodation including 62 sleeping berths and a 72-seater restaurant. Her shallow draught enabled her to use St Malo at most states of the tide.

She continued on the various services until nearly the end of 1939, when she was switched to the Folkestone–Boulogne leave service. This lasted until April 1940. The following month she became involved in

111

Brittany in Southampton Water in the late 1930s

evacuation from French ports and the Channel Islands. In September 1940 she was taken over by the navy for use as an auxiliary net-layer. In winter 1941-2 she was refitted at Rosyth and during the next thirty months encircled Africa on active service, being at Bombay for part of 1942 and in the Mediterranean in 1943 and early 1944. She then returned to Portsmouth. She was returned to the SR in 1945 and was restored to her original services in 1947.

It was normal for her to maintain the connections all the year round, though only once weekly in winter, and she would often return to Southampton afterwards. On these occasions she could and frequently did

Alandsfarjan (ex-*Brittany*) in her new owner's colours. Note how the front of the superstructure has been built up

carry passengers, though the sailings were not advertised. During her annual overhaul, in January and February each year, she was replaced by TSMV *Winchester,* a cargo ship with accommodation for twelve passengers. As an experiment during the winter months for a couple of years up to 1961, the sailing of the mail ship from Weymouth to the Channel Islands was extended to St Malo, while *Brittany* had her overhaul and leave period increased to what can only be described as a 'lay-up'. This experiment was not a success, and in the winter of 1961 *Brittany* was restored to regular winter service. 1962 was her last year in service and she was withdrawn and laid up at Southampton on 30 November. In 1963 she was sold to Alandsfarjan A/B of Aland for use as a car ferry, and left for Aland renamed *Alandsfarjan* on 21 April.

On arrival in Finland, alterations were carried out to the ship's accommodation so that she could carry a total of 780 passengers, with a restaurant (150 seats), bar and cafeteria (180 seats) and lounge (125 seats). She can also carry thirty-eight cars, but it is not clear whether or not she has been given drive-on facilities. Since then she has been in general service linking Swedish and Finnish ports with Mariehamn in the Aland Islands. She is still operating, her colours being green boot-topping, mustard hull and funnel, white upper-strake and superstructure, green lifeboat covers, black top to the funnel, and on the mustard of the funnel appears a red 'shield' motif and a red band. Altogether a most attractive scheme.

TSMV ELK
TSMV MOOSE

BUILT	1959 by Brooke Marine Ltd, Lowestoft
GROSS TONS	795
DIMENSIONS	228 ft x 39 ft 6 in x 13 ft 5 in
MACHINERY	Two 2-stroke single acting 6-cyl diesels by Sulzer Bros Ltd
SPEED	14 knots
ROUTE	Weymouth-Channel Islands
	Southampton-Channel Islands/Le Havre, St Malo

Registered in Southampton, these ships were built to replace the steamers *Ringwood* and *Haslemere.* They have a total cargo capacity of 72,774 cubic feet, and are equipped to carry containers and palletised cargo. Livestock can also be carried. From the beginning they usually served from Southampton, but, following the withdrawal of the steamers *Roebuck* and *Sambur* from the Weymouth station, they have served from the latter port on many occasions, particularly during the flower and tomato seasons. When off for overhaul in the early part of the year they

H   113

have been frequently replaced by MV *Brest* of SNCF, while at other times chartered ships have substituted. Each ship has a two-berth cabin available only for cattle drovers. They still maintain a fairly regular service between Southampton and Jersey and Guernsey.

From 3 July to 10 September 1967 and from 3 June to 12 September 1968, the ships worked alternately for two weeks at a time on the Weymouth–Channel Islands route carrying passengers' cars. For the other two weeks they reverted to the Southampton service to give their crews some home leave. To replace them at Southampton BR chartered *Jacob Becker* in 1967, and *Frauke Danz* in 1968, owned respectively by Kustenschiffahrt Bauer & Hauschildt KG of Hamburg, and by Peter Dohle.

Elk leaving Guernsey August 1965

7: WEYMOUTH

Prewar services from Weymouth to the Channel Islands were operated by the GWR, whose funnel colours were red with black top. The two passenger ships *St Helier* and *St Julien,* and the two cargo ships *Roebuck* and *Sambur,* maintained the regular sailings, usually nightly in each direction all the year round. When extra sailings were needed during peak holiday seasons, or to take over relief duties in winter, it was the practice to transfer one of the Fishguard ships, usually *St Patrick* (1930), to operate from Weymouth.

During the war all ships were taken over for active service in one capacity or another, *St Patrick* alone being lost. Services to the Islands were suspended until the Germans had left. Cargo services were restored in 1945, passenger services in 1946.

The new *St David* acted as third and relief ship during October and November 1947, but in February 1948 *St Patrick* (1947) took over, and was associated with the Weymouth station from then until 1963. In 1959 *St Patrick* was officially transferred from the Fishguard & Rosslare Railways & Harbours Co (her original owners) to the Railway Executive. Thus the prewar pattern of sailings from Weymouth was reinstated and maintained in postwar years until the end of the 1950s. It was at this time that plans were being made to discontinue passenger sailings to the Islands from Southampton, and to replace *St Helier* and *St Julien* by two larger ships.

After agreement had been reached with the Jersey authorities to deepen the channel there so that bigger ships could enter and leave regardless of tide, orders were placed with J. S. White at Cowes for the new ships. The old steamers were withdrawn in September 1960, and *St Patrick* maintained the service until the first of the new ships, *Caesarea,* appeared the following December. From May 1961 a new one-class service was intended, so *St Patrick* was sent to South Wales to be brought into line. These two ships officially opened the new service on 13 May 1961, aided by *Isle of Guernsey,* late of Southampton, until the new *Sarnia* took up the run some four weeks later. Although the withdrawal of services from Southampton was a sad affair, there can be little doubt that it was economically justifiable. Between May and September 1960 a total of 181,385 passengers used the Weymouth and Southampton routes served by six ships. In a similar period in 1961 passengers, using the three ships based on Weymouth alone, totalled 200,955.

From 1961 to 1963 *Caesarea, Sarnia* and *St Patrick* ran on the service, but further economies and the need for ships elsewhere in the region led to the last-named making her last regular sailing between the Channel Islands and Weymouth in October 1963. She was missed in subsequent years not only on the main service, but also because it had been her practice to run day trips to Guernsey from Weymouth and Torquay. She did return in 1964 to carry out some excursions from Weymouth, and also to operate the odd nightly run to St Malo, but this was her final

115

link with the port.

The service to the Islands is still operated all the year round, but the frequency has been reduced so that, since January 1964, winter runs have, for reasons of economy, been operated only twice a week in each direction with sometimes as few as thirty people on board. Since 1964 the summer service has been run by only two ships, and further cuts seem unlikely.

On the cargo side of the trade, *Roebuck* and *Sambur* continued to operate on a fairly regular daily schedule, aided by chartered ships when necessary. *Roebuck,* the last of them, was withdrawn early in 1965, and since then *Winchester,* from Southampton, has been associated with the Weymouth station. The Southampton cargo ships *Elk* and *Moose* served the Weymouth–Channel Islands route during the holiday seasons in recent years especially to carry passengers' cars.

There is a possibility of a third ship for the 1969 season ; *St David* has been suggested.

TSS ROEBUCK
TSS SAMBUR

BUILT	1925 by Swan Hunter & Wigham Richardson Ltd, Tyneside
GROSS TONS	866/861
DIMENSIONS	210 ft x 35 ft 8 in x 12 ft 8 in
MACHINERY	6-cyl triple-expansion by Swan Hunter & Wigham Richardson
	Oil-fired boilers
SPEED	12 knots
ROUTE	Weymouth-Channel Islands/occasionally French ports

With these vessels, the fashion of naming ships after animals, adopted by the GWR for its Weymouth ships in the 1880s was revived. They were the only ships so named after the turn of the century. Launched on 24 March and 9 April 1925 respectively, they were each delivered one month later and could carry livestock (usually horses, outwards in spring and inwards in early autumn) on the 'tweendecks fore and aft, and some 600 tons of cargo. The deckhouse amidships contained the officers' quarters and two double-berth passenger cabins, one of which was later taken over for use by the officers. Further dormitory accommodation was provided below for six passengers, but, since the war, little use has been made by passengers of any of this accommodation.

In the war, between 1940 and 1943, both served as barrage balloon vessels, based on Sheerness, being renamed *Roebuck II* and *Toreador.* Afterwards, they reverted to the Weymouth station and *Sambur* restored

116

the postwar Weymouth–Channel Islands cargo service on 18 September 1945.

After 1948 however, they frequently sailed from Southampton. *Sambur* was the first to be withdrawn, making her last Guernsey–Weymouth sailing on 29 March 1964. Two days later she sailed to Southampton and was laid up, being offered for sale at once. Bought by Frank Rijsdijk-Holland of Hendrick-ido-Ambacht for breaking, she left Southampton in tow on 10 June. *Roebuck* continued for another year, making her last return sailing to Weymouth on 27 February 1965. It was not until July that a reasonable offer was made for her, when Lacmots Ltd, Queenborough, Kent, bought her for scrap. She sailed for Sheerness on 29 July, but two months later work on her had still not started, and it was announced the following November that she had been resold for breaking by Brussels Scrapping Co. They were not replaced at Weymouth by any railway-owned ship for any length of time, their work being shared between *Elk, Moose, Winchester* and several chartered vessels, all of which have operated from Weymouth from time to time.

Roebuck at Weymouth 21 August 1960

TSS ST JULIEN
TSS ST HELIER

BUILT	1925 by John Brown & Co (Clydebank) Ltd
GROSS TONS	1,943/1,949
DIMENSIONS	291 ft 3 in x 42 ft 6 in x 13 ft 1¼ in
MACHINERY	4 turbines by John Brown, SR geared
	Oil-fired boilers
SPEED	18 knots
ROUTE	Weymouth-Guernsey/Jersey

It is rare for railway-owned ships to be substantially altered, no matter what age they may be, but these two were exceptions to the general rule. When launched in May and June 1925 respectively to replace the steamers *Ibex* (1891) and *Reindeer* (1897), *inter alia,* each had two funnels (the aft one being a dummy), a high docking bridge aft and an all-black hull. In 1927 the dummy funnel and docking bridge were removed. Ten years later a new cowl-topped funnel was fitted and this and other alterations combined to increase the gross tonnage slightly from its original 1,885, the increase being less on *St Helier*. During this period they could carry 589 first-class and 459 second-class passengers.

During the war *St Julien* served as a hospital ship, appearing at

St Helier arriving Weymouth 6 September 1955

118

Dunkirk, Cherbourg and Boulogne during the evacuation. In 1943 she went to the Mediterranean and was at the Anzio landings. By early 1944 she was back in the UK preparing for the Normandy landings. *St Helier* was engaged throughout in general transport services, putting in particularly good service at the Dunkirk evacuation, making four trips in all and picking up over 3,500 personnel on the first two. In 1942 she was fitted out as a landing ship infantry (hand-hoist) with the pennant number 4.255, and could carry 180 troops and 6 assault landing craft, being part of the Southampton Assault Group J2.

Both ships were returned to the GWR in 1945, and their refit for public service included the removal of the funnel cowl, and the plating in of the forward part of the superstructure. After the war they returned to normal service at Weymouth and *St Helier* restarted the postwar Islands service in June 1946. On nationalisation, they became part of the Western Region, but were transferred to the Southern Region on 1 November 1948. It was during this year that the upper parts of their hulls were painted white. After the war they had accommodation for 950 passengers.

Both *St Helier* and *St Julien* made their final sailings in 1960, on 21 September and 27 September respectively. *St Helier* was sold to Belgian breakers and arrived at Antwerp on 19 December in tow of the tug *Schowenbank*. She was bought by Van Heyghen Frères but resold to Jos. de Smedt. *St Julien* was not sold until the following March when Van Heyghen Frères took her for scrap. She arrived in Ghent 12 April 1961. Late in 1963 she was reported to have been seen, stripped of her trappings, in use as a rest home and recreation centre for dockyard workers at Walcheren. She may still be there.

TSS CAESAREA
TSS SARNIA

BUILT	1960/1961 by J. White & Co Ltd, Cowes
GROSS TONS	4,174
DIMENSIONS	322 ft x 53 ft 8 in x 13 ft 7 in
MACHINERY	2 turbines by J. S. White, DR geared
	Oil-fired boilers
SPEED	20 knots
ROUTE	Weymouth-Channel Islands

These ships came as a welcome relief to passengers who had had to travel frequently to the Channel Islands on the old steamers *St Helier* and *St Julien*. As the new ships were very much larger than any predecessor on the route, the harbour at Jersey had to be specially dredged. *Caesarea* was launched on 29 January 1960 and made her maiden commercial voyage on 2 December 1960. *Sarnia* was launched on 6 September 1960 and entered service 17 June 1961. There are two continuous decks, main and upper, a promenade deck, boat deck, and navigating bridge deck. The hull below the main deck is divided by eleven watertight bulkheads. The staircases from deck to deck are particularly impressive, being spacious, well-lit, and furnished in light oak veneer.

The ships are fitted out for both night and day crossings, and provide total covered seating accommodation for 1,400 one-class passengers. Public rooms include restaurant seating 110, and three lounges together seating 396. Sleeping accommodation consists of two 2-berth cabins-de-luxe with private bathroom on the promenade deck, twenty-five double- and twelve single-berth cabins forward, two 22-berth sleeping lounges one each for ladies and gents respectively, and dozens of comfortable reclining seats distributed in the lounges, some fully lit, some with subdued lighting. Navigational and other features include Denny-Brown stabilisers, radio-telephone, bow-rudder and the extensive use of fire-proof materials.

Caesarea had to return to her builders in June 1961 to have vibration remedied, but, minor matters apart, the ships have given singularly reliable service. *Sarnia* had a novel change of duty from 19 November 1962 to 30 January 1963 when she served between Dover and Calais on the 'Golden Arrow' run. *Caesarea* followed suit from December 1966 to January 1967, relieving *Invicta*. *Sarnia* made at least one sailing from Folkestone at Easter 1967.

These ships are probably the last conventional cross-channel passenger ships to be built for any UK operator, and we believe that they embody the very finest ideas of our marine architects. We can pay no better compliment.

Caesarea leaving Dover for Calais 4 January 1967

TSMV WINCHESTER

BUILT	1947 by Wm. Denny & Bros Ltd, Dumbarton
GROSS TONS	1,149
DIMENSIONS	251 ft 6 in x 37 ft 9 in x 12 ft 9 in
MACHINERY	Two 2-stroke single acting 5-cyl Sulzer diesels by Denny
SPEED	15 knots
ROUTE	Southampton/Weymouth-Channel Islands

Ordered by the SR as part replacement for war losses, *Winchester* was launched on 21 March 1947. She carries 650 tons of general cargo (50,000 cu ft), can easily be adapted for large numbers of livestock, and accommodates twelve passengers in eight single- and two double-berth cabins amidships on the lower deck adjacent to the dining saloon. There is no lounge-bar.

Her principal service from the beginning has been from Southampton to the Channel Islands, but April to June each year usually sees her running into Weymouth from the Channel Islands with flowers and tomatoes. After *Sambur* and *Roebuck* were withdrawn in 1964 and 1965, she appeared more often at Weymouth at other times of the year. Over the years she has relieved *Brittany* on the Jersey–St Malo run for about a month from mid-January during the latter's refit. When *Brittany* was withdrawn in November 1962, *Winchester* spent most of that winter on the St Malo service. This was repeated in winter of 1963-4 and again in winter 1964-5 up to 18 December. On that date she made the last sailing from Jersey, and on the following day the last sailing from St Malo. Since then the service has not been operated by BR in winter. Since early 1965, following the withdrawal of *Roebuck*, *Winchester* has been based

Winchester leaving Jersey July 1967

principally at Weymouth. In January 1965 she visited St Sampson's Harbour, Guernsey, for damage repairs to be carried out by Messrs John Upham Ltd, possibly the only visit ever made to this port by a BR vessel. Heavy weather had caused some rivets in her plates to work loose, and the repairs were carried out at low tide over a weekend. A further novelty came at the end of August 1966, when she replaced *Darlington* on the daily Folkestone–Boulogne unit-load service for a few weeks, before returning to Weymouth.

In Autumn 1966 her radar mast was re-sited on the foremast. In 1967 there was talk of her having accommodation for twenty-five passengers fitted, presumably for winter sailings, but nothing has yet come of this.

THE WESTERN REGION

All services operated by the former GWR came under the Western Region on 1 January 1948. However, on 1 November that year the Weymouth–Channel Islands service was transferred to the Southern Region.

The standard buff funnel with black top was applied to vessels at Dartmouth and Plymouth and to the Waterford steamer *Great Western,* but not to the three Rosslare passenger ships. The latter were owned (one still is), by the Fishguard & Rosslare Railways & Harbours Co and they retained their red funnels with black tops. Likewise, when the new BR livery was applied to *Great Western* in 1965 it was not applied to the Rosslare ships, which were given the white letters 'FR' on the funnels instead of the 'double-arrow' BR motif.

Although the Rosslare service is still publicised by the Western Region, marine control has been carried out by the London Midland Region at Euston since 1950, being included in the overall title 'Irish Shipping Services'.

8 : DARTMOUTH

The ferry service between Dartmouth and Kingswear was operated after 1908 by TSS *The Mew,* built that year for the GWR Company by Cox and Co Ltd, Falmouth. She had a gross tonnage of 117, and could carry 543 passengers and 5 cars. Although she was sent to help in the Dunkirk evacuation she was never used and returned to service on the Dart, continuing after 1948 with BR Western Region.

When off for overhaul, usually in October each year, *The Mew* was replaced by PS *Totnes Castle* (91 tons, built 1923), chartered by BR from the River Dart Steamboat Co Ltd, Dartmouth. This paddler was fitted with a specially strengthened foredeck so that she could carry cars, and in fact had acted as relief annually since 1924. The last refit on *The Mew* was carried out in May 1954, and she was withdrawn towards the end of the year. Cars ceased to be accommodated thereafter.

No replacement for *The Mew* had even been ordered at this time, so further charters were necessary to keep the service open. MV *Lady Elizabeth* (15 tons, built 1927) owned by Millbrook Steamboat and Trading Co Ltd, served until late March 1955, when she was replaced by the same company's MV *Devon Belle* (22 tons, built 1925). From May 1955 to June 1957 MV *Seymour Castle* (36 tons, built 1938) owned by RDS served regularly on bareboat charter, being replaced during her overhaul by yet another RDS motor vessel *Berry Castle* (49 tons, built 1949).

Car Ferry *The Mew.* Note clear deck-space aft for cars

At long last, in June 1957, the British Transport Commission provided its own tonnage in the form of two small motor vessels *Humphrey Gilbert* and *Adrian Gilbert*. Built by Blackmore and Sons Ltd, Bideford, they have Dorman oil-engines and accommodate 150 passengers, cabin accommodation being provided. The service is normally worked by only one vessel, the other acting as relief and extra. During peak periods both vessels are used. The threat of the axe has been hanging over this service for some time, but so far it still operates.

---

9 : PLYMOUTH

The tender service at Plymouth was inaugurated by the GWR in 1873. A happy system of naming vessels after well-known sea captains was chosen. It has been remarked that the design of the tenders, particularly the later ones, bore a strong resemblance to that of the Mersey ferries, and it is conceivable that the design of the latter was deliberately copied because of valuable experience they had provided in handling large numbers of passengers in restricted waters. Indeed, one Birkenhead Corporation ferry PS *Cheshire* actually found its way into the Plymouth fleet in 1905, remaining there for about six years.

The use of tenders in the excursion trade has been a common feature throughout, trips being run to places like Salcombe, Looe, Fowey and the Eddystone Lighthouse. After the 1939-45 war these excursions were less numerous, and as the years passed and the total number of tenders based at Plymouth was reduced, the season gradually shortened. In 1949, for example, this season lasted from April to September, while in 1960 trips were run only in August. In the following year three weeks in July were added, but there were no excursions at all in 1962. Two 'farewell' cruises to the Eddystone were run by *Sir Richard Grenville* in late summer 1963, and there have been none since.

In the late 1930s there were four tenders engaged in full-time excursion and tender duties, *Sir Walter Raleigh, Sir Francis Drake, Sir John Hawkins* and *Sir Richard Grenville*. All survived the war, though *Sir Walter Raleigh* was not considered worth renovating, having been severely cut up and altered for wartime duties. She was sold out of the Great Western fleet in 1947 and some twelve months later was put into service at Cherbourg as a tug/tender named *Ingenieur Reibell*, owned by Cherbourg Salvage and Towing Co. She is still there, though not quite so active as she used to be.

The other three ships returned to normal tender duties after their post-war refits. However, the number of calls being made by ocean liners was rapidly decreasing yearly. In the 1930s there were often as many as eighty calls a month, but by the mid-1950s there were fewer than 200 in a whole year. In 1954 *Sir Francis Drake* was declared redundant and sold for breaking up. Latterly, the main callers were ships of the French Line and the Ellerman Group, the former making up by far the larger share of the trade, but after *France* entered service in 1961 no further calls were made by this company. In 1962 there were in all only eighty-two visits, and *Sir John Hawkins* was sold for breaking up in that year. Clearly the service was doomed.

In mid-1963 it was announced that the tender service would be withdrawn at the end of October, and accordingly the one remaining tender, *Sir Richard Grenville,* was laid up and subsequently sold. She also is still in service as a passenger/car ferry named *La Duchesse de Normandie* operating in Channel Islands waters.

There is one other Plymouth tender still with us. The iron TSS *Sir Richard Grenville,* built by Laird Bros in 1891, was sold out of the Plymouth fleet when the new vessel with that name appeared in 1931. She became a tender at Dover, named *Lady Savile,* and remained there until 1947, when she was resold for service as a club-house in Essex. She was towed from Dover to Leigh-on-Sea in September 1947, and subseqently beached at Chalkwell. Her engines and boilers were removed shortly afterwards. She is now the club-house of the Essex Yacht Club and lies on a narrow strip of sand between the railway line and the water near Chalkwell. Her funnel and part of her superstructure have been removed but her hull is unaltered, and is kept in sparkling condition in black paint on which a white line is painted along the upper strake.

TSS SIR FRANCIS DRAKE

BUILT	1908 by Cammell Laird & Co Ltd, Birkenhead
GROSS TONS	478
DIMENSIONS	148 ft 10 in x 38 ft 8 in x 9 ft 11 in
MACHINERY	6-cyl triple-expansion by Cammell Laird
	Coal-fired boilers
SPEED	11 knots
ROUTE	Plymouth tender/local excursions

Built for the Plymouth tender service of the GWR, *Sir Francis Drake* remained on station throughout until the second war. She was requisitioned on 25 August 1939 for examination duties at Plymouth. Under the White Ensign she was sent to Scapa on 2 August 1941 for similar duties. Early in the war a makeshift wheelhouse was fitted for protection, but was removed in 1946. After the war she was refitted at Southampton and returned to service in June 1946, making her first excursion on 2 July, and her first tender duty on 23 July. A permanent wheelhouse was fitted in

1948. She could carry 555 passengers. During the years following the war callers at Plymouth became fewer and fewer and so, being the oldest of the three tenders, *Sir Francis Drake* was the first to go. She made her last excursion, to Looe and Fowey on 1 September 1953 and made her last tender call, to Blue Star's *Paraguay Star,* on 8 October. She was then laid up and sold in June 1954 for breaking up by Demmelweek & Reading Ltd, Plymouth.

Her sister ship, *Sir Walter Raleigh,* had a similar career, but in 1941 was so considerably altered for war service, including the cutting away of her stern, that when she was returned to the railway in August 1946 she was not considered worth refitting, and was sold for breaking up in January 1947. She passed in turn to Risdon, Beazley Ltd ; to Overseas Salvage & Towing Co Ltd, and finally to Cie Cherbourgeoise de Remorquage et de Sauvetage within a very short time. She is still in service for the last-named as a tender at Cherbourg under the name *Ingenieur Reibell.*

Sir Francis Drake at Plymouth in 1933

TSS SIR JOHN HAWKINS

BUILT	1929 by Earle's Shipbuilding & Engineering Co Ltd, Hull
GROSS TONS	930
DIMENSIONS	180 ft x 45 ft 3 in x 12 ft 9 in
MACHINERY	6-cyl triple-expansion by Earle's
	Coal-fired boilers
SPEED	13 knots
ROUTE	Plymouth tender/excursions

Launched in July 1929, *Sir John Hawkins* replaced TSS *Smeaton* (1883) which was sold to Belfast buyers soon after her arrival. The Plymouth tender service was a venture of the GWR, and a very successful one too, particularly in the inter-war years when passengers who disembarked at Plymouth could get to London quicker by train than by going further on by ship.

Little of note marked her career until the war, during the first few months of which she remained at Plymouth and was given a temporary, though solidly built, wheelhouse. In January 1941 she was requisitioned, armed at Plymouth with two 'strip-Lewis' machine guns (later replaced with four Oerlikons), and sent to Scapa on personnel ferry duties. She had her postwar refit at Penarth, being handed back to the railway in October 1945.

She made her first postwar tender trip to the liner *Argentina* on 6 November 1945 and on 22 April the following year began her long series of postwar summer cruises. In 1948 a permanent wheelhouse was fitted. In May 1952, while being overhauled at Southampton, she was badly damaged by fire and subsequent refitting included modernisation of the passenger accommodation, though she remained a coal burner. She had accommodation for just over 800 passengers and carried a crew of 13. Following this, she re-entered the excursion service on 16 August 1952.

In 1961, French Line ships stopped calling at Plymouth, and the resulting reduction in passenger traffic caused the redundancy of *Sir John Hawkins*. At the end of 1961 she was withdrawn, and offered for sale in March 1962. Two months later she left for Ostend, to be broken up by Dutch breakers.

Sir John Hawkins at Plymouth

TSS SIR RICHARD GRENVILLE

BUILT	1931 by Earle's Shipbuilding & Engineering Co Ltd, Hull
GROSS TONS	901
DIMENSIONS	180 ft x 44 ft 8 in x 12 ft 6 in
MACHINERY	6-cyl triple-expansion by Earl's Oil-fired boilers
SPEED	13 knots
ROUTE	Plymouth tender/excursions

Launched in July 1931, *Sir Richard Grenville* was the last tender built for the GWR. She replaced TSS *Sir Richard Grenville*, which, as already mentioned, served for a time at Dover before becoming a yachting clubhouse in Essex. *Sir Richard Grenville* was easily distinguishable from *Sir John Hawkins* by the size of funnel. On *Sir John Hawkins* it was tall, but on *Sir Richard Grenville* it was short, necessitating forced-draught boilers.

She was requisitioned for the examination service at Plymouth in August 1939, and was given a wheelhouse as some protection against air attack. In March 1941 she was sent to Scapa for ferry duties. After the war her temporary wheelhouse was removed, and she was refitted for civilian duties at Penarth, though she was not officially returned to the GWR until January 1946.

Her first postwar tender trip was on 22 February 1946, and just two

Sir Richard Grenville at Plymouth about 1950

months later she took up the excursion business again. A permanent wheelhouse was fitted in 1948.

After 1961, when *Sir John Hawkins* was withdrawn, she alone catered for the rapidly diminishing passenger traffic, and in July 1963 was on the sale list, available for delivery after the end of October in that year. She made two special 'Farewell' cruises to the Eddystone Lighthouse on 9 August and 4 September and was withdrawn on 31 October. Her surprise sale to the Devon Cruising Co Ltd came in mid-November, but she was resold on 23 December to Jersey Lines Ltd, a new small Channel Islands company which has proved to be both enterprising and successful.

Sir Richard Grenville left Plymouth on 2 May 1964 with her new name, *La Duchesse de Normandie* registered in Jersey. Alterations included the addition of radar and two steel, motorised lifeboats, and at this time she had a green hull and funnel, each in two shades. She took up regular sailings between Jersey and St Malo on 10 May. About a week later the tyres round her rubbing strake were removed. Since then she has been repainted in what have become Jersey Lines' standard colours of dark-blue hull, white superstructure and wine-red funnel with black top. She serves many ports in the Channel Islands and on the French mainland. Her car-lift was installed in 1966, and in 1967 her foredeck (car deck) was extended right forward to its maximum width, enabling two more cars to be carried. Her annual overhaul is usually carried out early in the year at either Plymouth or Cardiff. She can now carry 550 passengers and about 25 cars.

La Duchesse de Normandie (ex-*Sir Richard Grenville*) at St Helier, Jersey, July 1967 showing the foredeck extension

10: FISHGUARD

The ships serving between Fishguard and Rosslare have technically been owned by the Fishguard & Rosslare Railways & Harbours Co. This venture had been instigated in 1893 under a slightly different name jointly by the GWR and the Great Southern & Western Railway of Ireland. In 1925 the Irish share was transferred to the Great Southern Railway and in 1945 to the Irish Transport Board, or Coras Iompair Eireann, as it is better known. In 1948 the BTC took over the interest formerly held by the GWR. The ships had red funnels with black tops until 1965, when the white letters 'FR' were added on each side.

In 1939, there were two passenger services in operation from Fishguard. Waterford was served three nights per week by *Great Western* (1934) ; Rosslare nightly in each direction by *St Patrick* (1930), *St Andrew* (1932) and *St David* (1932), one of which took extra sailings. Efforts were made to keep up some sort of service during the early stages of the war until *St Patrick* was torpedoed on the run in June 1941. *St Andrew* and *St David* had been taken over earlier for use as hospital ships, the latter being sunk at the Italy landings in 1944. The Waterford service was kept open spasmodically by *Great Western,* but there was no pretence at regularity.

In 1946 the Rosslare service was reopened by *St Andrew.* Two new ships were ordered to replace war losses and *St David* entered service in July 1947, followed by *St Patrick,* though the latter ship generally served from Weymouth during the summer season. *Great Western* again took up the regular Waterford run.

Nothing occurred to upset the steady nautical life at Fishguard until early 1959, when it was announced that passengers would no longer be carried on the Waterford service after June that year. *Great Western* was refitted to carry more livestock and cargo, and re-entered the service, maintaining it up to the end of 1966, when she was withdrawn. During her last few months in service she did not sail regularly, but only when a fairly full load had accumulated. After 1959 there was no need for *Princess Maud* to relieve her during her annual overhaul, and so a cargo ship from either Holyhead or Heysham was used.

On the Rosslare service a daylight sailing was introduced in 1961. This ran on two days per week from each port during the peak season from 4 July to 7 September. The regular night ships were used, and the experiment was considered a success, 1,305 cars and 5,481 passengers having been carried. In the winter months, however, only three night sailings per week were given in each direction.

Interest was aroused in November 1963 when it was reported that BR was considering the possibility of increasing by some 30 per cent the car carrying capacity of one of the Rosslare ships. In the event, *St David* was altered to enable cars to be driven on at the side, certain berth alterations were carried out at Fishguard, and in the following season additional daylight services were run. Thus, in 1964, when the full summer timetable came into operation from 8 June, *St David* took the daylight sailing

131

from Fishguard and the night sailing from Rosslare, while *St Andrew* did the opposite. There was now both a daylight and a night-time sailing in each direction every day except Sunday. These efforts to improve patronage were successful, over 20,000 cars being carried compared with about 11,000 during the same period in 1963.

During 1964 cars were still being loaded by crane at Rosslare, and it was necessary to modify the rail bridge connecting the harbour with the mainland so that cars could be driven across instead of being carried on rail waggons as hitherto. This work completed, the 'drive-through' service was opened on 10 June 1965. During the 1965 peak season the night sailing (ie departing Fishguard 2.15 am) was dropped and the timings reorganised, so that there were now three sailings per day in each direction, *St David* taking the lion's share at 7.00 am and 5.00 pm and *St Andrew* making the 2.30 pm sailing. Again, the changes were successful, over 32,000 cars being carried by the end of September. Passenger carryings also increased by some 15 per cent. No doubt the new London–Fishguard car-carrier train with reserved passenger accommodation introduced in this year also helped to increase trade. One Sunday return sailing (by *St David*) was also introduced. In spite of this big boost in peak summer sailings, the service returned to a night sailing three times per week in each direction during winter 1965-6, though it should be mentioned that sailings are phased out gradually during the autumn, and increased gradually during spring.

A similarly ambitious programme was drawn up for the 1966 season. The night sailing was reintroduced at 2.00 am, and two daylight sailings and a Sunday sailing given, at times different from those in 1965. During the peak season the cargo ship *Slieve Donard* was borrowed from Holyhead for use as a car ferry to run alongside *St Andrew* on which all the passengers travelled. This was a surprise move, for she had already been used in this trade at Stranraer and been found wanting. In 1967 there was a maximum of four sailings per day.

Towards the end of 1966 it was learned that Heysham's *Duke of Rothesay* was to be converted to side-loading for the Rosslare service. *St Andrew* was subsequently withdrawn, and during the first few months of 1967 *St David* maintained the service alone until *Duke of Rothesay* joined her in May. There are now, therefore, two side-loading car ferries serving Rosslare.

The running down of the Fishguard–Waterford service in recent years has caused considerable consternation among Waterford people. In November 1964 a resolution drawn up by the Waterford Council of Trade Unions urged the Railways Board to provide a replacement for *Great Western* which, besides accommodating containers and livestock, should also provide berths for passengers. In the following February the law adviser to Waterford Town Council maintained that BR was under a statutory obligation to maintain a daily cargo and passenger service to Waterford, dating from an Act of 1898, and that the termination of the passenger service in 1959 by 'Gentlemen's Agreement' between BR and the Waterford authorities was out of order. At one stage there were high hopes that Waterford would win its case, but in March 1965 it became known that BR and CIE were considering a scheme to provide a new drive-on passenger/car ferry for the Rosslare run, harbour installations for stern-loading ships at both terminals, and a drive-on commercial-vehicle cargo and livestock vessel for the Waterford service. In spite of continued local protest, Waterford Corporation adopted by eight votes to five a committee recommendation accepting the terms of the Waterford Harbour Commissioners' agreement with BR for the replacement of *Great Western* by such a drive-on ship. At the time of writing there is no news of the advent of this new ship, though a unit-load ship has been chartered to replace *Great Western*. From late 1967 the regular Fishguard–Rosslare cargo service was discontinued in favour of that between Fishguard and Waterford, though some traffic continues on the former route.

TSS ST ANDREW

BUILT	1932 by Cammell Laird & Co Ltd, Birkenhead
GROSS TONS	3,035
DIMENSIONS	337 ft 9 in x 49 ft 1 in x 14 ft 8 in
MACHINERY	4 Parsons turbines by Cammell Laird, SR geared
	Oil-fired boilers
SPEED	21 knots
ROUTE	Fishguard-Rosslare

Launched on 10 November 1931, and delivered to her owners, F & R in February 1932, *St Andrew* was managed by the GWR up to 1947, after which she was managed by BR Western Region. Her sister-ship, *St David,* was lost on active service at the Italy landings in January 1944.

St Andrew originally had a gross tonnage of 2,702, this being increased to 3,035 during modifications in June 1947, and she could carry 1,026 first-class and 334 third-class passengers. The first-class accommodation was amidships in single- and double-berth cabins on the boat, promenade and main decks, while all present second-class cabins are aft. There were also public rooms for both classes in relevant parts of the ship.

In the early part of the war she served as a hospital ship, and rescued several hundred men during the Dunkirk evacuation. On 27 May 1940 with *St Julien* (hospital ship) and *St Helier* (transport), she was one of a noble convoy, which, escorted by two destroyers, made a special effort to get wounded and sick away.

In 1946 she reopened the civilian route to Rosslare, and since then has served there fairly consistently, though she has served elsewhere from time to time. For instance she served Holyhead–Dun Laoghaire from 29

September to 5 October 1952 and 6 October to 2 November 1964 ; Weymouth–Channel Islands in July 1961, and Harwich–Hook of Holland from 10 April to 1 June 1948. She has also made the odd special trip from Fishguard direct to Dun Laoghaire, eg on 12 March 1966 as a 'Rugby Special'. In 1955 her masts were removed and new ones of the tripod type were erected on the superstructure. This left large areas of deck space clear for the carriage of containers.

In anticipation of the arrival at the Fishguard station of *Duke of Rothesay* in spring 1967, *St Andrew* made her last regular sailing from Fishguard on 30 December 1966, and her last from Rosslare on 31 December. She was then moored in the harbour on a care-and-maintenance basis. She sailed again late in March 1967, and on 24 June arrived at Antwerp in tow of the tug *Dhulia* for scrapping by Jos. de Smedt.

St Andrew arriving Fishguard August 1966

TSS GREAT WESTERN

BUILT	1933 by Cammell Laird & Co Ltd, Birkenhead
GROSS TONS	1,742
DIMENSIONS	297 ft 6 in x 42 ft 5 in x 13 ft 3¼ in
MACHINERY	6-cyl triple-expansion by Cammel Laird
	Oil-fired boilers
SPEED	14 knots
ROUTE	Fishguard-Waterford

Delivered in January 1934, this single ship was designed for the Water-ford run and replaced the *Great Western* (1,339 tons, built 1902). Indeed, she has rarely sailed elsewhere. She could carry 450 passengers in two classes (250 first-class amidships ; 200 third-class in the poop), general cargo and considerable numbers of cattle. She was owned by the GWR and remained on the service through most of the war except for a period from April to August 1944 when she was engaged in cross-Channel trooping. With the exception of her conversion from coal burning in her spring overhaul of 1947, little variation marked her career until June 1959 when passengers ceased to be carried. She was then refitted at Penarth to carry more unit loads. Her third-class accommodation, deck-house and lifeboats at the stern were removed and the crew moved into the first-class accommodation. Her foremast and mainmast were replaced ; a new foremast was fitted on the superstructure forward of the funnel and new mainmast fitted at the after end of the boat deck. Total altera-tions had the effect of increasing her gross tonnage from 1,659 to 1,742.

Her annual overhaul came end of April to early June each year, and, due to lack of coaling facilities at Fishguard, she was usually replaced by an oil-burner. While the passenger service was operative she was replaced by *Princess Maud* in the years 1948-59. In 1960 *Slieve Donard* ran ; in 1961 *Slieve Bearnagh*. After then *Slieve Bawn* appeared each year.

Great Western in her passenger-carrying days

135

A welcome relief was provided from her routine in 1964 when BR won from Jenkinson & Archer Ltd an annual contract to carry Irish bacon to the London market. During the summer period, when the Fishguard–Rosslare passenger service is nightly, the passenger ships carried the goods, but in winter and spring, when there were only three sailings per week in each direction, *Great Western* made a special Saturday sailing between Rosslare and Fishguard. She began this work in October 1964 and continued it until withdrawn.

That she should be replaced had been urged for some years, and she was withdrawn on 2 January 1967 and sent to Holyhead to lay up pending her sale, being replaced by *Eden Fisher,* on charter. From 6 March to 18 May 1967, she relieved *Slieve Bearnagh* on the Heysham–Belfast cargo service and was then sent to Jos. Boel et Fils, Tamise, Belgium, for breaking up in June 1967.

TSS ST DAVID

BUILT	1947 by Cammell Laird & Co Ltd, Birkenhead
GROSS TONS	3,783
DIMENSIONS	321 ft 4 in x 50 ft 5 in x 13 ft 3 in
MACHINERY	4 turbines by Cammell Laird, SR geared
	Oil-fired boilers
SPEED	20 knots
ROUTE	Fishguard-Rosslare

Launched in February 1947 and delivered five months later, *St David* has been owned from the beginning by F & R, being managed by the GWR up to nationalisation, thereafter by the BR Western Region.

Originally she carried some 1,300 passengers in two classes, accommodation including one- and two-berth cabins and open berths in the saloons, and fifty cars, loaded by crane. She has remained on the Fishguard station throughout her career except for autumn 1947, when she operated between Weymouth and the Channel Islands for a time.

Little excitement cheered her life until 10 February 1964, when she returned to her builders for modifications to enable her to operate as a side-loading drive-on car ferry. Not a great deal of structural alteration was necessary, the main item being the installation of a power-operated hinged hatch which, when closed down, covers the well in the shelter deck which gave access to the aft hold on the main deck. Her gross tonnage was thereby increased from 3,352 to 3,783. Side doors were also fitted to allow cars to drive onto the shelter deck. Her passenger accommodation was improved at the same time, and also in May 1966 when, *inter alia,* a new second-class smokeroom was fitted out.

She opened the drive-on service from Fishguard in May 1964, but driving-off at Rosslare was not possible until June 1965. She made the first known postwar cruise from Fishguard on 11 May 1968, giving five hours around Cardigan Bay.

St David at Fishguard August 1966

TSS DUKE OF ROTHESAY

BUILT	1956 by Wm. Denny & Bros Ltd, Dumbarton
GROSS TONS	4,138
DIMENSIONS	376 ft 1 in x 57 ft 4 in x 14 ft 10 in
MACHINERY	2 turbines by Denny, DR geared
SPEED	21 knots
ROUTE	Fishguard-Rosslare

This vessel was built for the Heysham–Belfast route, but was selected for conversion to a side-loading car ferry for Fishguard–Rosslare when an extra ship was required there for the 1967 season.

The work of conversion was carried out by Cammell Laird (Ship Repairers) Ltd, Birkenhead, from February to April 1967, and cost about £250,000. The main deck was stripped of all bulkhead structures, passenger and crew cabins and cargo spaces, leaving only an inner island comprising engine and boiler room casing, stairways, air-conditioning machinery, etc. Additional underdeck girders and pillars were fitted to BOT

137

and Lloyds standards. Fore and aft cargo spaces were modified and flush watertight steel hatch covers fitted. The original side doors were retained, but fitted with watertight seals. Extensive electrical modifications were necessary. New steel stairways were fitted between the three passenger decks and the car deck. In all, 116 cabins were removed during the conversion.

New accommodation includes a second-class lounge at the after end of the promenade deck, and another lounge containing an enquiry bureau at the aft end of the upper deck. The cafeteria on this deck has been redesigned, access being by a new lobby. There is a modified smokeroom and bar on the lower deck aft, fitted with alcove seating and air-conditioning.

To provide the drive-on facility, watertight side sliding doors were fitted, operated by air-powered motors. She is able to load and discharge in 1 hr 20 min.

The work was completed at the end of April and she ran trials on 8 May. She sailed for Fishguard on 9 May, and entered service on the Rosslare run on 13 May 1967. Still owned by BRB, she is on charter to F & R.

Duke of Rothesay leaving Rosslare 28 July 1968

THE
LONDON MIDLAND REGION

On 1 January 1948, services from Holyhead, Heysham and Goole, the sailings on Lake Windermere and the Tilbury-Gravesend ferry, all previously operated by the LMS were taken over by the London Midland Region. Not long afterwards the Goole section was transferred to the North Eastern Region, and the Tilbury section to the Eastern Region.

In 1950 the Rosslare service from Fishguard, previously managed by the Western Region, came under Euston's administration. Two years later responsibility for the service from Stranraer was transferred to Euston on behalf of the Scottish Region, so that most Irish Sea cross-channel services were now co-ordinated under the title 'Irish Shipping Services—London Midland Region'. It may be remembered, in passing, that it was the manager of the Irish Shipping Services at Euston who was held partly responsible for the factors leading to the loss of *Princess Victoria* in January 1953. Near the end of 1960 control of the Stranraer service was transferred back to Gourock to operate under a new name.

11 : HOLYHEAD

After 1939 the cross-channel situation at Holyhead changed little until recently, when plans were put into force which are gradually transforming the port into a vehicle ferry terminal of some importance.

Immediately before the last war only one passenger service was in operation from Holyhead. This was a nightly service to Dun Laoghaire, operated by *Cambria* (1921), *Hibernia* (1920) and *Scotia* (1921).

Cargo services were run on a nightly basis to Dublin (North Wall) and three times a week to Greenore (the passenger service there having ceased in 1926). To cater for these there were generally four or five cargo ships available, *Slieve Donard* (1921), *Slieve Bloom* (1930), *Slieve More* (1932), *Slieve League* (1935) and *Slieve Bawn* (1936). The reason for so many cargo ships is that it was not the practice to send cargo by the nightly mail/passenger ships.

In 1939 two new motor ships were ordered from Fairfields, but the war caused these to be cancelled. It was intended that the new ships should carry cargo, and there was talk of their serving Dublin (North Wall) direct instead of Dun Laoghaire. Had war not intervened it is reasonable to suppose that the pattern of service from Holyhead would have altered considerably.

During the war the services were kept open as far as possible. *Hibernia* remained mainly on the Dun Laoghaire run whilst *Cambria* was posted to the Heysham–Belfast service for a period because all the Heysham ships had been called up. The Greenore cargo service was reduced to two sailings per week in 1940 and later to only one. After the war, only one ship, *Scotia,* lost in June 1940, failed to turn up for civilian duties. *Cambria* and *Hibernia* quickly brought the service back to near normal, and about the beginning of 1947 *Princess Maud* was transferred to Holyhead from Stranraer to replace *Scotia* as third ship. She took up the service at once but shortage of coal caused sailings of the older pair to be cancelled for odd periods.

In prewar days it was not unusual for one of the cargo 'Slieves' to be transferred to Heysham for a period, eg *Slieve Bloom* was there during 1938, and again during the late 1940s. The postwar Dublin (North Wall) service was run as before on a nightly basis, there being often two ships sailing in each direction every night for quite long periods. The Greenore service settled down to a regular schedule of one sailing only per week, but the steady decline in cargo offering ensured its final withdrawal in December 1951. Most of the 'Slieves' served on this route.

The two passenger ships ordered in 1939, but later cancelled, eventually appeared in 1949. They were ordered in 1946 from Harland & Wolff, not Fairfield. Replacing the two existing steamers, the new motor ships were named *Cambria* and *Hibernia* and they took up service to Dun Laoghaire. There was, presumably, no further thought of operating to Dublin direct, so there was still a need to provide cargo-only ships for the latter service. The mail service continued to be operated on a nightly basis all the year round, generally by the two motor ships, with *Princess Maud* relieving them for overhaul and joining them in high summer so that extra, daylight, sailings could be given.

In July 1963 it was decided to build a stern-loading drive-on vehicle ferry for the main passenger route, delivery being expected in early July 1965. Talks were held between the Irish Government and BR concerning the construction of special berths to accommodate the new ships. The Holyhead terminal was built beside the entrance to the Inner Harbour, while a temporary terminal for which the Irish Government paid £143,000, was erected at Dun Laoghaire's East Pier. Of this cost £25,000 of fittings and equipment was to be transferred to the permanent berth at St Michael's Wharf on completion. As detailed plans were being made for this building programme, further improvements to the service were announced in August 1964, namely that *Cambria* and *Hibernia* were to have a face-lift. This was carried out by Harland & Wolff Ltd over winter 1964-5.

By the end of June 1965 everything was set for the start of the big new season with modernised mail ships and new berths, but there was no car ferry. The new ship, now named *Holyhead Ferry 1*, was not ready, and it was necessary to borrow *Normannia* from Dover to open the new drive-on service in a blaze of glory on Friday 9 July. Shortly afterwards the new ship took up the run. The timings from Holyhead of this new service were 10.45 am and 8.15 pm on Fridays and Saturdays ; 10.45 am only on other days, including Sundays. As the season drew to a close sailings became less frequent until they were operated only on Fridays and Saturdays (10.45 am) during the first two weeks of October, after which it did not run. Clearly the service was to be seasonal only, the ship being transferred to Stranraer during the early part of 1966 and 1967. In 1966 the service ran from 20 May to 15 October on a daily basis with extra sailings on certain days between mid-June and mid-September. During the off-season months cars have to be crane-loaded onto the mail ships, but the latter do not accept cars when the car ferry is running.

The appearance of *Holyhead Ferry 1* rendered *Princess Maud* redundant as third ship, and, after spending most of the season running day excursions to Dun Laoghaire, she was withdrawn in September 1965. During the year she retained the old BR livery of black hull and buff funnel with black top.

Not all attention was being devoted to the Holyhead passenger service, however. Quietly, behind the scenes, improvements were also being carried out to the cargo services. From 1951 to 1954 the Dublin service was maintained by *Slieve Donard* (1922), *Slieve Bloom, Slieve More* and *Slieve League*. In that year the old *Slieve Donard* was withdrawn and replaced by *Slieve Bawn,* transferred from Heysham. In 1960 a new TSMV *Slieve Donard* took up the run, freeing *Slieve Bawn* to return to Heysham. The trade was turning more and more to the use of containers, and the older 'Slieves' had by now been modified to enable them to carry more of these. What was really needed was a proper container ship, but to avoid the expense of buying a new one the railways bought the motor vessel *Harrogate* from Associated Humber Lines Ltd, and had her specially converted. She entered the run in April 1965, *Slieve Bloom* being withdrawn in April and *Slieve More* the following month, and at about the same time *Slieve Bawn* was again transferred from Heysham to make up the full quota of four ships. Thus there were now generally *Harrogate, Slieve Donard, Slieve League* and *Slieve Bawn* in service together, the first two usually carrying containers only, while the other two took some containers, livestock and general cargo.

In September 1966 *Slieve League* was withdrawn, and subsequently chartered tonnage has been used to take her place. Indeed, the chartering of cargo ships has taken place from time to time ever since 1948, and has increased in recent years (see chapter on chartering).

There was a minor stir in 1965 when a publicity brochure entitled 'Cruise across to Ireland with British Rail' was published, carrying a photograph of the Eastern Region's *Avalon*. These were subsequently withdrawn because of possible misrepresentation. The brochure also carried a picture of *Lord Warden* which has never served anywhere but from Dover since built in 1952! This leaflet is therefore something of a collectors' item. But worse was to come. The Heysham–Belfast brochure for 1965-6 proudly bore a spectacular air-picture of one of the Holyhead–Dun Laoghaire mail ships which, like *Lord Warden,* had never served anywhere but on their original route.

The McKinsey Report of 1968 recommended that the use of Holyhead as a container port be intensified at the expense of Heysham. Two large new container ships are expected to serve both Dublin and Belfast.

TSS CAMBRIA
TSS HIBERNIA

BUILT	1920 by Wm. Denny & Bros Ltd, Dumbarton
GROSS TONS	3,462/3,467
DIMENSIONS	380 ft 7 in x 45 ft 2 in x 14 ft
MACHINERY	4 turbines by Denny, SR geared
	Coal-fired boilers
SPEED	25 knots
ROUTE	Holyhead-Dun Laoghaire

By the end of the first world war, the City of Dublin Steam Packet Company had held the Holyhead mail contract for longer than the London & North Western Railway cared to remember, and, when the war was over, orders were placed by the railway for four crack steamers in a determined effort to gain this contract. The Dublin company suffered severe losses in the war, and conceded victory to the railway in 1920. *Hibernia* was launched on 9 March, *Cambria* on 31 August 1920. The other two had relatively short histories ; *Anglia* was sold for breaking at Troon in 1935, *Scotia* was sunk by enemy action in May 1940. They were extremely fine ships, their speed being a particularly interesting feature, as they were predominantly night ships and there can have been no special advantages for passengers in arriving in Ireland any earlier than the crack of dawn.

There was accommodation for 956 first-class and 549 third-class passengers, though these figures altered from time to time. There were berths for about 220 first-class and 86 second-class, mostly on the main deck. After passing to the LMS in 1923, they underwent modernisation during winter 1931-2, including the fitting of a lounge under the bridge, and the enclosing with glass windows of the forward part of the superstructure at promenade deck level aft to a point just before the after funnel. It was about 1936 that the cowls were removed from the funnels, the forward one of which was always slightly narrower than the other.

Hibernia II in summer 1948

143

In the second war *Cambria* was confined, as far as was practicable, to maintaining the Irish Sea services, running from Heysham to Belfast during the latter years. *Hibernia* also was kept on station for most of the war.

The war over, replacements were ordered by the LMS, and in May 1948, the suffix *II* was added to the old pair so that their names could be used again. *Hibernia II* was towed to Barrow for breaking on 30 March 1949, and *Cambria II* to Milford Haven in mid-May also for breaking. T. W. Ward Ltd handled both.

TSS SLIEVE DONARD

BUILT	1921 by Vickers Armstrong (Shipbuilders) Ltd, Barrow
GROSS TONS	1,116
DIMENSIONS	299 ft 11 in x 39 ft 1 in x 12 ft 8½ in
MACHINERY	8-cyl triple-expansion by Vickers
	Coal-fired boilers
SPEED	16 knots
ROUTE	Holyhead-Dublin (North Wall)
	Holyhead-Greenore (to 1951)

Launched on 6 October 1921, *Slieve Donard* was the last ship built for the London & North Western Railway and replaced *Slieve Bloom* (1908), unhappily run into by an American cruiser off South Stack at night when she was travelling without lights.

Slieve Donard could carry some 400 tons of cargo, several hundred cattle and 242 passengers. She thus had more passenger accommodation

Slieve Donard in her later years

144

than the other cargo ships and was usually used for the Thursday midday sailing from Dublin, bringing home farmers who had attended the morning cattle sales there. This continued until the new *Slieve More* appeared in 1932, after which *Slieve Donard* was taken off this special sailing and her passenger licence lapsed. During the war she remained on Irish Sea cargo services.

After 1946, by which time the passenger services had been fully revived, she never carried passengers, and did not operate to Greenore after the service to that port was terminated in 1951. In January 1954 she was withdrawn, replaced by *Slieve Bawn* (qv) from Heysham, and eventually sold for breaking up at Troon, where she arrived on 21 May 1954 for scrapping by the West of Scotland Shipbreaking Co Ltd.

TSS SLIEVE BLOOM
TSS SLIEVE MORE

BUILT	1930/32 by Wm. Denny & Bros Ltd, Dumbarton
GROSS TONS	1,297/1,370
DIMENSIONS	310 ft/309 ft 6 in x 46 ft 10 in x 13 ft
MACHINERY	4 Parsons turbines by Denny, SR geared Coal-fired boilers
SPEED	16 knots
ROUTE	Holyhead-Greenore (to 1951)/Dublin

These two were the first of a series of five cattle/general cargo ships ordered by the LMS for the services from Holyhead and Heysham in the early 1930s, and throughout their careers they have remained fairly consistently at Holyhead.

Slieve Bloom was the first of the five, running trials on 17th December 1930. In postwar years each has appeared occasionally at Heysham on relief work, and, in fact, *Slieve Bloom* spent two years up to 1948 serving from Heysham. *Slieve Bloom*, when new, made small history by being the first cargo 'packet' to be fitted with electric deck cranes. She had no passenger certificate, but did, up to 1939, occasionally carry drovers who attended the 615 head of cattle she could carry. *Slieve More*, on the other hand, did have a passenger certificate. Her accommodation, situated amidships, included a dining saloon and two two-berth cabins, catered for seventy-five people, and was installed specially so that the ship could take over the Thursday midday sailing from *Slieve Donard*. During the war her certificate lapsed, and she did not thereafter carry passengers. She carried 623 head of cattle. Both ships were delivered with cowls on the funnels, but these were removed in the mid-1930s.

During the war both remained in normal service, as far as possible.

Shortly after the war their mainmasts were removed, but the new lighting regulations of 1954 caused them to have a second mast fitted immediately forward of the funnel. 25 to 28 containers could be carried. Each ship served intermittently on the Greenore run until it was terminated in 1951. 1964 was an exciting year for *Slieve More* in an otherwise stolid career. On 7 April she collided with the Ellerman steamer *Grecian* (3,284 tons, built 1949) just over a mile north of Holyhead and suffered extensive bow damage. In August she intercepted a yacht, stolen from Menai Bridge, in mid-channel, and with Admiralty permission placed some men aboard. The two ships then set off for Holyhead, *Slieve More* being replaced by a naval vessel en route.

The passage of years and the fact that they were still coal-burners ensured that 1965 was to see their final voyages ; *Slieve Bloom* made hers on 10 April and *Slieve More* on 12 May. They were then laid up in the outer harbour and offered for sale in July. Van Heyghen Frères bought them for scrap in September, *Slieve More* arriving at Bruges on 6 October and *Slieve Bloom* at Ghent on 7 October, both under tow.

Slieve More before mast alterations

146

TSS PRINCESS MAUD

BUILT	1934 by Wm. Denny & Bros Ltd, Dumbarton
GROSS TONS	2,917
DIMENSIONS	330 ft x 51 ft 3 in x 11 ft 6 in
MACHINERY	4 turbines by Denny, SR geared
	Oil-fired boilers
SPEED	21 knots
ROUTE	Holyhead-Dun Laoghaire

Built for the Stranraer–Larne service of the LMS, the *Princess Maud* was an all-round improvement on her predecessors. She had mechanical stokers (being at first coal-fired); was the first British-built ship to have automatic sprinkler and fire alarm protection against fire, and had superb public room accommodation. She was, in addition, the first LMS ship to be built without a cowl on the funnel. She originally carried 1,458 passengers, and was launched in December 1933 in thick fog—not an encouraging start! She made her inaugural voyage on 27 February 1934.

When war came she left Stranraer on 5 September 1939 for transport duties based on Southampton and then appeared at the Dunkirk evacuation. While approaching Gravelines on 30 May 1940 she suffered severe damage and the loss of several of her crew when a shell penetrated her engine-room. Having returned to Dover for quick repairs, she sailed yet again. Together with *Royal Sovereign* (Eagle steamers) she is said to have been the last passenger ship to leave Dunkirk on the morning of 4 June just before the port was closed. In later war years she served as an infantry landing ship, pennant number 4.414, with J2 Assault Group based on Southampton. During D Day operations she was attached to the US Task Force. In 1945 she did some leave-trooping between Channel ports, notably Calais–Folkestone, and was then returned to the LMS.

Her postwar duties were at first on her original route, until *Princess Margaret* returned to the run a few months later. Part of 1946 was also spent on the Stranraer station, and she made her first sailing from Holyhead on 19 February 1947. To assist in docking at the latter port she was fitted with an extra 'flying bridge' on her port side. In subsequent years she carried 1,200 passengers in two classes with berths for 223, including one- and two-berth cabins and two-berth cabins-de-luxe first-class, and two-, four- and six-berth cabins and open-berths second-class. She also had some 43,000 cu ft of cargo space. About 1947 some first-class accommodation, including the smokeroom, was given over to second-class.

After the war she was essentially a vagrant ship, being mainly involved in relief and extra sailings although her home was Holyhead and she had a Holyhead master and crew. Up to 1959 she undertook very much the same cycle of activity each year. January and February she sailed Stranraer–Larne (relieving *Princess Margaret*); March and April: Holyhead–Dun Laoghaire; May and June: Fishguard–Waterford (relieving *Great Western*); July to September: Holyhead–Dun Laoghaire (extra sailings); October and November she had her overhaul, usually at Holy-

Princess Maud arriving at Dun Laoghaire 6 August 1965

head; December she was spare at Holyhead. In 1946 she was converted to oil burning. Summer 1951 saw her unusually serving between Southampton and St Malo, while her place at Holyhead was taken by *Duke of York*. After 1959 she did not serve Fishguard, the Fishguard–Waterford passenger service having been terminated in that year, and so her various duties gradually became whittled down, though later on she served between Heysham and Belfast on two or three days, usually in July, as extra to the resident mail ships. Her last trip between these two ports was on 9 July 1965. Her last relief work at Stranraer was in 1961, *Princess Margaret*'s last year in service there.

The *Princess Maud*'s last few years in service were really very quiet, centring as they did on extra and relief sailings only from Holyhead, including providing cheap-day 'Four Hours in Dublin' excursions for trippers from North Wales towns. It was known in February 1965 that she was to be withdrawn in September that year, and she was actually bought by Lefkosia of Panama in August for service in Greek waters.

Venus (ex-*Princess Maud*) showing her present appearance after alterations in Greece

She made her last sailing for BR on Saturday, 4 September 1965, left their service entirely on 17 September and was shortly afterwards renamed *Venus* for her new owners. She was never given the new BR livery, worn by her running-mates during 1965. What a disappointing end to this fine ship's home-waters career!

As *Venus* she left Holyhead for a refit at Brest on 17 September, and on arrival in Greece later was further altered. Her present external appearance can be seen in the drawing. Internally her public rooms and cabins were refurbished, additional berths being fitted, and she was also provided with side-loading drive-on facilities. She left Piraeus on her first commercial voyage for her new owners on Wednesday, 15 June 1966, and operated until 10 October on the weekly Piraeus–Limassol–Haifa–Limassol–Piraeus–Brindisi–Piraeus circle. Her present gross tonnage is 3,032 and she is managed by Cyprus Sea Cruises (Limassol) Ltd.

TSMV HIBERNIA
TSMV CAMBRIA

BUILT	1949 by Harland & Wolff Ltd, Belfast
GROSS TONS	5,284
DIMENSIONS	397 ft x 56 ft 3 in x 14 ft 10 in
MACHINERY	Two 2-stroke single-acting 8-cyl Burmeister & Wain diesels by Harland & Wolff
SPEED	21 knots
ROUTE	Holyhead-Dun Laoghaire

These ships were ordered by the LMS as replacements for the ageing *Cambria II* and *Hibernia II*. *Hibernia* came first and was launched on 22 July 1948, entering service on 14 April 1949, and running with *Hibernia II* until the latter was replaced by the new *Cambria* in the following month. *Cambria* was launched on 21 September 1948. In these years they could carry some 2,360 passengers in two classes. Sleeping accommodation consisted of two-berth cabins-de-luxe with wc and bath ; one- and two-berth cabins with and without wc plus open berths for the first-class and two-, four- and six-berth cabins plus open berths for the second-class. Stabilisers were fitted in both ships in 1951.

In 1964 tenders were invited from British yards for the complete modernisation of the ships, and the contract went, appropriately enough, to their builders. *Hibernia* was off for refit from 28 September 1964, and *Cambria* from early January 1965, each refit lasting three months. *Hibernia* was replaced successively by *Princess Maud* and *St Andrew* ; *Cambria* by *Princess Maud*. The work involved the renewal of interior decoration, furnishings and fittings ; the removal of cabins from C deck (replaced by the new second-class lounges amidships and aft) and from D deck (re-

149

placed by the new second-class smokeroom and cafeteria). On B deck the original first- and second-class smokerooms have become a tearoom seating 146 ; the aft end of the main lounge has become a second-class lounge with 106 seats. The coal-fired galleys were replaced by new electrically-operated equipment. New lighting was installed in all the public rooms and seating is now provided for 425 first-class and 1,830 second-class. The gross tonnage was increased from 4,972 but the dimensions were not affected. Externally, the changes have been few. The white line has disappeared from the uppermost strake, and most important, the open sides of the after end of the promenade deck have been plated over, and a spirket plate has been fitted to the bows. Present sleeping accommodation consists of one- and two-berth cabins with and without wc plus open berths first-class, and two-, four-, and six-berth cabins plus open berths second-class.

Neither ship has been particularly accident-prone but on 24 September 1965 *Cambria* damaged her plates in collision with West Pier, Dun Laoghaire in thick fog. She was temporarily repaired on the spot with cement and a more permanent repair was carried out the following month on the Mersey by Harland and Wolff. Her place was taken by *Hibernia*, whose sailings were, in turn, taken by the *Duke of Rothesay* for a short time, as the usual relief ship, *Princess Maud,* had been delivered to foreign buyers just a week before it happened.

Hibernia served between Heysham and Belfast from 28 December 1967 to 13 January 1968, replacing *Duke of Argyll* which was in dry dock at Liverpool undergoing damage repairs. This was the first time either ship had served on the Heysham route.

Hibernia at the Heysham berth, Belfast, 29 December 1967

TSMV SLIEVE DONARD

BUILT	1960 by Ailsa Shipbuilding Co Ltd, Troon
GROSS TONS	1,598
DIMENSIONS	310 ft 3 in x 47 ft 3 in x 13 ft 1 in
MACHINERY	Two 2-stroke single-acting 8-cyl diesels by British Polar Engines Ltd
SPEED	14 knots
ROUTE	Holyhead-Dublin

Replacing *Slieve Donard* (1921), the present version has no sister and although specially fitted out for unit-loads, cattle and vehicles, has an attractive profile more in keeping with the grace of the thirties than the utilities of the sixties.

She made her maiden voyage in January 1960 between Holyhead and Dublin (North Wall) and has remained generally on that route, though she has made interesting excursions elsewhere from time to time. In spring 1960 she relieved *Great Western* on the Fishguard–Waterford run, and in that year as well as in 1961, relieved the unit-load ships on the Heysham–Belfast service. From 4 July 1964 to 24 August 1964 she ran on charter to the Caledonian Steam Packet Co (Irish Services) Ltd carrying passengers' cars between Stranraer and Larne, and on 29 August 1964 she sailed from Waterford for Holyhead with fifty-two containers of meat and cheese, the first known railway-ship link between the two ports. From 8 July 1966 to 30 September 1966 she ran between Fishguard and Rosslare with passengers' cars. Quite a widely travelled cargo ship!

She has no passenger accommodation; but carries up to 685 cattle, 639 tons of cargo and 63 containers. She can carry a total of just over 100 cars, driven on at the stern. The photograph shows that she has both masts positioned on the midships superstructure to leave the decks clear for cargo. Early in 1968 she served for some weeks regularly between Heysham and Belfast.

Slieve Donard at Fishguard August 1966

151

MV HARROGATE
MV SELBY

BUILT	1959 by James Lamont & Co Ltd, Port Glasgow
GROSS TONS	963
DIMENSIONS	232 ft 1 in x 39 ft 5 in x 13 ft 2 in
MACHINERY	4-stroke single-acting 7-cyl diesel by Ruston & Hornsby Ltd, Lincoln
SPEED	12 knots
ROUTE	Hull/Goole-Continent (to 1965)
	Harrogate Holyhead-Dublin *Selby* Heysham-Belfast

During 1958-9 six new general cargo ships were delivered for the Humber–Continent services of AHL to replace the gaggle of elderly steamers operating until then. *Harrogate* and *Selby* are two of this series, the others were similarly named after towns. None has consistently served a particular route for any length of time. There is some 93,000 cu ft of cargo space and no passenger accommodation.

Harrogate entered service on the Goole–Rotterdam run on 4 April 1959 and *Selby* on the Goole–Amsterdam run on 8 July 1959. Afterwards they served severally between Hull and Goole and Hamburg, Bremen, Antwerp, Amsterdam and Rotterdam. *Harrogate* paid rare visits to Copenhagen. By the end of 1964 services from the Humber had been reduced so much that the decision was taken to part with these two ships, and they were sold to BR London Midland Region, which was short of suitable unit-load tonnage. They were transferred in March 1965 and refitted at Immingham and Holyhead respectively, emerging in BR livery, suitably adapted for containers, including the provision of vertical steel framework along the sides to enable units to be carried on deck. *Harrogate* took up the Dublin (North Wall) run on 15 April 1965, *Selby* entered the

Harrogate at Dublin 1965

Belfast service about the same time. Each can carry about sixty-three containers.

On 1 January 1968, a through unit-load service from London and the Midlands to Dublin via Holyhead was introduced on a daily (Monday-Friday) basis. *Harrogate* was selected to operate the sea journey, leaving Holyhead at 8.30 am and Dublin at 7.00 pm daily, the crossing taking about six hours. She was specially adapted at Holyhead for this work to enable her to carry a total of twenty-eight 20 ft x 8 ft x 8 ft International Standards Organisation containers. The 'tween deck hatches were fixed in the open position and tonnage hatches closed resulting in the ship being remeasured as a single-deck cargo ship. Cells constructed of steel girders, capable of accommodating containers stacked three-high, were built into No 1 and No 2 holds. Six containers fit into two cells in No 1, and twelve in four cells in No 2. The MacGregor hatch covers have been reinforced to carry the extra weight of the other containers, which are secured to key plates.

TSS HOLYHEAD FERRY I

BUILT	1965 by Hawthorn Leslie (Shipbuilders) Ltd, Hebburn-on-Tyne
GROSS TONS	3,879
DIMENSIONS	369 ft x 57 ft 2 in x 12 ft 9 in
MACHINERY	2 sets Pametrada turbines by Hawthorn Leslie (Engineers) Ltd, DR geared
	Oil-fired boilers
SPEED	19½ knots
ROUTE	Holyhead-Dun Laoghaire

Launched on 17 February 1965, this ship is the railway's first specially built stern-loading car ferry to operate from Holyhead. Her name is an unhappy choice. The general manager of the region evidently felt that some defence was necessary, for after her launch, he is reported to have said that the name 'Was carefully chosen to identify the ship with the service, and to give some indication of future intentions'.

She was late entering service, being delayed by minor troubles on two occasions, and *Normannia* from Dover operated the Holyhead–Dun Laoghaire service from 9 to 19 July 1965 when *Holyhead Ferry I* was able to make her maiden voyage. There is accommodation for 1,000 one-class passengers, including 2 cabins-de-luxe, 12 one-berth, 15 two-berth and 6 three-berth cabins. Other facilities include smokeroom-bar (120 seats) forward on the shelter deck, self-service cafeteria (228 seats) on the upper deck, tea-bar/lounge (196 seats) on shelter deck amidships, and a lounge aft on shelter deck (232 reclining seats).

The ship is fitted with bow rudder, twin stern rudders, Vickers transverse bow propulsion unit and fin stabilisers. Access to the main (car) deck, holding 125 vehicles, is by hydraulically-operated stern ramp. From the main deck twenty-five cars can gain entry to the upper deck forward by hinged ramps. A 22 ft-diameter electrically-operated turntable near the stern aids handling.

In February and March 1966 and 1967 she relieved *Caledonian Princess* on the Stranraer–Larne service, but has served on no other route.

Holyhead Ferry I leaving Larne for Stranraer February 1966

12: HEYSHAM

Heysham was the most fortunate of all the major packet ports being the only one whose fleet came through the war intact. This was not entirely to its own advantage, however, because some ships were taken away after the war to fill vacancies elsewhere.

The summer season of 1939 was among the busiest ever on the Heysham–Belfast passenger route. Not only were the three regular 'Dukes' kept busy, but *Duke of York* and *Princess Margaret* (from Stranraer) were also pressed into frequent service. There were, on some nights, three sailings in one direction and two in another. Also on the same service was the cargo steamer *Slieve Bearnagh* although all passenger ships carried some cargo. *Slieve Bearnagh* was, in fact, the first cargo-only ship to be built specially for the route.

No other cross-channel route has been operated by the railways from Heysham since 1928, but a small twin-screw tug-tender named *Wyvern* (1905) was based latterly at Heysham and used for excursions to Fleetwood. She survived the war and took up excursions from Heysham in 1946, but lasted only a short time in this trade. She could carry 250 passengers.

After war broke out *Duke of York* was taken over fairly soon for active service, but the other 'Dukes' remained and efforts were made, not always successfully, to maintain the service. About 1942 the remaining 'Dukes' went to war, and the route thereafter was served, as far as was possible, by Holyhead's *Cambria* and a twin-screw steamer *Louth* (1906) chartered from the British & Irish Steam Packet Co Ltd. Cargo services of sorts were also kept up. An additional service to Greenore was run from 1941 to 1943 as a relief measure about twice a week.

After the war *Duke of Lancaster* was the first to be returned to the LMS and so went back into service, followed soon by *Duke of Argyll*. The other two, *Duke of Rothesay* and *Duke of York*, spent a short time trooping between Harwich and the Hook of Holland before returning to Heysham. *Princess Margaret* did not return at all, being needed at Stranraer during and after the war. In 1948 *Duke of York* was transferred to Harwich for good. Thereafter, the three sister 'Dukes' had to cope, helped by *Princess Maud* and, to provide additional sailings, daylight crossings were made. With *Duke of York* gone, a further cargo ship was required and *Slieve Bloom,* usually based at Holyhead, was transferred to run opposite *Slieve Bearnagh. Slieve Bloom* returned to Holyhead about 1950 in exchange for *Slieve Bawn*. The withdrawal of *Slieve Donard* near the beginning of 1954 meant that the Heysham–Holyhead cargo fleet was one ship down. To keep up numbers at the latter, *Slieve Bawn* returned there late in 1953, this time to take over *Slieve Donard*'s sailings. The vacancy thus created at Heysham was filled by the steamer *Maidstone,* moved from Folkestone. After September 1957 she seldom served, and in 1959 *Slieve Bawn* was again in service opposite *Slieve Bearnagh,* remaining on station until early 1965.

To revert to the passenger services, we find the three 1928 'Dukes' still in service up to 1956-7, when they were replaced by three new ships with the same names. One of these, *Duke of Lancaster,* was specially fitted out to undertake off-season cruises. She visited many far-distant places during the years she was cruising, but of particular interest was the revival of Western Isles cruises in 1959. Operated from Liverpool by Coast Lines Ltd in prewar years, these were reinstated in 1947 by that company's beautiful *Lady Killarney* but later abandoned because they were uneconomical.

During the peak holiday season in subsequent years the Belfast service run was operated by the 'Dukes' and *Princess Maud,* offering double nightly sailings each way and daylight sailings on odd occasions. After *Princess Maud* went at the end of 1965, only the extra 'Dukes' served in 1966, again offering a number of extra daylight passages and double nightly sailings in one direction only. This year was the last during which Western Isles and other cruises were operated by *Duke of Lancaster,* because in 1967 only she and *Duke of Argyll* remained to handle business, *Duke of Rothesay* having gone to Fishguard. What a contrast with 1939, when five ships were kept busy! It is extremely unlikely that Western Isles cruises will ever be revived by railway ships in any event. The places visited on the last *Duke of Lancaster* cruise were, in order of calls, Brodick in the Isle of Arran, Iona, Tobermory, Stornoway, Ullapool, Portree and Oban.

So much for the development of passenger services to date. While these have been somewhat reduced, the carriage of cargo, particularly in unit loads, has expanded. Early in 1958, *Slieve Bearnagh* was waving the flag for the railways largely on her own, supported from time to time by chartered tonnage. It was in this year that big developments came in the unit-load trade, when the region's first nightly through-unit-load service, using specially built ships, was started in October with *Container Venturer* and *Container Enterprise.* They proved successful, and early in 1965 *Selby,* formerly owned by AHL, joined them, enabling *Slieve Bawn* to return to Holyhead. *Selby* was originally a general cargo ship, but was altered to carry containers on deck before taking up her new duties. With three container ships and *Slieve Bearnagh* available it is possible to provide two cargo sailings nightly in each direction, and this is the general practice.

Frequent daylight passenger sailings were operated for the first time for many years between Heysham and Belfast during 1967 to cope with the holiday traffic. They were run on Saturdays and some Fridays during July, August and September.

TSS DUKE OF ARGYLL
TSS DUKE OF LANCASTER
TSS DUKE OF ROTHESAY

BUILT	1928 by Wm. Denny & Bros Ltd, Dumbarton
GROSS TONS	3,799/3,838/3,805
DIMENSIONS	349 ft x 53 ft 1 in x 14 ft 10 in
MACHINERY	4 Parsons turbines by Denny, SR geared
	Coal-fired boilers
SPEED	21 knots
ROUTE	Heysham-Belfast

Prior to the introduction of these three ships, the LMS had maintained services to Belfast from both Heysham and Fleetwood. Towards the mid-1920s it was decided that all sailings should be made from Heysham,

Duke of Lancaster leaving Belfast about 1955

157

and so the LMS ordered new ships for that station. *Duke of Lancaster,* launched on 22 November 1927, opened the new combined service from Heysham on 30 April 1928, with *Duke of Argyll* launched on 23 January 1928. *Rothesay,* Denny's hundredth turbine steamer, was launched on 22 March 1928. They were similar in layout, and could carry 1,500 passengers, 700 first-class and 800 steerage, with berths for 308 first-class and 104 third-class passengers. They were among the first cross-channel ships to introduce single-berth cabins which were not of the very expensive de-luxe type. Bathrooms were equipped with showers and both fresh and salt water were available. The first-class dining saloon, seating fifty, was forward on the upper deck, with kitchen underneath, and there were two lounges for ladies abaft the dining saloon. Woodwork in the public rooms was of mahogany, except for the smokeroom on the promenade deck aft which was oak. There were also stalls below decks for 296 cattle and horses.

Duke of Lancaster was seriously damaged by fire shortly before she was due to sail from Heysham on 28 November 1931. She heeled over to starboard and sank the following day. Saloon accommodation on four decks was gutted and it was January 1932 before she was raised. Her refit included the addition of the new type of bridge with end-cabs, which became a feature of LMS ships. The cowls originally on their funnels were removed from *Duke of Argyll* and *Duke of Rothesay* in 1935 and from *Duke of Lancaster* in 1937. In 1939 *Duke of Lancaster* again had bad luck, ramming the Liverpool coaster *Fire King* in mid-channel causing the latter to sink with the loss of one life.

After war broke out they remained on station and were not requisitioned until about 1942, when they took up transport duties. *Duke of Rothesay* became an assault transport, pennant number 4.421, and *Duke of Argyll,* which saw most war service, also became a landing ship, infantry, with the pennant number 4.42 (Exbury group) and then was in use as a hospital carrier for a time. *Duke of Lancaster* was returned to the LMS immediately after the war, and *Duke of Argyll* followed shortly after. *Duke of Rothesay* came last, having been engaged in trooping from Harwich. On her return to service she was given a deckhouse on the after end of the boat deck, the only one of the three to have this.

When in service before the war all the ships had a gross tonnage slightly less than shown above ; alterations for war service and refits early in 1946 and again in 1948 served to increase it by small but not uniform amounts each time.

Replacements for them were ordered in 1954 and in the same year each ship had the suffix *II* added to its name to free it for the successor. *Duke of Lancaster*, the first of the new ships, entered service in late summer 1956, the other two coming before the end of the year, by which time the old 'Dukes' had been withdrawn and sold for breaking up by T. W. Ward Ltd. *Duke of Lancaster* was towed to Briton Ferry in October 1956, *Duke of Rothesay* to Milford Haven in January 1957 and *Duke of Argyll* to Troon in July 1957. So far as can be discovered none of the

1928 'Dukes' served commercially on any route other than Heysham–Belfast during peacetime. *Duke of Lancaster* made her last sailing on 13 August 1956, *Duke of Rothesay* hers on 16 September, and *Duke of Argyll* made hers on 24 October.

TSS SLIEVE LEAGUE
TSS SLIEVE BAWN
TSS SLIEVE BEARNAGH

BUILT	1935/1937/1936 by Wm. Denny & Bros Ltd, Dumbarton
GROSS TONS	1,369/1,573/1,485
DIMENSIONS	*Slieve League* 309 ft 6 in x 46 ft 10 in x 12 ft 10 in
	Slieve Bawn/Slieve Bearnagh 309 ft 6 in x 47 ft 4 in x 13 in
MACHINERY	4 Parsons turbines by Denny, SR geared
	Slieve League Coal-fired boilers
	Slieve Bawn/Slieve Bearnagh Oil-fired boilers
SPEED	14–15 knots
ROUTE	*Slieve League* Holyhead-Greenore (to 1951)/Dublin
	Slieve Bearnagh Heysham-Belfast
	Slieve Bawn, all the above routes

These well-balanced ships completed the series of five built for the LMS Irish Sea cargo services in the 1930s.

Slieve League was launched on 21 December 1934, delivered in February 1935, and had a restricted certificate for seventy-five passengers so that she could be used to relieve *Slieve More* on the Dublin–Holyhead livestock run on Thursdays. This certificate lapsed during the war and was not taken up again. She could carry between 25 and 28 containers and 655 cattle. She altered little over the years, with the exception of the resiting of the mainmast forward of the funnel, and remained a coal-burner to the last. She made history by being the last ship to serve Greenore, making the final voyage from that port on 29 December 1951. Neither *Slieve Bearnagh* nor *Slieve Bawn* ever had a passenger certificate, though the latter has carried a few passengers occasionally.

Slieve Bearnagh was launched on 7 March 1936, and inaugurated the Heysham–Belfast cargo-only service, all cargo having been carried hitherto in the holds of the passenger ships, and she has served on that route throughout, although in 1961 she did run from Fishguard to Waterford relieving the *Great Western.*

Slieve Bawn was the last of the five, being launched on 15 December 1936 and delivered in February 1937. She entered service on the Holyhead station and generally remained there until moving to Heysham in 1950. From 1953 to 1959 she served from Holyhead, and then she went back to

Heysham again for nearly six years. Since early 1965 she has been based at Holyhead, replaced at Heysham by *Selby* and in turn taking up the sailings previously operated by one of the first 'Slieves'. Each spring from 1962 she relieved *Great Western* on the Fishguard–Waterford service.

Slieve Bearnagh carries 735 cattle and *Slieve Bawn* 718, and each has 55,580 cu ft (bale) cargo space, and can carry 27 large containers. In 1953 mainmasts were resited, *Slieve Bearnagh*'s immediately aft of the funnel, *Slieve Bawn*'s forward of it. This change was made to leave the aft deck completely clear of obstructions to enable more containers to be carried. In 1960 *Slieve Bearnagh* was refitted to burn oil, and officer and crew accommodation was modernised. In the following year *Slieve Bawn* underwent an even more extensive refit which also included modernisation of accommodation and conversion to oil-firing. The superstructure was almost entirely rebuilt, the wooden cabs being removed from the bridge wings ; the companionway from the boat deck down to the main deck was removed ; and the front of the superstructure and sides of the boat deck were almost entirely plated in. These changes caused an increase in gross tonnage for *Slieve Bearnagh* of 34 gross tons from 1,451 and for *Slieve Bawn* of 109 gross tons from 1,464.

During the war all three maintained cargo services in the Irish Sea as far as possible. They were capable of a speed of 17 knots but do not make use of this power under normal service conditions.

Slieve League arrived at Holyhead after her last sailing on 29 September 1966 and was later offered for sale. In January 1967 she was bought by Van Heyghen Frères of Ghent for breaking up at a cost of about £14,000, and arrived at Bruges under tow on 27 February 1967.

Slieve Bawn at Dublin 1965

TSS MAIDSTONE

BUILT	1926 by D. & W. Henderson & Co Ltd, Glasgow
GROSS TONS	844
DIMENSIONS	220 ft 9 in x 33 ft 7 in x 12 ft 9¼ in
MACHINERY	6-cyl triple-expansion by D. & W. Henderson
	Coal-fired boilers
SPEED	15 knots
ROUTE	Folkestone-Boulogne (to 1953) Heysham-Belfast (from 1953)

Launched on 16 March 1926 *Maidstone,* like *Deal,* carried no passengers, but was specially fitted out for the carriage of horses (including race-horses) and perishable cargo. During the war she, like others of her

Maidstone at Folkestone 9 August 1945, the day cargo services
were restored

type, served as a transport for military personnel and equipment on, for example, the Stranraer–Larne route. This did not last more than a couple of years, and she was returned to civilian services to run on a variety of routes including Penzance–Scilly Isles. In 1946 she went onto the Boulogne run, until making the surprise move to Heysham in 1953. At this time there was a surfeit of cargo ships on the south coast, but a shortage at Heysham, following the transfer of *Slieve Bawn* to Holyhead to replace *Slieve Donard* in that year. She served fairly consistently from Heysham, though she was not particularly successful. She was laid up at Barrow from 27 September to 12 December 1957, after which she had another spell in service and finally arrived in Barrow on 22 April 1958 for lay-up following her last crossing. She lay there, on the sale list, until 14 December, when she was towed away by the tug *Poolzee* for Antwerp to be broken up by Boomse Scheepsloperij.

She made her first sailing from Heysham to Belfast on 22 July 1953, and her last on the route on 14 April 1958.

TSS DUKE OF ARGYLL
TSS DUKE OF ROTHESAY

BUILT	1956 *Duke of Argyll* by Harland & Wolff Ltd, Belfast *Duke of Rothesay* by Wm. Denny & Bros Ltd, Dumbarton
GROSS TONS	4,797/4,780
DIMENSIONS	376 ft 1 in x 57 ft 4 in x 14 ft 10 in
MACHINERY	2 turbines by Denny, DR geared Oil-fired boilers
SPEED	21 knots
ROUTE	Heysham-Belfast

These two ships are of the group of three similar ships (see also *Duke of Lancaster*) built to replace the 28-year-old Heysham steamers with the same names. Without doubt the three are the most attractively designed ships built for any of the regions since 1948, and are as impressive inside as outside, the second-class accommodation in particular being a vast improvement on anything which had previously appeared. It has been further improved during the winter overhauls of 1964-5. *Duke of Argyll* was the second of the three to enter service having been launched on 12 January 1956, followed by *Duke of Rothesay* three months later, and she was the first 'Duke' to get the new BR colours in October 1964 at Belfast.

The ships load port-side only, have bow rudders, are fitted with stabilisers and have 77,510 cu ft (bale) cargo capacity. 1,800 passengers can be carried, 600 in the first-class and 1,200 in the second-class. Sleeping accommodation consists of 240 first-class berths in 4 two-berth cabins-de-luxe with bath facilities, and one-, two-, and four-berth cabins and 214 second-class berths in two- and four-berth cabins. Open berths with rug and pillow are available in both classes. The deck layout is similar to that of *Duke of Lancaster* (qv). A number of cars can be carried in two holds forward and 'tween decks fore and aft and are loaded by dockside crane. The mail and baggage are carried in special compartments aft. The annual overhaul is usually done at Heysham, and dry-docking at Holy-head. *Duke of Argyll* has, to date, served no other route, but *Duke of Rothesay* has served between Holyhead and Dun Laoghaire on two occasions so far. From about 25 September to 11 October 1965 she relieved the damaged *Cambria,* and for a few weeks in January and February 1966 she was on relief work. *Duke of Rothesay* was converted to a side-loading car ferry in February and March 1967 by Cammell Laird for service between Fishguard and Rosslare. Accommodation was modernised and the main deck for the most part stripped and she can now carry 100 cars.

Duke of Argyll arriving at Belfast 9 July 1966

TSS DUKE OF LANCASTER

BUILT	1956 by Harland & Wolff Ltd, Belfast
GROSS TONS	4,797
DIMENSIONS	376 ft 1 in x 57 ft 4 in x 14 ft 10 in
MACHINERY	2 turbines by Harland & Wolff, DR geared
	Oil-fired boilers
SPEED	21 knots
ROUTE	Heysham-Belfast West Highland and Continental
	cruises

Duke of Lancaster was the first of the three new ships built for the Heysham station at this time (see also *Duke of Argyll*). This one is like the others in nearly every respect when operating the night Belfast service, but was specially designed to undertake cruises also. Her structure consists of two complete steel decks, a lower deck forward and aft of the machinery space, boat deck and navigating bridge deck joining forward and aft bridges. The hull is divided into eleven watertight compartments. Peaks and double bottom carry water ballast, and there are lubricating-oil drain tanks below the turbines. Oil fuel and fresh water are carried in tanks built into the structure on top of the double bottom. First-class public rooms consist of a dining room seating seventy-six on the upper deck, and shop, smokeroom and bar adjoining the main lounge on the promenade deck. Second-class passengers have for their use a cafeteria

Duke of Lancaster passing through the Kiel Canal on a cruise
in 1963

seating ninety-six and a lounge on the upper deck and another lounge and ladies' room on the main deck.

When *Duke of Lancaster* is required for cruising big changes take place in the matter of only a few days. Many cabins are transformed into bathrooms for adjacent cabins ; double-berth cabins convert to singles with special drawer and wardrobe space ; lounges have seating removed and become recreation room and ballroom ; the second-class cafeteria becomes a proper dining room and is redecorated to be the same as the first-class dining room, and one cabin is altered to a ladies' hairdressing salon. When thus converted she carries 350 first-class passengers only and sleeping accommodation consists of double-berth cabins-deluxe, single-berth cabins inside and outside on A and B decks, doubles inside and outside on B deck and doubles also on lower decks. The crew is obtained from other ships on a voluntary basis, so that the service can be reckoned second to none. Up to six cruises have been run each year since 1958, using a variety of base ports in England, and visiting a wide range of Scottish, Scandinavian and Continental ports. Cruises have been run during the 'off' season, during May and June and again in September. It is of little value to detail all her cruises fully, but the following points may be of interest:

First cruise: Left Southampton 7 June 1958 for Amsterdam, Ostend, Rouen. (6 days).

First West Highland Cruise: Left Heysham 19 September 1959 for, *inter alia*, Oban, Skye, Iona. (10 days).

First from Harwich: 6 June 1961 for Amsterdam, Antwerp, Ostend. (6 days).

First to Oslo and Copenhagen: Left Heysham 10 May 1962. (12 days).

First to Spain (Corunna) and Lisbon: Left Southampton 4 June, 1964. (13 days).

First from Plymouth: 18 May 1965 for Corunna, Lisbon, etc. (13 days).

Last cruise: Left Heysham 14 September 1966 for Western Isles. (10 days).

Other points of interest are that when on passage from Heysham to Southampton on 31 June 1958 she called at Dun Laoghaire, and did so again on the return trip on 30 June ; on 16 September 1962 she made her only call at Ramsey Bay, Isle of Man.

Since 1966 she has made no more cruises because *Duke of Rothesay* was converted to side loading for another route and *Duke of Lancaster* was therefore required to maintain the night mail service along with *Duke of Argyll. Duke of Lancaster* has not served on any other crosschannel route to date.

MV CONTAINER ENTERPRISE
MV CONTAINER VENTURER

BUILT   1958 by Ailsa Shipbuilding Co Ltd, Troon
GROSS TONS   982
DIMENSIONS   262 ft 9 in x 42 ft x 10 ft 9 in
MACHINERY   2-stroke single acting 8-cyl diesel by British Polar
                    Engines Ltd, Glasgow
SPEED   12½ knots
ROUTE   Heysham-Belfast

Delivered in April and October 1958 respectively these unlovely, though intensely practical, ships inaugurated at the end of October a nightly unit-load service to Belfast. This was the first completely BR-owned service of this kind to operate anywhere. Designed for containers only they carry sixty-five large B-type units, and rarely carry other.

There is no accommodation for passengers. They have never served on any other route, and when off for overhaul are usually replaced by unit-load ships of other companies, eg MV *Race Fisher* owned by James Fisher and Sons Ltd in 1963 and 1964. *Slieve Donard* from Holyhead replaced them in 1960 and 1961.

Container Enterprise at her Belfast berth 9 July 1966

13: LAKE WINDERMERE

During the years leading up to the second world war there were generally four vessels in full-time summer service on the lake, with one or more in reserve. Those sailing in 1939, all of which are still in service, were as follows:

TSS *Tern,* 120 tons, built 1891 by Forrest, Wyvenhoe, 633 passengers.
TSS *Swift,* 203 tons, built 1900 by Seath, Rutherglen, 781 passengers.
TSMV *Teal,* 251 tons, built 1936 by Vickers, Barrow, 877 passengers.
TSMV *Swan,* 251 tons, built 1938 by Vickers, Barrow, 855 passengers.

Also available for extra duties was the twin-screw motor vessel *Cygnet,* built as a steamer in 1879 at Barrow and given new engines in 1924, but she did not last long after the war, being sold to private buyers.

In postwar years the services quickly regained their former regularity, with Lakeside, the southern rail-head, as the base for trips to Ambleside via Bowness. As time passed car-borne patrons became more numerous than those travelling by rail, so that Bowness, being near Windermere and near fairly good roads, gradually assumed greater importance as the base from which people made the sailings, and the rail link between Ulverston and Lakeside was finally closed early in September 1965.

Bow view of *Tern* 31 July 1964, showing decoration. The low fore-deck is allocated to first-class passengers

In 1947 the old coal-fired steamers did not sail because of the fuel shortage, so *Cygnet* joined *Swan* and *Teal,* and all were kept busy. Later, however, with *Cygnet* taken off, both *Tern* and *Swift* returned to duty. In summer 1956 *Swift* was laid up with boiler trouble, but she reappeared in 1957 with a modern funnel fitted and re-engined with a pair of Gleniffer oil engines. This conversion was successful, and early in 1958 *Tern* was similarly refitted and took up service with her new engines on 18 May. The latter vessel's passenger accommodation was refurbished at the same time, and the first-class saloon is beautifully decorated. Carpets, curtains and upholstery are a deep wine-red, and walls, ceilings, pillars, and light fittings are off-white with linings picked out in gold. Although short-sea and inland water-way motor ships are often derided, it is true to say that as far as *Tern* is concerned the usual disadvantages, vibration, smell, etc, do not apply.

Passenger carryings on Windermere have not altered appreciably over the years. 1937, over 492,500 passengers ; 1955, over 453,240 passengers ; 1956, over 400,000 passengers ; 1964, over 500,000 passengers (probably a record).

Comparisons are odious they say, but none the less can be interesting. Loch Lomond, the much-vaunted 'Largest lake in Britain', situated near the vast metropolis of Glasgow and connected to it by frequent rail services, can, in spite of intensive publicity, muster at best less than half this Windermere record figure. Until recently between 100,000 and 150,000 passengers was normal. By contrast, Windermere is a long way away from the nearest conurbation, and has not been the subject of any particularly

TSMV *Swan* showing high bridge structure 31 July 1964

168

aggressive sales campaign, and now has no rail link. Perhaps the Sasse-nachs are not quite so apathetic as sometimes labelled!

Besides these services and ships on Lake Windermere the LMS also ran excursions on Lake Coniston with steamer *Gondola* (1859) and *Lady of the Lake* (1908) in prewar years. After war broke out sailings were gradually withdrawn and the ships disposed of. No railway-owned vessels have worked on this lake since.

THE SCOTTISH REGION

On nationalisation the Railway Executive (Scottish Region) took over the former LMS ships operating from Stranraer ; those on the Kyle ferry run ; the former LNER Clyde ships and the LMS/LNER jointly-owned Loch Lomond fleet. The Caledonian Steam Packet Co Ltd continued to own and operate its fleet from Gourock under the BTC as it had done under the LMS. Standard BR livery of buff funnel and black top was applied to all ships at Stranraer, on Loch Lomond and on the Clyde in 1948.

As the years passed changes in administration were made. From 1952 to 1960 responsibility for Stranraer was in the hands of Euston, but in the latter year was returned to Scotland and assumed by the CSP (Irish). Since early 1967 this company has been dormant, the *Caledonian Princess* being transferred to the British Railways Board. Management is now carried out at Gourock under The CSP.

In an effort to unify the Clyde, Loch Lomond and Kyle vessels under one central control, the surviving ex-LNER ships were transferred to The CSP in 1951, and the Kyle ferries and the Loch Lomond steamer were transferred in 1957.

14: STRANRAER

Stranraer made history in 1939 by being the first west coast port to be equipped with a ramp over which vehicles could be driven on board ship at any state of the tide. Similarly, the LMS made history by putting into service the first specially built drive-on stern-loading cross-channel vehicle ferry to operate in UK waters. Named *Princess Victoria,* this twin-screw motor-vessel (another innovation) entered service between Stranraer and Larne on 7 July 1939, using ramps financed by the railway at both terminals. On her introduction she took up an early evening departure from Stranraer, and a mid-morning one from Larne. The mail ship *Princess Maud* had an early morning departure from Stranraer, and evening departure from Larne. The arrival of the new ship caused *Princess Margaret* to be transferred to Heysham. Thus, during the few months leading up to the outbreak of war there were two passenger ships serving the route. There were no cargo-only ships on the service.

In September 1939 the approach of war caused *Princess Victoria* and *Princess Maud* to be called up for mine-laying and trooping respectively. *Princess Margaret* was thereupon called back to Stranraer and again took up the mail sailings which she maintained throughout the war. This was the only cross-channel route which retained anything like its normal schedule during the war. Great use of the route was made by army personnel, and a variety of railway ships appeared on it from time to time, notably the three Dover train ferries, from July 1940 ; *Biarritz ; Canterbury ; Maid of Orleans ; Glen Sannox ; Whitstable and Maidstone,* to name but a few. These were mostly used to carry troops, and usually followed the mail steamer, while the train ferries, which could use the existing ramps, carried tanks and vehicles.

When the war was over *Princess Margaret* returned to the mail service in 1946, and she and *Princess Maud* each seem to have served for a few months at a time until early in 1947 when the latter was transferred to Holyhead on a permanent basis, except for returning to Stranraer on relief duties. From then on *Princess Margaret* was solely responsible for the mail sailings, except for overhaul periods, until December 1961.

Meantime, a replacement was ordered for *Princess Victoria* (1939), mined off the Humber in May 1940. The new ship was like her predecessor in most respects, given the same name, and took up similar sailings in March 1947. The prewar equilibrium had again, quite quickly, been regained and things went smoothly enough until mid-1952, when a flutter was caused by news of novel plans for the service. It was suggested that the mail sailings should go direct to Belfast, and a daily all-year-round vehicle-ferry service should operate to Larne. Objections caused the plans to be dropped ; there seem to have been fewer bureaucratic steam-rollers in those days.

The sinking of the new *Princess Victoria* in heavy weather at the end of January 1953 has been well recorded. Her loss caused the train ferry *Hampton Ferry* to be transferred from Dover in time to take up sailings from June 1953. In subsequent years this ship sailed regularly on the route in summer, June to September only, up to and including 1961.

After 1952 the responsibility for the operation of the Larne service rested with the manager, Irish Shipping Services, based at Euston, instead of with the Scottish Region. During 1960 plans were made to create something approaching a new authority to run the service. The decision was taken in November 1960, and from January 1961 Gourock took over responsibility. In December 1960 the Clyde and Campbeltown Shipping Co Ltd (by now without any ships), was renamed the CSP (Irish), and during 1961 technically chartered the ships in service from Stranraer. Since early 1967 the newly-named company has been dormant, but management continues from Gourock.

In January 1957 it was announced that a replacement for *Princess Victoria* would be ordered, but she was a long time coming. Not until December 1961, in fact, did the new ship appear. Named *Caledonian Princess,* she was the first and so far the only, ship owned by the newly renamed company. A stern-loading ship like her predecessors, she introduced double sailings each way daily and at one and the same time rendered *Princess Margaret* redundant and made the future seasonal appearance of *Hampton Ferry* unnecessary.

The new ship was kept very busy, particularly at the height of the season, and when extra tonnage was needed in the summer of 1964 to cope with increased traffic the Holyhead cargo ship *Slieve Donard* was chartered to run from 4 July to 24 August. The latter is a stern-loader, so cars could be driven on, but passengers had to travel on the *Caledonian Princess.* She was not a success, and in the following year a German car carrier MV *Lohengrin* was chartered to operate the service from 7 June to 25 September. Again, passengers could not travel on this ship, and like *Slieve Donard,* she was not a success.

Two features made 1965 an important year ; on 17 November the new modern terminal at Stranraer, costing £35,000, was officially opened, and in the following month the announcement was made that tenders were to be invited for a new ship. This was a decision which was long overdue, for as far back as September 1964 it was understood that a second ship was to be ordered. Hawthorn Leslie Ltd obtained the contract in March 1966, and the new ship was delivered in November 1967. Meanwhile, following the failure of Wallenius Line's *Lohengrin* in 1965 yet another ship had to be chartered. Again the company 'went foreign', and took over the Stena Line's *Stena Nordica* better known as 'The Londoner' which had traded between Tilbury and Calais in 1965. Her charter started in February 1966 and was expected to last until the new ship entered service. *Stena Nordica,* a Swedish ship, can carry about 950 passengers and 120 cars and is popular on the service. She and the *Caledonian Princess* on 2 May 1966 introduced twice-daily sailings in *both* directions, with the *Caledonian Princess* taking the early morning departure from Stranraer, and *Stena Nordica* taking the departure from Larne, so that there were then four sailings in each direction during the summer season. A new modern terminal at Larne, costing £33,000, was opened on 7 November 1967.

It is usual for *Caledonian Princess* to have her overhaul in the early part of the year, and from 1963 to 1965 inclusive *Shepperton Ferry* from Dover was taken over as relief. As she is a much slower ship timetables had to be altered. In 1966 and 1967, however, *Holyhead Ferry I* did this duty, with no alteration in the timings. *Stena Nordica* was overhauled in 1967 at the Garvel Graving Dock, Greenock, arriving there on 9 January, and was given BR funnel colours.

Princess Margaret at Larne in the early 1950s

TSS PRINCESS MARGARET

BUILT	1931 by Wm. Denny & Bros Ltd, Dumbarton
GROSS TONS	2,838
DIMENSIONS	325 ft 1 in x 49 ft 3 in x 11 ft 8 in
MACHINERY	4 turbines by Denny, SR geared
	Oil-fired boilers
SPEED	20½ knots
ROUTE	Stranraer-Larne

Each successive ship which has appeared on the 'Short Sea Route' to

Macau (ex-*Princess Margaret*) showing the way she was built up after arriving at Hong Kong

Ireland over the years has been a noticeable improvement on its predecessor. The *Princess Margaret* was no exception. She was the first on the route to have the forward part of the superstructure completely plated in, enclosing an observation lounge on the boat deck, and was also the first to offer berths for third-class passengers. She was the largest built up to that time, and carried 1,250 passengers, with 107 first-class berths and 54 third-class. When she entered service on 1 April 1931 a new express train service was inaugurated between Glasgow and Stranraer. The cowl on her funnel was removed in about 1935.

In 1939, on the appearance of the car ferry *Princess Victoria,* she was transferred to Heysham to help out on the busy Belfast service. When war broke out, *Princess Victoria* was requisitioned, and *Princess Margaret* returned to Stranraer to operate the mail service to Larne on her own, as *Princess Maud* was also called up for war duties. As *Princess Victoria* was sunk by a mine in May 1940, *Princess Margaret* was retained at Stranraer afterwards, and was joined by the new *Princess Victoria* (1947) in March of that year. In postwar years *Princess Margaret* did not revive the coastal cruises and trips to Bangor, etc from Larne which she operated during the season in the late 1930s.

Princess Margaret was reconditioned and converted to burn oil fuel in 1952. When *Princess Victoria* was lost at sea on 31 January 1953, the

174

fact that she had no radio telephone was considered to have been a contributory cause of the confusion during rescue operations, and a similar fault in *Princess Margaret* was remedied in the following month.

When responsibility for the Larne service was transferred to Gourock near the end of 1960, *Princess Margaret* was technically chartered by the CSP (Irish) from January 1961 until her withdrawal on 17 December of that year in favour of the new *Caledonian Princess*. She lay at Stranraer until being moved to Greenock early in January and was sold two months later to the Shun Tak Co Ltd of Hong Kong, being handed over at the end of March. She was dry-docked for voyage modifications and left Greenock under her own steam on 25 April for Hong Kong. Further alterations increased her gross tonnage to about 3,670 and, renamed *Macau,* she entered service on the Macau route on which she has proved to be a popular and comfortable sea-boat, many people preferring her steady passage to a quick voyage on hydrofoils which operate on the same route. The way in which she has been built up is well seen in the illustration.

TSMV PRINCESS VICTORIA

BUILT 1946 by Wm. Denny & Bros Ltd, Dumbarton
GROSS TONS 2,694
DIMENSIONS 309 ft 9 in x 48 ft 2 in x 16 ft 8 in (depth)
MACHINERY Two 2-stroke single acting Sulzer diesels by Denny
SPEED 19 knots
ROUTE Stranraer-Larne

The LMS made nautical history in 1939 by ordering the first specially-designed drive-on cross-channel car ferry on UK routes. Named *Princess Victoria* she was novel in being fitted with diesels, other railway companies and subsequent authorities preferring steam-turbine machinery. The ship was very short-lived, being mined off the Humber on 21 May 1940.

Our *Princess Victoria* was basically the same as the 1939 model, though she incorporated a number of improvements. She was launched on 27 August 1946 and entered service early the following year. Accommodation was provided for about 1,500 passengers, 70 tons of cargo and about 40 vehicles. Cars were driven on over the stern and there was a 20 ft diameter turntable to accelerate the loading and unloading of vehicles. In addition she was also fitted with stalls for livestock below the car deck, reached by a walk-down from the latter. On the boat deck there were six single-berth staterooms and the officers' cabins. Her annual overhaul usually took place about April each year, when she was dry-docked at Holyhead ; no other drive-on ship replaced her.

It was on 31 January 1953 that she met her doom, being caught in a storm after leaving Stranraer on the 7.45 am sailing. She sank shortly after 2.0 pm with the loss of about 128 persons including her master, Captain James Ferguson; 34 passengers and 10 crew were saved. No similar ship was ordered to replace her until more than six years later and in the meantime the train ferry *Hampton Ferry* was borrowed from Dover to operate from Stranraer during the summer months only.

Princess Victoria at Larne about 1949

TSS CALEDONIAN PRINCESS

BUILT	1961 by Wm. Denny & Bros Ltd, Dumbarton
GROSS TONS	3,630
DIMENSIONS	353 ft x 57 ft 2 in x 12 ft
MACHINERY	2 turbines by Denny, DR geared
	Oil-fired boilers
SPEED	20½ knots
ROUTE	Stranraer-Larne

Following the loss of *Princess Victoria* in 1953, the train ferry *Hampton Ferry* served on this route for passengers and cars each summer up to and including 1961. The appearance of *Caledonian Princess* was therefore extremely welcome, particularly to those who used the route often. The decision to build the new ship was announced as early as January 1957, but she did not take to the water until 5 April 1961, making her maiden voyage on 16 December. She was, in fact, due to enter service on 9 October, but during her trials in September a defect was found in her starboard turbine gearing and she was sent back to Denny's to have it rectified. She was finally delivered to her owners the CSP (Irish) on 24 November.

She can carry some 400 first-class and 1,000 second-class passengers.

Caledonian Princess arriving at Larne in May 1966

Berth accommodation is 82 first-class berths in 2 two-berth cabins-de-luxe and one- and two-berth cabins, and 94 second-class berths in two- and four-berth cabins. On the boat deck are the first- and second-class lounges, on the promenade deck are the first- and second-class smokerooms, a first-class restaurant seating 50 and a second-class cafeteria seating 140. Her structure consists of two complete decks, main and promenade, part upper deck above main deck, a lower deck forward and aft, boat deck and navigating bridge deck. Vehicles are driven on at the stern, the main deck accommodating 103 vehicles or 29 trailers and 53 cars. Turn-round is assisted by a 22 ft electrically-operated turntable aft capable of handling loads of up to 24 tons.

She operates on this service twice daily and had not served on any other route before 1968. During annual overhaul early in the year, usually February and March, she was replaced from 1962 to 1965 inclusive by *Shepperton Ferry,* but in 1966 and 1967 she was relieved by *Holyhead Ferry I.*

When new she had a yellow funnel with black top, a red lion rampant on the yellow portion, white superstructure and black hull with a narrow white band round the waterline and a thicker one just above the rubbing strake. She retained this livery until her 1965 overhaul, from which she appeared with funnel unchanged, but with grey masts and a blue hull with only the lower white line remaining. After her 1966 overhaul she re-entered service with the new BR red funnel with white motif.

There are two items of commercial interest connected with this ship. On 28 January 1965 she took from Stranraer to Larne the first batch of new Rootes cars, which had arrived from Coventry via Johnstone on goods train and road transport. On 3rd August 1966 she carried the first BR 'Freightliner' container (27 ft long, payload 20 tons) to cross the Irish Sea. On the following day it returned by the same route containing 12 tons of Gallaher's cigarettes.

Early in 1967 she was transferred to the BRB, but continued to be managed from Gourock, though under The CSP. In 1968 she made her first sortie elsewhere when she operated between Holyhead and Dun Laoghaire from early July to early August. On 26 June 1968 she was chartered to run a day trip from Stranraer to Douglas (I.o.M.) by Galloway Pageant Committee.

TSMV ANTRIM PRINCESS

BUILT	1967 by Hawthorn Leslie (Shipbuilders) Ltd, Hebburn-on-Tyne
GROSS TONS	3,630
DIMENSIONS	369 ft x 349 ft 6 in x 12 ft
MACHINERY	Two S.E.M.T.-Pielstick 16-cyl diesels by Ateliers et Chantiers de Bretagne
SPEED	19¼ knots
ROUTE	Stranraer-Larne

Launched on 24 April 1967, this vessel is unique in being the first BR vessel to have both bow and stern doors, and is unusual in having diesel engines although the railway authorities have in general preferred steam turbines for this kind of vessel. The main deck can accommodate commercial vehicles, and the 'gallery decks' private cars and light commercials. There is total space for 170 cars or a ratio of commercials and private cars. Vehicles of axle loads up to 11 tons and up to 14 ft 3 in in height can be carried. The stern opening is 20 ft wide and is closed by a watertight hydraulically-operated door hinging upwards ; the bow visor opening has an inner watertight steel door. Hydraulic ramps are fitted to each end of the gallery decks, which hinge up against the vessel's sides when not in use. She has bow and stern rudders, a bow thrust unit and stabilisers.

Major public rooms of both classes of passenger accommodation are on the shelter deck. First-class is placed forward and includes a large elliptical lounge, seating over 100, with an observation gallery fitted with tables and chairs, aft of which are the smokeroom and restaurant separated by a cocktail bar with 42 seats. Second-class facilities include a lounge and tearoom with windows on three sides and 112 reclining seats plus about 60 others, a cafeteria seating 104 and smokeroom-bar.

The ship was delivered to her owners, the British Railways Board, on 27 November 1967, and arrived at Stranraer on 10 December. She left on her maiden voyage to Larne on 20 December.

Antrim Princess on trials

179

15: THE CLYDE

In the years immediately preceding the second world war, there were three companies operating on the Clyde whose ships eventually came within the embracing arms of the BTC, namely the Clyde & Campbeltown Shipping Co Ltd, the LNER and The CSP. Each of these had its own fleet of ships serving on more-or-less specific routes, many of which were abandoned as a direct result of the onset of war. We propose here to take a look at each in turn and at the former company of Williamson-Buchanan Steamers Ltd.

Clyde & Campbeltown Shipping Co Ltd

This company, so named in 1937 (though it and its predecessors dated back much further), was a subsidiary of David MacBrayne Ltd until the end of September 1949. In service before the war were three cargo steamers, *Minard, Ardyne* and *Arran,* generally running between Glasgow and Rothesay and other Clyde piers, and the passenger, mail and cargo ships *Davaar* and *Dalriada,* maintaining the Campbeltown link, generally daily, from the upper Firth. This passenger service was closed on 16 March 1940, and both ships were subsequently summoned for war duty. *Davaar* was finally broken up in 1943 and *Dalriada* was sunk in the Thames in 1942, her wreck being dispersed with explosives after the war.

All three cargo ships survived the war and afterwards continued to ply on the Clyde, though their services were reduced. There were, incidentally, two more cargo steamers during and after war years in the fleet, *Marie* owned by the company, and *Empire Tulip* chartered, but neither was there in late September 1949.

The Company was taken over by the BTC Railway Executive, on 1 October 1949, and the remaining ships served between Ardrossan, Millport and Brodick, and Glasgow and Rothesay. As time passed the ships aged and were gradually withdrawn, their duties having been taken over by road transport or the new car ferries, so that all had gone by early 1958.

The Company was not wound up, however, but was renamed the CSP (Irish) in December 1960 to operate the Stranraer–Larne service.

London & North Eastern Railway Company

The LNER's base on the Clyde was latterly Craigendoran and from here paddlers served *inter alia* Rothesay and the Kyles, the Holy Loch, Greenock and Dunoon and Arrochar. Available in 1939 for these runs were *Lucy Ashton, Marmion* (1906), *Jeanie Deans* and *Talisman*. There was also a fifth named *Waverley* (1899), but apparently she was laid up during that year. During the war *Lucy Ashton* alone remained on the Clyde, serving Kilcreggan, Kirn and Dunoon from Craigendoran, while the others were called up for active service. *Marmion* and *Waverley* were both lost, the former in 1941, the latter at the Dunkirk evacuation in 1940.

Jeanie Deans re-entered Clyde service in 1946, followed by *Talisman* soon after. This gave *Lucy Ashton* a chance to have a much needed overhaul. Services to several piers, eg the Gareloch, were terminated during and after the war, but the main routes were kept open and continue to operate today. The one-time base pier Helensburgh, was closed to regular sailings in 1951, and by this time steamers from Craigendoran were generally calling at Gourock; the ferry service changed from Greenock Princes Pier to Gourock during the war. In 1947 a new paddler appeared named *Waverley,* and she revived the Arrochar excursions in June of that year. Thus, LNER services were back to normal. There were never any screw ships based at Craigendoran until new ships appeared in 1953, because of shallows requiring the use of ships with a draught of 6 ft 6 in or less.

All four ships were operational when the LNER was taken over by the Railway Executive in 1948, and passed to the Scottish Region. Early in 1949 *Lucy Ashton* was withdrawn. In 1951 other changes came which affected ex-LNER services in an effort to rationalise Clyde sailings. Calls at Greenock were dropped. On 5 November the three remaining ships were transferred to The CSP.

It was not until 1964 that the next LNER steamer was withdrawn. *Jeanie Deans* was taken off in September 1964, leaving *Talisman* and *Waverley* to carry on. Both these ships continued to ply, *Waverley* usually from Craigendoran, though occasionally further afield, and *Talisman* mainly between Wemyss Bay, Largs and Millport, until the latter was withdrawn in 1966, leaving only *Waverley* in service.

The Caledonian Steam Packet Co Ltd

This concern, controlled by the LMS, owned in 1939 a fleet of four small motor ships, five turbine steamers, and nine paddlers, one of which, *Glen Rosa,* originally owned by the Glasgow & South Western Railway Company, was withdrawn in that year. The turbine steamers *Duchess of Argyll, Glen Sannox, Duchess of Montrose,* and *Marchioness of Graham,* and the paddler *Marchioness of Lorne* remained on Clyde service during the war. The paddlers *Mercury* and *Juno* were lost in active service, while PS *Duchess of Rothesay,* though returned, was not considered worth renovating.

By 1946 The CSP services were getting back to normal, and available ships were, in that year, generally serving as follows:

PS *Duchess of Fife*: Wemyss Bay–Millport
TSS *Duchess of Argyll*: Greenock–the Kyles
TSS *Glen Sannox*: Ardrossan–Arran
TSS *Duchess of Montrose*: Gourock–Arran
TSS *Duchess of Hamilton*: Gourock–Campbeltown or Inveraray
PS *Caledonia*: Gourock–Dunoon ; Wemyss Bay–Rothesay
PS *Marchioness of Lorne*: Gourock–Holy Loch

181

TSMV *Wee Cumbrae*: Largs–Millport
TSS *Marchioness of Graham*: Ardrossan–Arran
TSMV *Arran Mail*: Ardrossan–Arran
PS *Jupiter*: Gourock–Dunoon ; Wemyss Bay–Rothesay
TSMV *Ashton*: Gourock–Dunoon
TSMV *Leven*: Gourock–Dunoon

From the above it will be seen that the main bases of The CSP ships were Gourock, Wemyss Bay, Largs and Ardrossan.

As the years passed cruises were reintroduced and ships were withdrawn. Unlike the LNER, the LMS (The CSP) ordered no new ships after the war to replace those lost. There was no immediate change in the fleet when the company became a subsidiary of the BTC in 1948. The first to go was *Arran Mail* in 1951, followed by *Duchess of Argyll* in 1952, *Duchess of Fife* and *Wee Cumbrae* in 1953, *Glen Sannox* in 1954, *Marchioness of Lorne* in 1955, *Jupiter* in 1957, and *Marchioness of Graham* in 1958. The reason for the massive shake-out during and soon after 1953 was the long-overdue arrival of four new small motor ships and three drive-on car ferries in 1953 and 1954, followed in 1957 by another larger car ferry, *Glen Sannox,* specifically for the Arran service. In 1952 there arrived on the Clyde the Loch Awe motor vessel *Countess of Breadalbane,* owned by The CSP and which since then has remained in service on the Clyde.

Many piers were closed to The CSP ships during postwar years, notably Colintrave 1946, Govan 1953, Lamlash 1954, Kilchattan Bay 1955, Strone 1956, Whiting Bay 1961, Kirn 1963, Hunters Quay 1964 and Lochgoilhead 1965. The termination of calls at piers over the years has meant a reduction in services and consequently fewer ships are needed to maintain the services. There is now, on the Clyde, a total of fourteen vessels, compared with about thirty of all companies before the war (excluding MacBrayne's own fleet). Drop in patronage also helps this deterioration, which in all probability will continue to take place, except for car ferries.

As early as March 1963 plans to terminate the Holy Loch service were announced, and reiterated in May 1964. But it is still operated, usually by one of the 'Maids'. In recent years certain other alterations have been made, particularly to the excursion routes. Special economy moves led to the withdrawal of trips from Ayr and Troon, the reduction of Bridge Wharf sailings by taking off the Saturday one, and the reduction of frequency of sailings to Inveraray and Campbeltown after the 1964 season. These and other moves enabled the company to withdraw *Jeanie Deans, Duchess of Montrose, Ashton* and *Leven*. Plans to alter the summer-only Ardrossan–Arran service after 1965 to operate from Fairlie did not materialise. In April 1965 the Largs-Millport early morning mail service was taken over by a local operator.

Although many services have been reduced in frequency, and calls at certain piers cancelled altogether, the general pattern on the Clyde is still very much as it was in later prewar years with certain notable exceptions like the Stranraer visits. It is still possible to sail by passenger ship to outlying places like Campbeltown, Inveraray and Tighnabruaich, and the railway-terminal piers of Craigendoran, Gourock, Wemyss Bay, Fairlie and Ardrossan are still busy in the height of the season, in many cases largely due to the introduction of the new car ferries.

Williamson-Buchanan Steamers Ltd

In addition to the three companies which eventually become part of the nationalised group, there had also been another named Williamson-Buchanan Steamers (1936) Ltd, which did not survive to be taken over, though two of its ships did. Since 1935 controlled by the LMS, this company owned five ships in 1939, all of which had been owned by The CSP for a short time after October 1935 until being transferred to the new Williamson-Buchanan concern on 16 June 1936. Of these ships only one, PS *Kylemore*, did not survive the war, but two more, PS *Eagle III* and PS *Queen Empress,* were not considered worth renovating afterwards.

On 4 March 1943 the ships existing in the fleet at the time were transferred to The CSP, for the last time, and the Williamson-Buchanan concern was then wound up. Both the other steamers, *King Edward* and *Queen Mary II* remained on the Clyde during the war, the former mainly on troop-tender duties, the latter in normal service from Gourock. These were the only ships of the Williamson-Buchanan fleet to be in service after the war, though they were then integrated in The CSP fleet.

The predecessors of Williamson-Buchanan Steamers (1936) Ltd, were associated with several particular routes, Glasgow–Clyde Piers (notably Rothesay), Kyles of Bute, cruises to the Arran Coast and through their associates, Turbine Steamers Ltd, Gourock–Campbeltown/Inveraray. It was fitting that the two remaining Williamson-Buchanan ships should revive one of these routes after the war, ie the Glasgow–Rothesay sailings. In prewar years *Queen Mary II* usually ran on this route, as did *King Edward*. In June 1946, *King Edward* reinstated the 11.0 am sailing from Glasgow to Rothesay and the Kyles, and remained on this seasonally until the end of the 1950 season. In 1951 she was mainly on the Rothesay–Arran Coast run. Also in 1946 *Queen Mary II* took up her prewar 10.0 am sailing from Glasgow to Rothesay and the Arran Coast, but from 1951 replaced *King Edward* on the 11.0 am sailing to Rothesay and Kyles. She has remained on this ever since.

For the 1965 season the fleet was, for the most part, given a new livery of blue hull with red lion rampant on the yellow part of the funnel.

It was announced on 3 February 1967, that the MOT had refused permission for the company to withdraw the Gourock–Kilcreggan–Blairmore–Kilmun service, but had permitted withdrawal of the winter Gourock–Craigendoran run from 1 October 1967.

183

PS LUCY ASHTON

BUILT	1888 by T. B. Seath & Co, Rutherglen
GROSS TONS	224
DIMENSIONS	190 ft x 21 ft 2 in x 7 ft 3 in (depth)
MACHINERY	2-cyl compound-diagonal by A. & J. Inglis Ltd, Glasgow
	Coal-fired boiler
SPEED	15 knots
ROUTE	Craigendoran-Gourock, Dunoon, etc.

Lucy Ashton, the oldest Clyde steamer inherited by the BTC, has a full and interesting history. With an original gross registered tonnage of 271, she was built for the North British Steam Packet Co's services from Craigendoran to Dunoon and the Holy Loch and later the Gareloch, and originally was fitted with a Hutson & Corbett single-cylinder diagonal engine which was discarded in favour of A. & J. Inglis' more modern machinery in 1902. In the following year her saloons also were modernised. During the first World War she remained at Craigendoran on Gareloch services, and in 1923, on passing to the LNER celebrated that event by being re-boilered. In common with those of her running-mates, her hull was painted light grey in 1936.

When the second war came she was again retained on Clyde runs,

Lucy Ashton leaving Craigendoran 25 March 1948

serving the Gareloch until 1942, Kilcreggan, Kirn and Dunoon, and, after July 1945, Innellan and Rothesay. It was during these years that the most extensive alterations were carried out, notably the building of the wheelhouse abaft the funnel in 1944 and the fitting out of a tearoom aft. In postwar years she had a Class V certificate for 903 passengers.

At a ripe old age she was withdrawn in February 1949 and laid up in Bowling harbour, where she remained until being towed by the tugs *Metind II* and *Flying Falcon* to Faslane on 10 December 1949, for breaking by Metal Industries Ltd. She was stripped to the hull, and then fitted out by Denny, Dumbarton with Rolls Royce jet engines for use by the British Ship Research Association in its experiments in hull design. Her hull was finally broken up at Faslane in 1951. She thus served only one full season with the Scottish Region, and for that period was given a buff funnel with black top.

TSS KING EDWARD

BUILT   1901 by Wm. Denny & Bros Ltd, Dumbarton
GROSS TONS   502
DIMENSIONS   250 ft 6 in x 30 ft 1 in x 6 ft
MACHINERY   3 turbines by Parsons, Newcastle-on-Tyne, direct drive
                 Coal-fired boiler
SPEED   19 knots
ROUTE   Glasgow (Bridge Wharf)-Rothesay-Kyles of Bute

A lengthy book could be written about this, the world's first commercial passenger turbine steamer, but curiously it has not yet been done. She was fitted originally with five screws, but the inner set of two was removed from the wing shafts in 1905. The high pressure turbine drove the centre shaft, and the two low pressure turbines the side shafts. In the same year the upper deck was built on, the boats being moved further aft. She was launched on 16 May 1901, and ran trials for her owners, The Turbine Steamer Syndicate, on 26 June, achieving a reputed speed of 20.48 knots. She burned coal at the rate of 18 tons per day. From 1902 to 1927 she was owned by Turbine Steamers Ltd being taken over in the latter year by Williamson-Buchanan Steamers Ltd. At the end of the 1935 season she came under The CSP banner, retaining her white funnels with black tops, and in 1936 she was re-decked. The old deck still showed markings where paddle sponsons were to be fitted should she have failed as a turbine steamer. On 16 June 1936 she was transferred to Williamson-Buchanan Steamers (1936) Ltd and having been given yellow funnels in December 1939, was on 4 March 1943 again transferred to The CSP under whose control she thereafter remained.

185

King Edward passing Bowling 18 April 1949 with BR house-flag

So much for her various owners, but what of her services? In her first year she ran between Greenock and Campbeltown in succession to the old *Strathmore,* but in the following year she was switched to the Ardrishaig run. She served both Ardrishaig and Inveraray from 1903 to 1910, when she reverted to the Campbeltown run, taking in Gourock, Dunoon, Wemyss Bay and Fairlie en route. This lasted until 1926 with the exception of the war years. From February 1915 to 1918 she served first as a transport, linking Dover, Folkestone and Southampton with Calais, Boulogne, Dieppe, Le Havre, Rouen, Cherbourg and the Channel Islands. After this she served for a few months as an ambulance transport during which time she visited the White Sea. It was in 1927 that she began her long career on the 'All the Way' service from Glasgow to Dunoon and Rothesay, etc. Until 1933 she took the 10.0 am sailing to the Arran Coast, calling at Dunoon, Rothesay, Largs and Millport (Keppel Pier), but from 1933 to 1939 she operated the 11.0 am run to the Kyles, Loch Striven or round Cumbrae.

During the second war she remained on the Clyde, operating important links, and occasionally became involved in troop movements though she was not officially placed under the control of the Sea Transport Officer until January 1945. In the closing years of the war she was mainly on the Gourock–Dunoon and Wemyss Bay–Rothesay services.

Her postwar overhaul was carried out by Scott's at Greenock, and on 1 June 1946 she again took up the 11.0 am sailing from Glasgow to Kyles of Bute. This lasted until the end of the 1951 season, during which she ran mainly to the Arran Coast, when she was withdrawn and laid up at Greenock.

In March 1952 she was reported sold to Belgian breakers, but in the event she was bought by the British Iron & Steel Corporation, who allocated her to the West of Scotland Shipbreaking Co Ltd, Troon, where she arrived for breaking up on 10 June 1952. Quite rightly parts of this famous ship have been preserved. The high pressure turbine was sent to the Kelvingrove museum, as was her bell. In her latter years she could carry a maximum of 1,966 passengers.

PS DUCHESS OF FIFE

BUILT	1903 by Fairfield Shipbuilding & Engineering Co Ltd, Glasgow
GROSS TONS	329
DIMENSIONS	210 ft 4 in x 25 ft x 8 ft 6 in (depth)
MACHINERY	4-cyl triple-expansion by Fairfield Coal-fired boilers
SPEED	15 knots
ROUTE	Wemyss Bay-Millport (to 1952)-Rothesay (1953) Gourock-Holy Loch Cruises from Gourock (1953)

This paddler was the first such Clyde vessel built by Fairfield, and gained a speed of over 17 knots on her trials on 5 June 1903. Her owners, The CSP, placed her on upper Firth railway connection services from Gourock and Wemyss Bay. Her tonnage then was 336, but this was later reduced. Her work was essentially seasonal at first, but from 1908 she was kept in commission almost the whole year round. In the first war she served as a mine-sweeper based at Grimsby and Dover between early 1916 and summer 1919. Afterwards she returned to normal service, and by the end of the 1920s had extended her sphere of operations to include Tarbert and Kilchattan Bay. By 1937 she was beating a regular pattern between Wemyss Bay and Millport. In September 1939 she was requisitioned again for use as a mine-sweeper. At the Dunkirk evacuation she brought back at least 1,500 personnel. Serving under her own name, she was attached to the 12th Mine-Sweeping Flotilla based at Harwich, with the pennant number J115. In 1941 she had a spell as a training ship for mine-sweeping personnel at Port Edgar on the Forth.

She was returned to her owners in time to take up regular sailings in 1946, when she ran to the Holy Loch, carried out cruises from Gourock and served between Wemyss Bay and Millport. In 1952 she introduced the afternoon cruise from Millport and Largs to Rothesay. Her last day in service was 6 June 1953, and two days later she was officially withdrawn and laid up in Albert Harbour, Greenock, being towed away on 15 June for breaking up at Port Glasgow. Her bell is still in use as a fog bell on Millport's Old Pier. In postwar years she could carry up to 1,101 passengers.

Duchess of Fife moving astern about 1951

TSS DUCHESS OF ARGYLL

BUILT	1906 by Wm. Denny & Bros Ltd, Dumbarton
GROSS TONS	594
DIMENSIONS	250 ft x 30 ft 1 in x 10 ft 1 in (depth)
MACHINERY	3 turbines by Denny, direct drive
	Coal-fired boiler
SPEED	20 knots
ROUTE	Greenock-Rothesay-Kyles (1948-9)-Campbeltown (1949)
	Gourock-Arran (1951); railway connections from Gourock or Wemyss Bay (1950-1)

This ship, the first turbine steamer built for The csp, succeeded the paddler *Duchess of Hamilton* (1890) on the Ardrossan-Arran service, remaining thereon until being laid up throughout 1909 following an agreement by rival concerns to pool their resources on the Arran services. She returned in 1910 and 1911, but in 1912 was diverted to the

188

Greenock/Gourock-the Kyles-East Arran run for a long spell lasting twenty-four years apart from war service.

In the first war she served as a channel transport from February 1915 to August 1919, during which she carried out a dramatic rescue when the transports *Archangel* (Great Eastern Railway) and *Queen Empress* (Capt John Williamson) were in collision with escorting destroyers. She towed the latter ship to Boulogne, and saved 1,600 men from *Archangel*. In all she made some 655 trips during these years.

After the war she went back to the Clyde, and in 1936 she took up the long distance runs from Gourock, alternating between Inveraray and Campbeltown, until again war came her way. This time, however, she stayed on the Clyde, and although occasionally used by the Sea Transport Officer for troop movements she spent most of the time on essential services, particularly 'ferry' runs from Gourock, Wemyss Bay and Fairlie.

In 1945 she ran to Rothesay, extending to the Kyles in 1946. This lasted until 1949. Her last full season in service was 1951 and she was offered for sale. Her sale to the Admiralty was announced in March 1952, and since 1955 she has been in use at Portland Harbour for experimental work. Her superstructure has been altered, but the fine lines of her hull are unspoiled. She could carry 1,512 passengers.

Duchess of Argyll off Gourock 31 July 1948

TSS GLEN SANNOX

BUILT	1925 by Wm. Denny & Bros Ltd, Dumbarton
GROSS TONS	690
DIMENSIONS	249 ft 10 in x 30 ft 1 in x 10 ft 1 in (depth)
MACHINERY	3 turbines by Denny, direct drive
	Coal-fired boiler
SPEED	20 knots
ROUTE	Fairlie/Ardrossan-Arran

Not unlike previous turbines built for service on the Clyde, *Glen Sannox* appeared on the Ardrossan–Arran service in 1925 for the LMS, replacing a fast paddler with the same name withdrawn in September 1924. She could originally carry 1,720 passengers, but by her latter years this was reduced to 1,622. She was transferred to The CSP in spring 1936 so that she could inaugurate and carry on a service to Campbeltown via West Arran, as ships owned directly by the railway company were not permitted to serve this port. In prewar days she also, on occasion, in spring and autumn, served railway connections from Gourock. During the war she remained on civil service, mainly Fairlie–Arran, though she did do some trooping between Stranraer and Larne for a short time. Afterwards, resplendent in new paint and with a varnished wooden wheelhouse added in 1948, she reverted to the Ardrossan–Arran run until being withdrawn in April 1954 and laid up at Greenock. Her service was taken over by *Marchioness of Graham,* and she was towed away to Ghent at the end of July by the tug *Turmoil* for breaking up.

Glen Sannox

SS ARDYNE
SS MINARD

BUILT	1928/1926 by Scott & Sons Ltd, Bowling
GROSS TONS	242/241
DIMENSIONS	*Ardyne* 135 ft 2 in x 25 ft 2 in x 9 ft 10 in
	Minard 143 ft 2 in x 25 ft 2 in x 10 ft 3 in
MACHINERY	2-cyl compound by Aitchison Blair Ltd, Glasgow
SPEED	10½ knots
ROUTE	Glasgow-Rothesay and Clyde ports

Both these ships were built for Clyde Cargo Steamers Ltd, and passed to the Clyde & Campbeltown Shipping Co Ltd in 1937. This company, which continued legally to own the ships, was taken over by the BTC on 1 October 1949. They were predominantly cargo ships but in prewar days could carry up to fifty passengers; after the war twelve only were carried. *Minard,* successor to *Minard Castle* of 1882, ran trials on 19 January 1926, and, up to 1948, was mainly associated with services to Loch Fyne, being switched to the Rothesay service in 1949. *Ardyne* on the other hand, was an additional vessel to the existing ships at that time, ran trials on 22 May 1928, and was retained on the Dunoon, Holy Loch and Rothesay route fairly consistently throughout. Both ships on occasion served Arran.

The arrival of the new general-purpose motor vessels in 1953 and 1954,

Minard in Kingston Dock, Glasgow, in 1954
191

and the inauguration of the Glasgow–Rothesay (via Wemyss Bay) cargo service, led to the redundancy of the two old steamers, and both were withdrawn in the latter year. *Ardyne* was withdrawn in September 1954 and sold in April 1955 to J. Lee of Belfast, but was resold for breaking up at Troon by the West of Scotland Shipbreaking Co Ltd. *Minard* was withdrawn in October 1954 also having been laid up in Albert Harbour, Greenock, and was sold in the same month for breaking up, going to Smith & Houston's at Port Glasgow.

TSS DUCHESS OF MONTROSE

BUILT	1930 by Wm. Denny & Bros Ltd, Dumbarton
GROSS TONS	794
DIMENSIONS	273 ft x 32 ft 3 in x 7 ft 2 in
MACHINERY	3 Parsons turbines by Denny, direct drive
	Oil-fired boiler
SPEED	18 knots
ROUTE	Long distance excursions from Gourock to Inveraray, Arran via Kyles and Campbeltown, etc.

Designed mainly for The CSP summer excursion trade, *Duchess of Montrose* replaced PS *Jupiter* (1896) and was the first Clyde steamer to cater for one class only. She was altered slightly a number of times during her career including the substitution of a full length mainmast for her stumpmast in 1934, and in spring 1956 the conversion to oil burning and saloon alterations involved a decrease in her gross tonnage from 802 to 792. Her original tonnage was 787 and was probably altered to 802 during the war.

Duchess of Montrose in the Kyles of Bute about 1948

Up to the end of 1936 season she sailed principally on 'round' trips, such as Round the Lochs, Round Arran and Round Ailsa Craig, and included sailings to Stranraer. From 1937 Stranraer was dropped and she operated instead to Inveraray.

She was not called up during the war, spending most of the time maintaining the service between Wemyss Bay and Rothesay.

Re-entering the excursion trade in 1946 she sailed on the Arran via the Kyles route and thereafter she concentrated on such long distance excursions as required her size and speed. In 1948 her wooden wheelhouse was fitted and in 1956 she was converted from coal to oil burning at Glasgow. In 1960 radar was installed. Her maximum summer passenger capacity was 1,854, but on her occasional sorties on the direct Arran connection she was restricted to 400. Having completed thirty-five years of faithful but unspectacular service on the Clyde, she made her last commercial sailing on 30 August 1964 on an afternoon cruise from Gourock to Lochranza Bay. On the next day she was laid up and was offered for sale at the end of March 1965. In August she was sold to Van Heyghen Frères of Ghent for breaking up, and two days behind schedule, due to gales, she left Greenock for Ghent on 19 September in tow of the Antwerp tug *Georges Letzer* arriving there five days later.

TSS DUCHESS OF HAMILTON

BUILT	1932 by Harland & Wolff Ltd, Govan
GROSS TONS	801
DIMENSIONS	272 ft 3 in x 32 ft 3 in x 7 ft 2 in
MACHINERY	3 Parsons turbines by Harland & Wolff Ltd, Belfast, direct drive
	Oil-fired boiler
SPEED	19 knots
ROUTE	Long distance excursions from Gourock

Similar in most respects to *Duchess of Montrose*, *Duchess of Hamilton* was also principally an excursion vessel, and replaced PS *Juno* (1898) in The CSP fleet. Unlike *Duchess of Montrose* she had a full-length mainmast from the beginning, and in prewar years was chiefly engaged in excursions from Ayr, Troon and Ardrossan and also operated sailings from Gourock to such places as Ardrishaig, Inveraray and Campbeltown. She, also, underwent a number of minor changes in appearance, including the fitting of cross trees to the mainmast in 1939, the addition of a gaff in 1957 (removed six years later), the addition of a wheelhouse in 1948, the fitting of radar in 1960 and of new all-welded funnels (by Lamonts) during winter 1963-4. In spring 1956, like *Duchess of Montrose*, she was converted to oil burning instead of coal, and structural changes increased her tonnage from 795. In 1939 she was placed at the disposal of the Sea Transport Officer, Clyde, and spent the early years of the war trooping between Stranraer and Larne and then tendering to ships anchored in the Clyde. After the war she appeared in 1946 on the Gourock to Campbeltown and Inveraray sailings, and, since 1948, was closely associated with the Campbeltown run, but included also trips to Arran and Ayr. In April 1965 she appeared in the new colours and, since her running-mate *Duchess of Montrose* had been withdrawn, she spent her time during the 1965 season fairly evenly distributed between the Campbeltown and Inveraray runs interspersed with occasional sailings to Arran via Kyles, *inter alia*. Her summer maximum capacity is 1,918 passengers.

Duchess of Hamilton passing Erskine Ferry in May 1965

PS JEANIE DEANS

BUILT   1931 by Fairfield Shipbuilding & Engineering Co Ltd
GROSS TONS   839
DIMENSIONS   257 ft 10 in x 59 ft x 6 ft 1½ in
MACHINERY   3-cyl triple-expansion by Fairfield
                 Oil-fired boiler
SPEED   15 knots
ROUTE   Craigendoran-Kyles
                 Arran via Kyles
                 Round the Lochs, etc

Launched on 7 April 1931 by Miss Rhoda Forbes (daughter of the chairman of the LNER) *Jeanie Deans* has been eulogised so much as to leave an impression in the mind as romantic as the Waverley novels themselves. After trials on 8 May 1931, she made her maiden voyage on 15 June on the Arrochar run, and thereafter, during peacetime, made Craigendoran her base for, usually, middle-distance excursions, though she has been to Campbeltown. She made frequent trips to Arrochar before the war, but did not appear on this station afterwards until the late 1950s. The extension of her Kyles run to include a 'Round Bute' cruise came early in 1950. As she was an LNER ship, she was owned after 1948 by the BTC Scottish Region and not by The CSP, but she was transferred to the latter on 5 November 1951.

Late in 1939 she was requisitioned for service as a paddle mine-sweeper,

Jeanie Deans arriving at Dunoon 3 September 1957

Queen of the South (ex-*Jeanie Deans*) off Greenwich

leader of the 11th Mine Sweeping Flotilla, which included the Clyde paddlers *Mercury, Juno, Jupiter* and *Caledonia*. Her pennant number at this time was J108. In 1941 she was converted to an AA ship serving on the Thames, and was credited with three 'buzz-bombs' and several aircraft. She was apparently the only ship in the flotilla with wooden floats and was known as 'Old Wooden Wheels'. The cynics were put to shame on one occasion when she is said to have beaten to the defence position the Eagle Steamers' flier *Royal Eagle*. She was returned to the LNER in 1945, and soon afterwards took up the sailings between Craigendoran and piers on the south bank, and to Dunoon and Rothesay and as far as Tighnabruaich.

During her lifetime she has undergone a remarkable number of alterations which successively increased her gross tonnage from 540 to 635, then to 814 and finally to 839, so that she was then the largest paddler owned by the railways, or their associates. When new she had two short funnels of equal height, one small deckhouse forward and one aft. In time for the 1932 season her forward funnel was increased by 6 ft, the aft one by 4 ft, an observation lounge was fitted forward of the bridge, and her aft deckhouse was extended.

At her postwar refit, she received two new funnels of equal height, new and larger deck shelters for and aft on which were fitted four lifeboats slung on new davits, her wheelhouse was enclosed and mainmast fitted. In 1953 her saloons were repainted white, instead of brown, and in 1954 a cafeteria replaced the conventional tearoom. The big change to oil burning came in 1957, and at the same time alterations were made to her public rooms, a dining saloon was fitted out on the main deck aft and a small cafeteria in the after deckhouse. In postwar years she could carry a maximum of 1,840 passengers.

Her colours were those of the LNER with black hull until 1936, when it was repainted grey. This she kept until the war. Afterwards, in 1946 and 1947 she had the LNER funnels with a black hull, but in 1948 adopted the standard BTC yellow funnels with black tops.

She made her last sailings for The CSP on 28 September 1964 on the Wemyss Bay–Rothesay service, and was laid up in Albert Harbour, Greenock. She lay there until being sold to a syndicate of businessmen for service 'Somewhere on the south coast'. She changed hands on 29 September 1965 and after being inspected at Port Glasgow left the Clyde under her own steam for the Medway, arriving there on 14 November.

After years of success on the Clyde, there now begins a disastrous tale. Her new owners, now known to be the Coastal Steam Packet Co Ltd, announced that she would serve Thames resorts from Tower Pier from Saturday 28 May 1966. She ran an inaugural trip for invited guests on 26 May and opened her season on the intended date. From then on there was nothing but trouble, including broken paddles, faulty boilers and lack of catering staff. In all she made only eight trips, her last being on 6 August from Tower Pier to Southend, though she failed to return on the same day even then, and her passengers went back to London by train. After this, she lay in the Pool for about two weeks and on 23 August was towed to Chatham to await disposal.

In 1967 she again appeared in service, but again was not successful, and made her last public sailing on 12 July. She was officially withdrawn the following day and laid up off Erith later in the month. Early in August a writ was served upon her for non-payment of debts, and she was subsequently offered for quick sale by the Admiralty Marshal, on 5 December. Bought by Belgian breakers, she arrived at Antwerp in tow of the tug *Dhuli* on 29 December.

Auxiliary A/A Vessel HMS *Jeanie Deans,* still with minesweeping
pennant number up

197

SS KILDONAN

BUILT	1933 by Ardrossan Dockyard Ltd
GROSS TONS	208
DIMENSIONS	120 ft 5 in x 23 ft 2 in x 9 ft 10 in
MACHINERY	2-cyl compound by Aitchison Blair Ltd, Clydebank
	Coal-fired boiler
SPEED	10½ knots
ROUTE	Ardrossan-Brodick-Millport

Kildonan, whose original name was *Arran,* was launched for Clyde
Cargo Steamers Ltd, on 31 July 1933, and replaced an earlier *Arran* built
in 1926. She was a cargo-only steamer with no passenger accommodation.
Throughout she had been primarily concerned with the Glasgow–Arran
cargo runs, though she appeared elsewhere from time to time. From
1937 she was owned by the Clyde & Campbeltown Shipping Co Ltd,
which, from 1 October 1949 was controlled by the BTC. She was renamed
Kildonan in 1953 to clear her name for one of the new motor vessels.
Her cargo runs to Arran were particularly important after TSS *Glen
Sannox* was withdrawn in April 1954 since the passenger ship *Marchioness of Graham* which then took up the run was short of the necessary
cargo space. However when the new *Glen Sannox,* a general purpose
ship, entered service in July 1957, *Kildonan* was rendered redundant and
she was withdrawn early in that month. She was sold for breaking up
at Port Glasgow by Smith & Houston Ltd, and arrived there on 3
February 1958.

Kildonan in Brodick Bay 11 August 1953

TSS QUEEN MARY II

BUILT	1933 by Wm. Denny & Bros Ltd, Dumbarton
GROSS TONS	1,014
DIMENSIONS	263 ft 4 in x 37 ft x 6 ft 9 in
MACHINERY	3 Parsons turbines by Denny, direct drive
	Oil-fired boiler
SPEED	19 knots
ROUTE	Glasgow-Dunoon, Rothesay and Arran Coast (to 1950)
	Rothesay, Kyles (from 1951)

This steamer, originally named *Queen Mary,* was designed for the Glasgow (Bridge Wharf) sailings of Williamson-Buchanan Steamers Ltd, and at that time could carry over 2,000 passengers. Her maiden voyage took her to Loch Long and Loch Goil, and included a call at Craigendoran, her only visit there so far as is known. This was a special trip for the benefit of Denny workers. Thereafter she operated on the Bridge Wharf–Arran Coast sailings, taking over the 10.0 am sailing from *King Edward.* She remained on this run until the end of the 1939 season. From late 1939 to 1945 she usually served the run between Gourock and Dunoon all year round and was not requisitioned for war service. In 1946 she reverted to the Arran Coast run and in 1951 she ran to the Kyles. From the 1952 season she took the only 'all the way' sailing then operated—this was a sailing at 11.0 am for Rothesay and the Kyles.

When Cunard's new giant liner was named *Queen Mary* the directors of Williamson-Buchanan Steamers Ltd were prevailed upon to alter the

Queen Mary II silhouetted against a background of Gourock and a steam train 10 May 1965

199

name of their Clyde ship, and Captain Buchanan's suggestion that the suffix *II* be added was accepted and became operative from July 1934. She was unusual among Clyde vessels in having a companionway up the front of the superstructure, leading from the foredeck to the boat deck. She was transferred to The CSP in October 1935, retained her original white funnels with black tops but was given silver vents. In the summer of 1936, she was again transferred, this time to Williamson-Buchanan Steamers (1936) Ltd, a new subsidiary of the LMS. From 1940 to early 1946 she served in naval grey being again finally transferred in 1943 to The CSP.

She was altered internally from time to time, the most significant post-war change being the substitution of a cafeteria for her tearoom in 1954. In the same year her mainmast was fitted. In 1957 came the greatest overall changes. Structural alterations involving the replacement of her original funnels by one larger one, conversion to oil burning and re-boilering, increased her tonnage to 917, from its original 870. From 1965 the Saturday sailing 'Doon the Watter' was withdrawn, and *Queen Mary II* then took up relief and extra sailings on the ferry routes and also made cruises from Gourock. She has an enclosed promenade deck, a dining saloon on the main deck forward and can carry a maximum of 1,820 passengers.

PS CALEDONIA

BUILT	1934 by Wm. Denny & Bros Ltd, Dumbarton
GROSS TONS	623
DIMENSIONS	230 ft x 62 ft x 5 ft 7 in
MACHINERY	3-cyl triple-expansion by Denny
	Oil-fired boilers
SPEED	14 knots
ROUTE	Ferry services based on Gourock and Wemyss Bay
	Cruises and excursions from Ayr, Ardrossan and Troon
	Sailings and cruises from Craigendoran

Caledonia, launched on 1 February 1934, replaced her namesake (1889) in The CSP fleet, but did not operate on the same routes. Her near sister *Mercury* was lost during the war.

Throughout her career on the Clyde, *Caledonia* has been mainly used on ferry services from the railway piers at Gourock and Wemyss Bay, and to a lesser extent from Largs, and was so employed during the years 1934-5, and 1946-53. Interspersed with these runs she also undertook cruises, and in some periods this was her main occupation. From 1936 to 1939, succeeding *Duchess of Argyll,* she frequently sailed to Arran via the Kyles starting at Greenock.

Her wartime service saw her requisitioned in November 1939, and placed in the 11th Mine Sweeping Flotilla. She served on the Clyde and elsewhere with the pennant number J125 as HMS *Goatfell*. In 1942 she was converted to an AA ship and is credited with two enemy aircraft. She was returned to her owners in 1945 and after extensive refit by Denny's re-entered Clyde service on 20 May 1946.

From 1954, having been largely displaced on the ferry runs by the new motor vessels, she was engaged in high-season excursions from Ayr, Troon and Ardrossan (in succession to *Marchioness of Graham*); early and late season excursions from Glasgow to the Kyles, and occasionally, long distance from Gourock. During these years she was also relief ship on the Brodick and Whiting Bay (Arran) run. Local interest was aroused in October 1960 when soundings were carried out at Craigendoran to see if she could use the pier. These were successful, but in spite of rumours to the contrary, she remained principally in the lower Firth until the end of the 1964 season when cruises from Ayr and Troon were terminated, her last cruise from Ayr being to Millport on 2 September. She was the first excursion ship to appear in the new colours at Easter 1965, and she then took up sailings from Craigendoran (previously mostly operated by *Jeanie Deans*), to Arran via the Kyles, round Bute, etc. These routes are now her main stamping grounds.

As with most vessels of her type, alterations were carried out from time to time. In her 1954-5 winter overhaul she was converted to oil burning and re-boilered at Troon; in 1956 the conventional tearoom was replaced by a cafeteria; in 1959 she was equipped with radar and in 1961 five inflatable life-rafts were fitted. She now carries a maximum of 1,730 passengers.

Caledonia passing down the Clyde on an evening charter 12 May 1965

201

TSMV WEE CUMBRAE

BUILT	1935 by Wm. Denny & Bros Ltd, Dumbarton
GROSS TONS	35
DIMENSIONS	59 ft 7 in x 12 ft 6 in x 4 ft 3 in (depth)
MACHINERY	2 diesels by Gleniffer Engines Ltd, Glasgow
SPEED	c. 10 knots
ROUTE	Gourock-Dunoon/Craigendoran

The first motor vessel in the Caledonian Clyde fleet, *Wee Cumbrae* was built for The CSP, and introduced a new ferry service between Largs and Millport only. She carried sixty passengers, inside in saloons and, from 1936, outside on seats on the fore and aft saloons. From late 1939 she was engaged on tender duties in the examination service based on Rothesay for most of the time, and returned to her original Millport service in April 1946. She remained thereon until late 1948 when she was replaced by *Ashton* and *Leven,* and in the following year she ran between Gourock and Dunoon. From 1950 to 1952 she operated between Gourock and Craigendoran, but by the end of the latter year had become redundant due to the frequent calls now being made at Gourock by vessels based on Craigendoran. She was sold in February 1953 to Marine Craft Constructors Ltd, Dumbarton, re-engined at Dumbarton, and then shipped to Brunei in North Borneo for use as a tug for towing timber rafts.

Wee Cumbrae leaving Craigendoran 24 May 1952

TSMV COUNTESS OF BREADALBANE

BUILT   1936 by Wm. Denny & Bros Ltd, Dumbarton
GROSS TONS   106
DIMENSIONS   95 ft 5 in x 18 ft 2 in x 3 ft 6 in
MACHINERY   Two 4-stroke single acting 6-cyl diesels by Gleniffer
               Engines Ltd, Glasgow
SPEED   9 knots

This vessel was designed for cruises on Loch Awe, operated by The CSP and, having been assembled at her builders' yard, was then dismantled and taken to the Loch in sections and assembled again. At this time her hull was painted white, waterline green and boot-topping blue. She has no funnel, the exhaust fumes being carried out of the stern, but there is a galley chimney. The promenade deck extends the full length of the ship, towards the forward end of this is an observation lounge with large windows. On the lower deck aft is machinery space, 'midships is the dining saloon and forward another lounge originally fitted with windows but replaced by portholes in 1952. In the same year the wooden wheelhouse was fitted, and her hull was painted black until 1961 when she appeared in a white hull. She was re-engined in 1956 with the same type as originally.

She remained in service on Loch Awe each season until 1951 apart from being laid up from 1940 to 1947 inclusive. Early in 1952 she was brought overland from the Loch by two tractors and refitted at Denny's for the winter Holy Loch service in particular. She was unpopular there

Countess of Breadalbane visiting Strone on a society charter

203

and in succeeding years has served a variety of routes, has run excursions and has been chartered. After 1954 she was particularly associated with the Largs-Millport or Rothesay route. She carries a maximum of 200 passengers. In spring 1965 a ticket office was incorporated in her wooden wheelhouse, and the following year a new stairway was fitted.

TSS MARCHIONESS OF GRAHAM

BUILT	1936 by Fairfield Shipbuilding & Engineering Co Ltd, Glasgow
GROSS TONS	585
DIMENSIONS	230 ft 7 in x 32 ft 7 in x 7 ft 3 in
MACHINERY	4 Parsons turbines by Fairfield, SR geared
	Coal-fired boilers
SPEED	18 knots
ROUTE	Ardrossan/Fairlie-Ardrossan

Built for The CSP, with service to Arran in mind, *Marchioness of Graham* was launched on 6 March 1936 and was provided with a large clear space immediately abaft the funnel for about six cars. The two deckhouses contained observation lounges, there being a separate deck over each, and the main deck accommodation included first-class dining

Marchioness of Graham arriving at Millport about 1951

saloon aft and general lounge forward beneath which was the third-class dining saloon. Also on the main deck were a smokeroom and a tea lounge.

Through most of the war she served Millport and Brodick from Fairlie, but in 1946 she returned to Ardrossan serving Brodick mainly as relief and extra ship.

From 1947 to 1953, in addition to Arran services, she operated the Ayr excursions, but from 1954 to 1957 she remained consistently running between Ardrossan and Arran in the summer only and Fairlie and Arran all the year round, with periods running to Millport. She could carry a maximum of 1,300 passengers, and was popular, but 1957 was her last full season in service. No buyer was found until December 1958, when the Greek owner Nicholas Diapoulos bought her and named her *Theo*. She was delivered to her new owners early in 1959, and was in the same year fitted with two new 8-cylinder single-acting 4 stroke oil-engines by Masch. Augsburg-Nurnberg A.G. of Augsburg. She was then renamed *Hellas,* this being changed to *Nea Hellas* in 1963 and *Galaxias* the following year.

After she was bought by Nicholas Diapoulos structural alterations increased her gross tonnage to 1,115. This was further increased to 1,131 in about 1964 and to 1,164 about a year later. It appears that she is now registered as a private yacht operated in the Aegean by Gouneleas Travel Office, Athens, by whom she was renamed *El Greco* near the end of 1965. In 1966 she was operated by Delphi Cruises S.A. with the name *El Greco,* cruising from Genoa every Saturday during the season taking in Barcelona, Ibiza and Palma. Her subsequent activities are not known. The picture shows the ship as *Galaxy* (1964) ; anglicised Greek names are frequently used on ships of this type.

Galaxy (ex-*Marchioness of Graham*) in 1964
205

PS MARCHIONESS OF LORNE

BUILT	1935 by Fairfield Shipbuilding & Engineering Co Ltd, Glasgow
GROSS TONS	427
DIMENSIONS	199 ft 6 in x 27 ft 1 in x 7 ft 6 in
MACHINERY	3-cyl triple-expansion by Fairfield
	Coal-fired boilers
SPEED	12 knots
ROUTE	Gourock-Holy Loch
	Wemyss Bay-Millport-Rothesay

Although a paddler, *Marchioness of Lorne* was similar to *Marchioness of Graham,* and shows how successful The CSP was in disguising its paddlers. Her deckhouses, unlike those of *Marchioness of Graham,* did not support extra decks, and she was introduced to replace the *Marchioness of Breadalbane* (1890) on the Holy Loch run from Greenock and Gourock. During the war she remained on the Clyde and until 1948 served the Holy Loch from the South Bank.

After the Clyde fleets were nationalised in 1948 the authorities found it desirable to alter ships' routines from time to time, one result being that *Marchioness of Lorne* was the first hitherto Gourock-based Caledonian (LMS) ship to use the former LNER stronghold Craigendoran. In

Marchioness of Lorne about 1948

206

1949 she sailed from Craigendoran to the Holy Loch calling at Gourock en route. In 1953 she was transferred to the Wemyss Bay–Millport–Rothesay service to replace *Duchess of Fife*, but was found to be rather too slow and was replaced by *Talisman* in June 1954 and laid up. Two months previously she had already been offered on sale, and she was taken in for breaking up on 24 February 1955 by Smith & Houston Ltd at Port Glasgow. Her enclosed wooden wheelhouse was fitted in 1948 and in her later years she could carry up to 1,233 passengers.

DEPV TALISMAN

BUILT	1935 by A. & J. Inglis Ltd, Pointhouse
GROSS TONS	544
DIMENSIONS	227 ft 6 in x 54 ft x 5 ft 9½ in
MACHINERY	Four 4-stroke single acting, 8-cyl diesels by British Polar Engines Ltd. Connected to an electric motor
SPEED	15 knots
ROUTE	Craigendoran-Rothesay and Kyles
	Wemyss Bay-Millport, Rothesay
	Excursions

Launched on 10 April 1935 for the LNER, *Talisman* originally had a gross tonnage of 450 and served the Craigendoran–Rothesay–the Kyles route up to mid-1939 when she was withdrawn and laid up, her original engines, made by English Electric, having given so much trouble.

She was requisitioned for war service in June 1940 and served as an AA ship and escort ship under the name HMS *Aristocrat*, seeing service at the North Africa landings and defending Mulberry Harbour. She entered Antwerp with the first convoy after liberation.

The war over, she returned to the Clyde in February 1946 and a refit by her builders included the installation of a mainmast, a wooden wheelhouse and two lifeboats on top of the forward deck. Her deckhouses were redesigned and accommodation generally improved. Later alterations included the painting of deckhouses white in 1952 ; paddle boxes white in 1956 and radar equipment fitted in 1958. She could carry a maximum of 1,252 passengers. A few cars could be carried on the promenade deck, which extended the length of the ship, abaft the funnel.

She re-entered service from Craigendoran in 1946 in LNER colours, being given BR livery in March 1948. She was the last ship to call regularly at Princes Pier, Greenock, before it was closed to Clyde passenger sailings in 1951. She remained on the Craigendoran–Rothesay–the Kyles

Talisman arriving at Gourock from Rothesay 10 May 1965

all-year-round service until July 1953, when the appearance of the new 'Maids' rendered her redundant, though only temporarily so. She was laid up on 5 July in Albert Harbour, Greenock. In May 1954 at Glasgow she was re-engined with British Polar Diesels and she took up the Wemyss Bay–Millport–Rothesay sailings in the following month replacing *Marchioness of Lorne*. Since then she usually served from Craigendoran or Wemyss Bay and she introduced the 'Round Bute' cruise in September 1961.

Until 1951 she was owned by the BTC (Scottish Region), but on 5 November that year she was transferred to The CSP with other ex-LNER vessels.

She made her last sailing on 17 November 1966, and was subsequently sold for breaking up by Arnott, Young & Co Ltd, at Dalmuir, where she arrived under tow on 17 October 1967.

TSMV ARRAN MAIL

BUILT	1936 by Wm. Denny & Bros Ltd, Dumbarton
GROSS TONS	137
DIMENSIONS	95 ft 1 in x 20 ft 1 in x 8 ft 6 in
MACHINERY	Two 6-cyl diesels by Gleniffer Engines Ltd, Glasgow
SPEED	10 knots
ROUTE	Ardrossan-Brodick

A curious little craft, with engines aft, *Arran Mail* was an 'extra' ship built for The CSP to operate an early morning mail-and-cargo run to Arran to stave off complaints by Islanders who previously had had to await the arrival of the first passenger ship for their goods. This entailed a departure from Ardrossan at 6.45 am, the crossing taking her just over 1¼ hours. She had a single long hatch and her turtle-decked forecastle was a notable feature. She could carry twelve passengers, hence the two large life-boats on the deckhouse aft. During the second war she was occupied mainly in tendering off Gourock. Towards the close of 1949 she was withdrawn, being considered of no further use, and laid up. She was sold in December 1951 to a Mrs F. M. D. Honnilow and resold in 1954 to the Allen Shipping Line (Guernsey) and renamed *Saint Ernest*.

As *Saint Ernest* she was engaged principally in the tomato and vegetable trade between the Channel Islands and South Coast ports, and it was en-route from Alderney to Newhaven on 19 January 1962 that she met her

Arran Mail in service 1946

Saint Ernest (ex-*Arran Mail*) at Guernsey in September 1961

untimely end. Shortly after she left, the weather worsened and it was presumed that she had foundered with the loss of all five on board.

PS JUPITER

BUILT	1937 by Fairfield Shipbuilding & Engineering Co Ltd, Govan
GROSS TONS	642
DIMENSIONS	230 ft 7 in x 62 ft 1 in x 7 ft 1¼ in
MACHINERY	3-cyl triple-expansion engine by Fairfield
	Oil-fired boilers
SPEED	13 knots
ROUTE	Gourock-Dunoon
	Wemyss Bay-Rothesay etc
	Excursions

A typical CSP 'disguised' paddler, *Jupiter,* whose sister *Juno* was bombed and sunk in the Thames in 1941, was launched on 9 April 1937 for general railway-connection services from Gourock and Wemyss Bay, and, in fact, she deviated little from these mundane duties throughout her career. Between her funnels there was a clear space for vehicles and goods.

In 1939 she was requisitioned for duties as a mine-sweeper and renamed HMS *Scawfell* (*Juno* was called HMS *Helvellyn*) and joined the 11th Mine Sweeping Flotilla with the pennant number J103. From 1942, as an AA ship, she served in the Thames and at Mulberry Harbour. She was returned to her owners in 1945, and was reconditioned by D. & W. Henderson Ltd, Glasgow.

Of the Clyde steamers which saw wartime service she was the first to resume peacetime sailings, taking up the Holy Loch service from Gourock in February 1946. Shortly afterwards she resumed the Dunoon and Rothesay services and remained thereon until 1953. In 1954 she concentrated mainly on the Wemyss Bay–Rothesay service, introducing the 'Round Cumbrae' from Rothesay the following year. On occasion during this period she ran relief trips to Arran, and in 1956 revived the Glasgow (Bridge Wharf)–Dunoon–Lochgoilhead Sunday excursions. In this year she was converted to oil burning and given a self-service cafeteria. She could carry 1,509 passengers and was withdrawn from service at the close of the 1957 season. No buyers were forthcoming and she was laid up for three years before making any move. In May 1960 The CSP sold her to Ulster Agencies Ltd, Belfast but continued to provide a watchman. She was sold eventually for breaking up by Hammond Lane Foundry Co Ltd, Dublin, whither she went in April 1961.

Jupiter near Wemyss Bay 4 September 1957

211

TSMV ASHTON
TSMV LEVEN

BUILT	1938 by Wm. Denny & Bros Ltd, Dumbarton
GROSS TONS	38
DIMENSIONS	60 ft x 13 ft 6 in x 5 ft 1 in (depth)
MACHINERY	Two 4-stroke single acting 8-cyl diesels by Gleniffer Engines Ltd, Glasgow
SPEED	c. 10 knots
ROUTE	Largs-Millport, Gourock-Holy Loch

These twins entered service making short river cruises from Glasgow, with white hulls and passenger accommodation for 112. Their hulls were repainted black in spring 1939. *Leven* served for a short time in 1939 from Gourock but shortly after war broke out both were taken over by the Sea Transport Officer (Clyde) for use as tenders. From 1946 *Leven* and *Ashton* ran as supplementary ships between Gourock and Dunoon and switched to the Largs–Millport run, succeeding *Wee Cumbrae*, in 1948 and 1949 respectively. There they remained, with forays elsewhere, especially the Gourock–Holy Loch winter run, until withdrawn early in 1965 and laid up in Albert Harbour, Greenock. Their passenger accommodation was reduced to seventy-two in 1962 and they were owned by The CSP throughout. *Ashton* was sold in July 1965 to R. Ritchie Ltd, Gourock,

Ashton arriving at Gourock 21 June 1947

for their Gourock–Helensburgh service. She was overhauled and given new colours, cream superstructure and dark blue hull, and took up the run, with no name shown, on 31 July. *Leven* was sold also in July to Thomas Jack & Co (Shipping) Ltd, Larne, but was resold soon afterwards to Western Steam Navigation Co Ltd and took up service on the excursion trade from Paignton to the River Dart etc, still registered in Glasgow. Her landing platform was removed before she left the Clyde. She was subsequently renamed *Pride of The Bay*.

PS WAVERLEY

BUILT	1947 by A. & J. Inglis Ltd, Pointhouse
GROSS TONS	693
DIMENSIONS	239 ft 11 in x 58 ft x 5 ft 9 in
MACHINERY	3-cyl triple-expansion by Rankin & Blackmore Ltd, Greenock
	Oil-fired boiler
SPEED	15 knots
ROUTE	Mainly services and excursions from Craigendoran

Launched on 2 October 1946, *Waverley* ran trials on 5 June 1947 and replaced a paddler with the same name built in 1899 for the North British Steam Packet Company and lost at Dunkirk. As she was an LNER ship,

Waverley off Gourock in August 1965, dressed for a Fleet Review

Waverley was owned by BTC (Scottish Region) from 1948 but on 5 November 1951 she was transferred to The CSP. In 1953 her deck saloons were painted white, in 1957 she was converted from coal burning and two years later her paddle boxes also were painted white. Her builders fitted a new forward funnel in February 1961 and a new after funnel a year later. She can carry a maximum of 1,350 passengers.

Throughout her career she has been based primarily on Craigendoran, serving Arrochar regularly up to 1952. In the following year sailings there were reduced to three or four per week, which enabled the ship to operate 'Round Bute' cruises. She was replaced on the Saturday Arrochar run by *Maid of Argyll* taking instead an Arran via the Kyles, or Rothesay–Arran sailing. In 1954 she was occupied on the Arrochar and Arran sailings and in the following year took up an additional excursion, namely 'Round the Lochs'. After *Jupiter* was withdrawn in 1957, *Waverley* took over her Saturday Wemyss Bay–Rothesay sailings and also did some up-river trips to Glasgow. Since then she has continued to operate on similar runs based on Wemyss Bay and Craigendoran.

TSMV ARRAN
TSMV COWAL
TSMV BUTE

BUILT	*Arran* 1953 by Wm. Denny & Bros Ltd, Dumbarton
	Cowal and *Bute* 1954 by Ailsa Shipbuilding Co Ltd, Troon
GROSS TONS	568/568/569
DIMENSIONS	185 ft 10 in x 36 ft 6 in x 7 ft 2 in
MACHINERY	Two 2-stroke single acting 6-cyl diesels by British Polar Engines Ltd, Glasgow
SPEED	15 knots
ROUTE	Gourock-Dunoon
	Wemyss Bay-Rothesay/Millport
	Ardrossan/Fairlie-Brodick

Launched on 22 September 1953, 20 January and 28 September 1954, and entering service 4 January, 9 April and early December 1954, respectively, these ships, built for The CSP, came as a welcome relief from the archaic conditions for motorists which had prevailed hitherto. No longer was it necessary to drive over slippery steep planks, nor wait for hours on end while each elderly steamer took its handful of cars. Here at last was a realistic system using a solid steel ramp over which cars could be driven more or less horizontally at any state of the tide, and then moved to the car deck by lift. True, they have not the serenity or freedom from vibration which generally characterised the older paddlers or turbine steamers, but none the less they serve their purpose well.

Arran opened the Gourock–Dunoon link on her maiden voyage, and *Cowal*, after running for some months with *Arran*, opened the Wemyss Bay–Rothesay service on 1 October 1954. Combined with the latter was a new through cargo service from Glasgow to Rothesay via Wemyss Bay, which caused the closure of the direct Glasgow–Rothesay cargo service and the withdrawal of *Ardyne* and *Minard*. *Bute* made her maiden voyage on the Rothesay run. *Arran* opened a cargo service between Wemyss Bay and Millport in 1957, replacing one previously operated from Ardrossan.

All three have served Gourock–Dunoon, Wemyss Bay–Rothesay and Fairlie–Brodick, the last usually being on relief or extra sailings. Very occasionally they also carry out cruises and serve on passenger-only routes, but they are not very satisfactory for these purposes. *Arran* was the last Clyde ship built by Wm. Denny & Bros Ltd.

They can carry a maximum of 650 passengers in saloons on two decks forward of the lift. Originally twenty-six cars could be carried and fifty tons of cargo, and for the latter a hold was provided aft to give access to the after end of the car deck. Derricks attached to sampson posts were also provided for cargo handling. However, in practice it was found that the cargo could be handled equally well by using the car lifts, so during overhauls of all ships, in spring 1959, the sampson posts were removed and the holds plated over. Tripod masts replaced the sampsons. This move increased car capacity on each ship to thirty-five. They have been very successful, and at the time of going to press there is talk of more to come.

Bute leaving Gourock 10 May 1965

TSMV MAID OF ARGYLL
TSMV MAID OF ASHTON
TSMV MAID OF CUMBRAE
TSMV MAID OF SKELMORLIE

BUILT	*Argyll* 1953 by A. & J. Inglis Ltd, Pointhouse
	Ashton 1953 by Yarrow & Co Ltd, Scotstoun
	Cumbrae 1953 by Ardrossan Dockyard Ltd
	Skelmorlie 1953 by A. & J. Inglis Ltd, Pointhouse
GROSS TONS	508
DIMENSIONS	164 ft x 30 ft x 5 ft 8 in
MACHINERY	Two 2-stroke single acting 6-cyl diesels by British Polar Engines Ltd, Glasgow
SPEED	13–14 knots
ROUTE	General passenger services eg:
	Craigendoran/Gourock-Holy Loch
	Wemyss Bay-Largs-Millport
	Craigendoran-Rothesay/Kyles
	Excursions eg:
	Gourock-Arrochar
	Round Cumbrae
	Short-distance cruises eg to Loch Striven

These most attractive little ships came as part of the Clyde fleet modern-

Maid of Ashton leaving Gourock 10 May 1965

isation plan, being economical to run and able to serve all piers, having a shallow draught. They can carry a maximum of 627 passengers and 13 officers and crew, the last having accommodation on the lower deck aft. There is no dining saloon proper, but there is a pleasant tearoom-lounge and another saloon on the main deck and a further saloon on the lower deck forward. Each has a landing platform fitted over the navigating bridge for use at low tide and also so that any of the ships can be called upon to act as a tender to liners calling off Gourock. The very high masts give them a singularly yacht-like appearance, and to reduce top-hamper the outer funnel is of aluminium. During their winter 1958-9 overhauls radar was fitted. Launchings and first commercial voyages were as follows:

Maid of Argyll: Launched 4 March 1953, maiden voyage 5 June 1953, Holy Loch

Maid of Ashton: launched 17 February 1953, maiden voyage 25 May 1953, Holy Loch

Maid of Cumbrae: launched 13 May 1953, maiden voyage July 1953, Glasgow–Dunoon

Maid of Skelmorlie: launched 2 April 1953, maiden voyage June 1953, afternoon and evening excursions

Maid of Ashton was threatened with withdrawal towards the end of 1964, but in the event *Maid of Argyll* was selected and was laid up at Greenock during winter 1964-5. The company requested permission from the MOT to withdraw the Holy Loch service, but as no decision had been announced by early 1965 the ship was overhauled in April and subsequently re-entered service. To date all four are still in service, and the Holy Loch service still operates.

TSMV GLEN SANNOX

BUILT	1957 by Ailsa Shipbuilding Co Ltd, Troon
GROSS TONS	1,107
DIMENSIONS	256 ft 6 in x 46 ft 3 in x 7 ft 6 in
MACHINERY	Two 2-stroke single acting 8-cyl diesels by Sulzer Bros Ltd, Winterthur
SPEED	17 knots
ROUTE	Ardrossan (summer only)/Fairlie-Brodick (Arran)

Entering the Arran service for which she was specifically designed in July 1957, *Glen Sannox* succeeded and rendered redundant *Marchioness of Graham* and the cargo steamer *Kildonan* in one blow. Her name revived that of her famous turbine predecessor, and paddler before that. She can carry a maximum of 1,100 passengers, 40 tons of cargo and 45-50 vehicles loaded by ramp and lift as on the 'Arran' class of 1953. Cargo is usually handled in containers.

The CSP crest is affixed to her stem. In June 1964 she was given a red lion rampant on each side of her funnel, and during her overhaul at Troon in February 1965 was given the new blue hull, though the white line above the strake was not removed until the following month. Her annual overhaul is usually carried out early in spring each year, and she is replaced by one of the smaller 1953-built car ferries. She has rarely served elsewhere, though she did visit Millport on 5 March 1966. She was the first Clyde vessel to be repainted in the new blue livery.

TSMV *Glen Sannox* at Brodick, Arran 11 August 1966. Note large deck-crane

MV KEPPEL

BUILT	1961 by J. S. White & Co Ltd, Cowes
GROSS TONS	213
DIMENSIONS	110 ft x 27 ft x 4 ft 6 in
MACHINERY	6-cyl unidirectional Lister Blackstone oil engine Voith-Schneider propeller
SPEED	9 knots
ROUTE	Largs-Millport

Built for the Tilbury-Gravesend passenger-ferry service with the name *Rose*, this vessel was acquired by The CSP from the BRB on 11 April 1967 as a replacement for *Countess of Breadalbane* to serve between Largs and Millport.

She left Tilbury on 24 April 1967 for the Clyde, via the east coast, and arrived at Greenock on 15 May. Here alterations were put in hand to fit her for her new work, including the building up of the bow to promenade deck level, the extension forward of the promenade deck, the replacement of the hydraulic gangways by railings, the fitting of a shelter aft on the promenade deck and the erection of a landing deck abaft the bridge. She should have been ready by 28 May, but she was late, and entered service from Largs on 12 June, still bearing her old name *Rose*. She was renamed at Greenock during a check-up six days later.

MV *Rose* (now *Keppel*) at Largs 12 June 1967

16: THE SCOTTISH LOCHS

Since 1948 the Railway Executive has run steamer services on two Scottish Lochs, namely Loch Awe and Loch Lomond. In 1939 there were railway cruises on Loch Tay, but these were abandoned at the close of that season and not revived.

Loch Awe

The cruises on Loch Awe were also suspended during the second world war. The only railway ship thereon at the time was The CSP *Countess of Breadalbane* running from Lochawe Pier to Ford. The war over, sailings were again taken up, and carried on seasonally until the end of 1951 season. *Countess of Breadalbane* was taken to the Clyde in the following year, and no railway ship has, since then, served on Loch Awe.

Loch Lomond

Available for service on Loch Lomond in 1939 were the paddlers *Prince George, Princess May*, and *Prince Edward*, with the two last named taking the main sailings between Balloch and Ardlui, and *Prince George* acting as relief. There had been no winter service since 1933, but the summer programme was kept up, even through the war years, and is still maintained, though in a much modified form.

Prince George was broken up in 1942, and thereafter the other two sailed alone until *Princess May* was withdrawn at the end of the 1952 season. To replace her a new ship was introduced in 1953, named *Maid of the Loch,* also a paddler. She and *Prince Edward* then ran for two seasons, the latter being withdrawn in 1954 and from 1955 the *Maid* has served alone. Passenger figures on the Loch have not, until recently, been very good and during the 1960s the ship has been under constant threat of withdrawal. In fact, in March 1963, a decision to terminate the Loch sailings was taken, but a reprieve was granted and great publicity efforts have succeeded in raising the patronage to reasonable figures. She should be safe for a few years yet.

Since the end of the 1963 season the pier at Ardlui at the northern end of the Loch has not been in use, and cruises in that direction have been substituted.

Maid of the Loch's original colours of white hull and buff funnel were not affected when alterations were carried out on the Clyde ships.

Prior to 1948 the Loch services had been operated by Group Committee No 4 of the LMS and LNER, but in that year, the two ships were taken over by the Scottish Region. *Maid of the Loch* was transferred to The CSP in May 1957.

PS PRINCESS MAY

BUILT	1898 by A. & J. Inglis Ltd, Pointhouse
GROSS TONS	256
DIMENSIONS	165 ft 6 in x 24 ft x 6 ft (depth)
MACHINERY	2-cyl double-diagonal, non-compound by Inglis Coal-fired boiler
SPEED	14 knots
ROUTE	Loch Lomond excursions and service runs

Launched on 11 October 1898, *Princess May* was sister to *Prince George* which was dismantled in 1942. She entered service in the summer of 1899 and was, at first, mainly relief and extra boat. In the years between the wars she and *Prince Edward* took the main sailings. She originally had one mast but this was removed shortly after the second war. She made her last voyage on 13 September 1952 and was broken up in 1953 at Balloch, being replaced that year by *Maid of the Loch*. Her spacious open promenade deck is well seen in the photograph, as are the large picture windows in forward and aft saloons. Latterly she could carry up to 871 passengers.

Princess May leaving Tarbert 31 May 1949

PS PRINCE EDWARD

BUILT	1911 by A. & J. Inglis Ltd, Glasgow
GROSS TONS	304
DIMENSIONS	175 ft x 22 ft 1 in x 6 ft (depth)
MACHINERY	2-cyl compound diagonal by Inglis
	Coal-fired boiler
SPEED	15 knots
ROUTE	Loch Lomond

Built for the Dumbarton & Balloch Joint Line Committee's Loch Lomond services, this steamer was, in 1911, the largest ever to be taken up the River Leven. She grounded on a sandbank just below Millburn, and horses and tractors were used to try to free her. They were not successful and she remained *in situ* until the following spring when a further attempt to refloat her was made. Her troubles, however, were still not over for it was found that, although she floated freely, she was unable to pass under Bonhill Bridge because there was too *much* water! Local children were invited aboard to act as ballast and, thus equipped, the ship finally gained the Loch. She entered service in July 1912.

From 1933 she was operated by the LMS AND LNER Group Committee No 4 until 1948, when BR (Scottish Region) took over. She was never owned by The CSP.

Prince Edward and *Princess May* at Balloch, September 1948 still with grey hulls but with the new BR buff funnels

During the second war she carried on her usual routine until the end of March 1941, when she became a temporary accommodation ship for blitzed Glasgow families.

Until 1948 she had a grey hull and red funnel with a black top, but nationalisation led to her funnel colour being changed to yellow and her hull colour to black. In spring 1953 her hull was repainted white but the funnel remained yellow.

She ran along with the new *Maid of the Loch* for two seasons, until being withdrawn at the end of the 1954 season, and was broken up at Balloch in March and April 1955. She could carry a maximum of 958 passengers.

PS MAID OF THE LOCH

BUILT	1953 by A. & J. Inglis Ltd, Pointhouse
GROSS TONS	555
DIMENSIONS	208 ft x 51 ft x 4 ft 6 in
MACHINERY	2-cyl diagonal-compound by Rankin & Blackmore Ltd, Greenock
	Oil-fired boiler
SPEED	12 knots
ROUTE	Loch Lomond pleasure cruises

Replacing the old paddler *Princess May* this ship is the largest inland steamer in the UK and had to be taken to Balloch in sections to be reassembled there. She took to the water on 5 March 1953, ran trials on 4 May and was officially named on 22 May. She made her maiden regular sailing on 25 May 1953 (Glasgow's Queen's Birthday Holiday).

She can carry a maximum of 1,000 passengers in good accommodation including a cocktail bar and excellent observation saloons with large windows. She has, in all, four passenger decks. On the lower one is a bar and tearoom ; the main deck has the dining saloon seating seventy and an observation lounge ; another observation lounge and the cocktail bar are on the promenade deck, while the top deck is open. Her funnel and superstructure are made of aluminium. She has retained her present colours throughout, and in 1957 was transferred from the Scottish Region to The CSP.

In the early 1960s in particular she was not very successful and lived from season to season under threat of withdrawal. However, imaginative plans to popularise the ship succeeded and in 1965, the first year in which these plans were put into operation, her passenger carryings increased by 65 per cent to 192,000 and her reappearance in 1966 was assured. She was running again in 1967 and 1968, but her future is still in doubt.

Maid of the Loch at Balloch Pier 9 May 1965

17: KYLE OF LOCHALSH

The Kyle of Lochalsh–Kyleakin ferry service has been railway-owned for decades, but until January 1945 was commonly leased to other operators. In that month the LMS took over responsibility and from then on ran the service itself. On nationalisation it passed to the Scottish Region, but in May 1957 the service and the ships thereon were transferred to The CSP.

The service operates all the year round, but until 1965 was not run on Sundays. In 1963 an attempt was made to run a Sunday service, but the Isle of Skye churches managed to squash the proposal. However, on 6 June 1965 MV *Kyleakin* introduced the first Sunday service to the Island amid a storm of protest. During the first four months of operation 4,300 cars and 10,400 people were carried.

Motorships in service 1945

Skye built at Glasgow	1922	6 net tons
Kyleakin built at Glasgow	1930	7 net tons
Moil built at Govan	1936	10 net tons
Cuillin built at Dumbarton	1942	11 net tons

*Passengers only

By 1956 all these had been withdrawn and the service was being run by three newer motor vessels named *Portree* (1951 ; 53 gross tons), *Broadford* (1954 ; 57 gross tons) and *Lochalsh* (1951 ; about 50 gross tons). In 1957 a new *Lochalsh* appeared, replacing her predecessor of the same name (now with *II* added as a suffix and disposed of in 1958). All these

Lochalsh approaching Kyleakin 24 July 1963

vessels could carry about six vehicles. On 11 July 1960 a new *Kyleakin* left the Clyde and sailed for Kyle of Lochalsh via the Crinan Canal. In 1965 and 1966 Lamonts' supplied two new vessels named *Portree* and *Broadford*. To make way for these, *Portree* (1951) had *II* added to her name early in 1965 and was sold later in the year to Irish buyers. It was understood that she was to be used on Strangford Lough, and she left the Clyde under tow for Belfast in September. In summer 1966 she was still laid up at Belfast. *Broadford* (1954) was renamed *Broadford II* in June 1966 and later offered for sale. The new ships have room for 10 cars, and are side-loading. *Broadford II* was sold in January 1967 to the Orwell & Harwich Navigation Co Ltd.

In 1965 *Broadford*, *Lochalsh* and *Kyleakin* were given the new blue livery, but *Portree II* was not, because of her pending disposal.

18: THE FORTH

In 1939 the LNER operated a ferry service between Granton and Burnt-island with TSS *Thane of Fife* (ex-*Snowdrop*, Wallasey Corporation 1936 ; built 1910). The service was suspended in March 1940 and formally abandoned in 1947.

The ferry service between North and South Queensferry, though owned by the LNER, was leased to Wm. Denny & Bros Ltd, Dumbarton, from March 1934. It was agreed that new ships were to be owned and operated by Denny, while the railway company could take a share of the profits.

Denny's at first provided *Queen Margaret* and *Robert the Bruce*, which were aided on the route by PS *Dundee* (1875) and bought by Denny in 1934 from the LNER. These three were in service up to and during the war. The two new ships had dimensions of 149 ft x 48 ft, a loaded draught of 5 ft and could carry about 30 cars and 500 passengers. They were propelled by independent paddle-wheels driven by diesel-electric motors. The ships were successful, but the onset of war prevented further orders until *Mary Queen of Scots* appeared in 1949, built on lines similar to the first two. A fourth, named *Sir William Wallace*, entered service in March 1956. She was slightly larger than the others, having a length of 153 ft and a gross tonnage of 277 compared with the 228 of the others.

The service has generally been run at 15 min intervals from March to

All four Forth ferries laid up after transfer to the British Railways Board

227

October, and every 20 min for the rest of the year.

When the Forth Bridge was opened, the ferry service was closed, and the last general sailings were made on 4 September 1964, *Robert the Bruce* making the last crossing. A ceremonial and religious sailing took place two days later. The four ships then became the property of the Railways Board, and were laid up at Burntisland on a care and maintenance basis. It was believed at this time that one or more might have been suitable for Clyde or Isle of Wight use, but in the event all four were put on the sale list in October.

Queen Margaret and *Mary Queen of Scots* went to T. W. Ward's yard at Inverkeithing for breaking up, arriving on 15 March 1965. *Robert the Bruce* was sold to Messrs P. & W. MacLellan at Bo'ness, arriving on 21 March, also for scrapping. *Sir William Wallace* was sold apparently for use as a cargo ship on Dutch waters, and in May 1965 was towed to J. S. White's, Southampton, for alterations. She remained there until 15 July, when she was towed away by the Bureau Wijsmuller tug *Hector*. Her present whereabouts are not known.

THE NORTH EASTERN REGION

The North Eastern Region, covering the area bordered roughly by the Humber, the North Sea, the Border and the Pennines, with headquarters at York, has now no ships under its aegis, and in fact was merged with the Eastern Region in 1967.

From 1948, the ships operating from Goole came within the sphere of the London Midland Region, while those operating from Hull were still technically owned by the two companies there which were in part controlled by the BTC. Management of the ships of all three was carried out by Associated Humber Lines of Hull.

In the early 1950s the old Goole ships were transferred to the North Eastern Region but continued to be managed by Associated Humber Lines until they were withdrawn and replaced by new motor vessels during the period 1957-9. In 1957 Associated Humber Lines Ltd was registered and the new ships were owned by this company throughout with the exception of the two Goole motor vessels on the Copenhagen run. These were the last ships to be owned by 'The Railway' (by now the BRB) and were sold in 1965 to Ellerman's Wilson Line Ltd.

The three Eastern Region Humber Ferries have been managed by AHL since 1959.

19 : HUMBER PORTS

From 1935, the services operated between Hull, Goole, Grimsby and the Continent by ships which were railway owned, or indirectly controlled by the railway through subsidiary companies, were managed by the Associated Humber Steamship Lines Control Committee, known in brief as Associated Humber Lines. This system continued to operate after the war for services based on Hull and Goole, the Grimsby sailings not being revived. War losses were not heavy. Up to the end of 1947 ownership of the various ships was vested in three concerns, the LMS, the Hull & Netherlands Steamship Co Ltd (a wholly owned subsidiary of the LNER) and the Wilson's & North Eastern Railway Shipping Co Ltd (in which the LNER had a majority holding, the rest belonging to the Ellerman's Wilson Line Ltd).

On nationalisation in 1948 the ships of the LMS, based on Goole, passed to the direct ownership of the BTC, while the ships of the two Hull-based concerns continued to be owned by those companies of which the BTC took control. Associated Humber Lines continued to manage the combined fleet which in 1948 consisted of the following steamers:

Based at Goole and all ex-LMS					Based at Hull		
Aire	built	1931	*Hebble*	built	1924	*Bury*	built 1910
Alt	,,	1911	*Hodder*	,,	1910	*Harrogate*	,, 1924
Blyth	,,	1931	*Irwell*	,,	1906	*Melrose Abbey*	,, 1929
Dearne	,,	1924	*Rother*	,,	1914	*Selby*	,, 1922
Don	,,	1924					

The frequency of services and the distribution of ships altered, from time to time, during these years, but for reasons of sound business efficiency rather than a direct result of change of ownership. In spite of the age of the fleet no new ships appeared until 1954, when two motor ships, the first in the fleet, named *Fountains Abbey* and *Whitby Abbey* took up service from Goole. Associated Humber Lines was still a managing company only and owned no ships until early 1957 when a new company Associated Humber Lines Ltd, was registered, BTC holding 91 per cent of the shares and Ellerman's Wilson Line 9 per cent, a representation of their share in the original Wilson's & North Eastern Railway Shipping Co Ltd. A number of ships, notably *Melrose Abbey*, *Fountains Abbey* and *Whitby Abbey* were transferred directly to AHL Ltd ownership, while most of the Goole ships, including the new *Byland Abbey* and *Kirkham Abbey* were retained by the BTC (North Eastern Region), management being entrusted to the new company. The Wilson & North Eastern Railway Shipping Company Ltd and the Hull & Netherlands Steamship Co were subsequently wound up.

During the years 1957 to 1959 the old steamers, most of which could carry up to eight or ten passengers and two of which could carry over a hundred (*Melrose Abbey* and *Bury*), were disposed of, and were replaced by modern cargo-only motor vessels. As each one appeared it was automatically registered as owned by AHL, with the exception of *Kirkham Abbey* and *Byland Abbey* which the BTC retained. Frequency of services was maintained over the years with only small alterations.

In 1961 rumours began to circulate that certain sections of the BTC interests were to be hived off to private enterprise. Further stages in what may be reasonably called 'de-nationalisation' were to be attempted. Clearly AHL was one such business. When the Transport Act 1962 appeared it was apparent that the rumoured wholesale hiving off would not materialise, but a definite step was taken to separate entirely certain sections of the shipping business (among others) from BTC control. In the event, control of AHL Ltd (see chapter on the Atlantic Steam Navigation Co Ltd) with Wilson's retaining its small holding, passed to the new Transport Holding Company on 1 January 1963. The Transport Holding Company Board was directly responsible to the MOT, but otherwise operated as any ordinary commercial holding company, instructing and advising on general financial and administrative matters but leaving the day-to-day running of the business entirely in the hands of the local people.

It was not until after the Transport Holding Company had taken over control of AHL, that service changes of any significance took place, the

MV *Leeds,* after conversion for unit-load work, alongside the sheer-legs in Albert Dock, Hull 1 May 1965

231

main feature being the reduction or termination of services altogether. At the close of 1962 the AHL fleet consisted of three passenger-carrying motor ships (*Bolton Abbey, Melrose Abbey* and *Whitby Abbey*) and six smaller cargo-only ships (*Darlington, Harrogate, Leeds, Selby, Wakefield* and *York*). Services, at least once weekly, were operated from Goole to Rotterdam or Amsterdam, Ghent or Antwerp, Bremen or Hamburg, and from Hull to Rotterdam, Ghent or Antwerp, Bremen or Hamburg. There was also an 'inducement' call made at Dunkirk from time to time by the Antwerp ship, or in special cases by a chartered ship. As is suggested above, it was normal practice for a ship to call at two ports on her round trip, but, if there were enough cargo offering out and back frequently only one would be served. In fact it was this very factor which caused the first sign of rationalisation of services. Frequently, even as late as 1959, one ship could sail, for example, to Rotterdam from Goole on one day and another ship to Amsterdam two days later, neither with full loads. To permanently combine the two calls was an obvious move, though not a new one.

The first change of significance took effect on 1 September 1963, when AHL and Germany's Argo Line began a joint passenger-cargo service between Hull and Goole and Bremen and Hamburg. *Whitby Abbey* was the only passenger-carrying ship available and she was put on the Hull service, joining Argo's *Mowe* and *Adler*. Sadly this was a short-lived venture as far as passengers were concerned, for before the end of 1965 Argo announced that its passenger ships were to be withdrawn and replaced by cargo-only vessels. The last passengers were carried in January 1966. This move therefore released *Whitby Abbey* for use elsewhere, and her place was taken by *Darlington* in September 1966. The joint Goole service was at first operated every eight or nine days, but from mid-May 1964 it was found necessary to increase the frequency to every six or seven days. Chartered or Argo ships have been generally used throughout, no passengers being carried. This also was short lived, for in December 1965 the Goole to Bremen link was closed, leaving only that to Hamburg operating weekly.

The next big alteration in the AHL programme came at the beginning of August 1964, when sailings between Goole and Holland were terminated altogether, the goodwill being turned over to the Holland Steamship Company which still maintains the service. It was also during 1964 that the railways decided to do without the third ship on the Copenhagen service. The third ship was always provided by AHL and was usually *York*. The sum effect of these moves meant that there were three ships available for disposal, *Darlington, Harrogate* and *Selby*, but not *York*. *Darlington* was, in fact, retained on the German run until being chartered to the BR (Southern Region), in September 1965, but the other two were sold outright to the London Midland Region in March 1965.

Although there was retrenchment on conventional cargo services, plans were being made to build up unit-load services by modifying certain ships and by providing new berths with the right sort of equipment. On 10

232

June 1965, *Leeds* inaugurated the twice-weekly unit-load service from Hull to Rotterdam, and in August 1966 she was joined by *Wakefield*, there being thenceforth four sailings per week in each direction. They were replaced by the lengthened 'Abbeys' in January and February 1968, and then opened a new Hull-Antwerp unit-load service.

In early 1965 it was anticipated that BR would rid itself of the Copenhagen service, thus leaving the North Eastern Region without any cargo or passenger ship. In fact, in 1967 the North Eastern Region was merged with the Eastern Region. The Copenhagen service, together with the two ships serving thereon, were disposed of to Ellerman's Wilson Line Ltd in September 1965. AHL were out of another job, though the Goole office continues to act as agents. An interesting point here is that while every year up to and including 1964, the Copenhagen service had been advertised in the AHL brochure, there was no mention of it in the 1965 edition. For this one service, BR issued its own illustrated pamphlet, and although it is only four years old it is already a 'collectors' item'.

New Argo Line roll-on ships were introduced to the Hull–Hamburg/ Bremen routes in August 1967, replacing AHL's *Darlington* and Argo's *Lumme*, which were then rendered spare. The Goole–Antwerp general cargo service was closed after the arrival of *York* at Goole from Antwerp on 31 January 1968, the new Hull–Antwerp unit-load service taking its place.

Thus were the fortunes of AHL to date. The fleet in August 1968 and the services operated by the company, were as follows:

Melrose Abbey *Bolton Abbey*	unit-load, general cargo, passengers, Hull–Rotterdam
Leeds *Wakefield*	unit-load, general cargo, Hull–Antwerp
*Antares **Arcturus*	roll-on, unit-load, general cargo, Hull-Hamburg/Bremen
*Albatros	unit-load, general cargo, Goole–Hamburg

Chartered vessel general cargo, Goole–Dunkirk—(or call on account)
    *Joint with Argo Line ; Argo ships

MV *Darlington*	Holyhead–Dublin—on charter to BR (LMR)
MV *York*	Laid up.

One final point, management of the Hull–New Holland ferry service was transferred to AHL on 1 January 1959 and the ships were subsequently given the company's colours of yellow and black top, with a red band but without the letters AHL on the red. The ships were given the new BR livery in 1965, but remained under AHL management.

If the 1968 Transport Bill becomes effective, it is expected that control of AHL will pass from the Transport Holding Company to National Freight Corporation control on 1 January 1969.

233

SS IRWELL

BUILT	1906 by Swan Hunter & Wigham Richardson Ltd, Tyneside
GROSS TONS	1,040
DIMENSIONS	255 ft x 36 ft 1 in x 15 ft 5 in
MACHINERY	3-cyl triple-expansion by Swan Hunter & Wigham Richardson
	Coal-fired boilers
SPEED	11 knots
ROUTE	Goole-Holland/Belgium/Germany

Irwell, and her sister *Mersey*, were built for the general cargo services out of Goole of the Lancashire & Yorkshire Railway Co, *Irwell* being launched in May 1906. She entered service in June, and with *Mersey* served Amsterdam and Rotterdam for a period. Both ships were used on a variety of services while owned successively by the London & North Western Railway in 1922, the LMS from 1923 and the BTC from 1948, though from 1935 they were managed by Associated Humber Lines.

Irwell at Goole in the early 1950s

In the second war, during which *Mersey* was lost in 1940 with the loss of fourteen lives, *Irwell* remained on commercial service until early 1940. In May of that year she appeared at Bordeaux, and afterwards took up the Cardiff–Clyde coal run. In 1941 she was involved in coastal convoys carrying general cargo, and in subsequent years she appeared in the North Atlantic and on services to Iceland.

The war over, she ran between Loch Ryan and Larne for a short time, and re-entered the Goole–Continental trade in 1946 mainly on the Holland route. In postwar years she also appeared occasionally on the Copenhagen service as third (extra) ship. She was still a powerful steamer right to the end. Following survey at Immingham in March 1954 she was disposed of at once to breakers, arriving at Gateshead on the Tyne on 3 April at the yard of J. J. King Ltd. She could carry eight passengers in four double-berth cabins.

SS BURY

BUILT	1910 by Earle's Shipbuilding & Engineering Co Ltd, Hull
GROSS TONS	1,686
DIMENSIONS	265 ft x 36 ft x 17 ft 11½ in
MACHINERY	3-cyl triple-expansion by Earle's
	Coal-fired boilers
SPEED	12 knots
ROUTE	Hull-Rotterdam

After *Accrington* and *Dewsbury*, the third ship of the series built for the Great Central Railway was *Blackburn*, launched on 8 September 1910. She had an early demise, having sunk after a collision with the Exmouth coaster *Rook* near the Dudgeon Lightship off the north Norfolk coast, on her maiden voyage on 8 December 1910. Fifty-eight passengers and crew of *Blackburn* were rescued by the Goole steamer *Aire*. The railway hurriedly ordered a replacement from Earle's, and *Stockport* appeared near the end of 1911. After a varied life, especially after 1935, she was torpedoed in the North Atlantic while on convoy rescue duties in February 1943.

Bury was the last of the original four to be completed, being launched on 3 November 1910. Her accommodation was similar to her predecessors. The first-class cabins were in the 'midships superstructure, including a de-luxe stateroom and several four-berth cabins on the main deck. The second-class accommodation was in the poop, and the third-class or steerage in the 'tweendecks. The first-class entrance, ladies' room and smokeroom were on the bridge deck. She ran between Grimsby and

235

Hamburg until she was unfortunate enough to find herself in Hamburg when the 1914-18 war was declared, and to be interned there with her running mates *City of Leeds* and *City of Bradford* (both 1903). After the war she reopened the Grimsby–Rotterdam service, on which she remained for a time, reverting to the Hamburg run before 1935. From then on she served Hamburg solely, with *Stockport* until October 1936, thereafter alone, being relieved for overhauls mainly by *Accrington*. She arrived in Grimsby after her last prewar crossing on 25 August 1939, thereby terminating the passenger service for all time. Later she did two rounds trips between Hull and Rotterdam, the second, her last prewar commercial voyage, being from Hull on 31 January 1940.

In common with her sisters, she was requisitioned for convoy rescue work, and came through unscathed. Details of the war work of any of the four are lacking, but it is believed that *Bury* and *Stockport* saved at least 170 and 240 lives respectively during Arctic convoys.

After the war *Bury* was modified as to accommodation and on 1 February 1947 took up the Hull–Rotterdam sailings, running opposite *Melrose Abbey*. She served thereon consistently for most of each year (generally April to November), until 1958. During this time she could carry 197 passengers in a variety of accommodation, comprising 101 saloon, 28 second-class and 68 steerage berths, the last being in dormitories reserved for juveniles. There was a two-berth stateroom, and some two- and three-berth cabins on the bridge deck, and two- and four-berth cabins on the main deck. She was possibly the last of our passenger ships

Bury in the Humber, arriving at Hull

to advertise steerage accommodation in name, which she did up to and including 1955. In early 1956 there was a further change in accommodation, when steerage was renamed second-class and the remaining accommodation, saloon and second-class became first-class. She made her last sailing from Hull on 28 May 1958, arriving back on 2 June. The new MV *Bolton Abbey* replaced her on the next scheduled sailing. *Bury* was put on the sale list and bought very soon afterwards by Dutch breakers. The local tug *Airman* towed her to the New Waterway, where she arrived on 1 July.

SS HODDER
SS ALT
SS ROTHER

BUILT	*Alt* 1911 *Hodder* 1910 by Wm. Dobson & Co Ltd, Newcastle
	Rother 1914 by Clyde Shipbuilding & Engineering Co Ltd
GROSS TONS	1,067/1,113/1,098
DIMENSIONS	240 ft x 34 ft 2 in x c. 15 ft 3 in (depth)
MACHINERY	3-cyl triple-expansion *Alt, Hodder* by Wallsend Slipway Co Ltd, *Rother* by Clyde Shipbuilding & Engineering Co Ltd
	Coal-fired boilers
SPEED	11 knots

These ships were part of a group of six similar ships built for the Goole general cargo services of the Lancashire & Yorkshire Railway Co. The others were *Dearne* and *Rye* (both lost in the first war) and *Ouse* which was lost after collision with SS *Rye* (1,048 tons, built 1924 and also a Goole steamer) off Beachy Head while on passage Goole–Cowes on 8 August 1940.

Hodder was launched in January 1910 and delivered the following month. She had accommodation for about eight passengers in two-berth cabins adjoining the saloon on the 'midships deckhouse. Before 1939 she was seen most often on the Bremen–Hamburg and Rotterdam–Amsterdam services and also operated the Goole–Channel Islands potato traffic from time to time. In 1940 she was in coastal general cargo convoys and from 1941 was engaged in the Icelandic fish run for a time.

Alt was launched on 25 October 1911, delivered at the end of the year and served several routes up to the second war, during which she ran most of the time in coastal convoys.

Rother, launched 18 March 1914, having refrigerated cargo space, was given a light grey hull, as opposed to the black of the other ships, and

237

was designed for the Copenhagen service on which she could carry dairy produce. She could also carry eight passengers amidships. During 1940 and 1941 she suffered the indignity of coal-running between the Bristol Channel and the Clyde, interspersed with odd general cargo runs elsewhere. After the war she had the honour of reopening the Copenhagen service on 28 October 1945, though now she had a black hull. She served mainly on this run thereafter, principally as third and relief ship, until her demise. She did, however, make one or two interesting trips elsewhere, including relieving the passenger ship on the Hull–Rotterdam service over the winter 1951-2, and in May and October 1954.

Hodder was running between Holyhead and Dublin for a time in 1946 and then reverted to the Humber, running principally from Goole to Holland from April 1947. She also did the odd Hull–Rotterdam relief run, notably early in 1955. *Alt* also mainly served Holland from 9 April 1946. The three ships in postwar years switched routes considerably, and although it is possible to trace these in detail the results would be of little value.

The entry of the new MV *Fountains Abbey* into the Holland trade in October 1954 rendered *Alt* redundant. She was withdrawn, and sold in December for breaking up by Shipbreaking Industries Ltd, arriving in tow of the tug *Masterman* at Charlestown, Fife on 10 January 1955. At about the time that *Alt* was withdrawn, *Hodder* was switched to other routes, and was finally taken off service early in 1956, arriving at Dunston for breaking up by Clayton & Davie Ltd on 15 November of that year. *Rother* also went there in 1956, arriving at Dunston on 27 September for breaking up.

Rother after the second world war

SS MACCLESFIELD

BUILT	1914 by Swan Hunter & Wigham Richardson Ltd, Tyneside
GROSS TONS	1,049
DIMENSIONS	250 ft 2 in x 34 ft 3 in x 16 ft (depth)
MACHINERY	3-cyl triple-expansion by Swan Hunter & Wigham Richardson
	Coal-fired boilers
SPEED	11½ knots
ROUTE	Hull/Goole-Bremen/Hamburg, Rotterdam, Antwerp, etc

Macclesfield and her sister *Chesterfield* were built for the Great Central Railway's Grimsby–Rotterdam service, catering mainly for cargo and livestock (particularly horses) but also having accommodation for twelve passengers. *Chesterfield*, launched 30 October 1913, had the misfortune to be torpedoed and sunk near Malta on 18 May 1918—a fact interesting if only because it shows how far our small ships travelled in troubled times. *Macclesfield*, launched in May 1914, was the last ship built for the Great Central Railway. Apart from the war years she was consistently on the Rotterdam run, with short breaks, until the formation of Associated Humber Lines in 1935 brought its own rationalisation. After this *Macclesfield* wandered somewhat, beginning with a spell of relief (for

Macclesfield in the Humber about 1957

239

Melrose Abbey) on the Hull–Rotterdam service in December 1935, her only prewar appearance on this run. She then ran between Grimsby and Hamburg for a time, and in the early part of 1937 she took up the Hull–Hamburg service as 'second fiddle' to *Stockport* which operated the main weekly passenger-cargo service. She arrived in Hull on 24 August 1939 after her last prewar crossing. During her overhaul, April 1939, her six double-berth cabins were modernised, reading lamps and new wash basins with hot and cold running water were installed, and other modifications were carried out, which resulted in an increase of her gross tonnage from 1,018 to 1,032.

Through most of the war she was engaged in coastal convoys, while in May 1940 her tonnage was again increased, this time to 1,049.

After the war she was mainly on the Goole trades, but did occasionally run between Hull and Rotterdam as relief between 1952 and 1956. She did not run to Copenhagen. When two new motor vessels entered service in 1958 she was made redundant, was withdrawn in November, and sold a few weeks later for breaking up in Rotterdam, whither she was towed by the Hull tug *Tradesman* arriving on 29 December. N. V. Vereenigde Utrecht Ijzerhandel were her buyers.

SS SELBY
SS HARROGATE

Selby

BUILT	1922 by J. Duthrie (Torry) Ltd, Aberdeen
GROSS TONS	1,063
DIMENSIONS	237 ft x 34 ft 2 in x 15 ft 7 in
MACHINERY	3-cyl triple-expansion by Amos & Smith Ltd, Hull Coal-fired boilers
SPEED	10 knots
ROUTE	Goole-Continent

Harrogate

BUILT	1924 by Ramage & Ferguson Ltd, Leith
GROSS TONS	1,113
DIMENSIONS	240 ft 5 in x 33 ft 11 in x 15 ft 10 in
MACHINERY	3-cyl triple-expansion by Ramage & Ferguson Coal-fired boilers
SPEED	11 knots
ROUTE	Hull-Continent

These ships were launched in October 1922 and 28 October 1924 respectively. They were built for the Hull–Continental cargo services of Wilson's & North Eastern Railway Shipping Co, and although built at different times and by different builders were very similar. The substantial difference between them was that *Selby* had far less superstructure forward of the funnel than did *Harrogate*, while the distance between the funnel and the well deck on both ships was about the same. Both were notable for their extremely ugly sterns, and very high vertical stove-pipe funnels. *Selby* had accommodation for four passengers (this was rarely used after the war) and *Harrogate* could carry up to twelve. They were scarcely affected by the alterations following the formation of Associated Humber Lines in 1935, though after that date they did, on rare occasions, serve from Goole in a relief capacity.

During the war both served in coastal convoys with general cargo and in the Cardiff–Newport–Clyde coal trade.

In postwar years *Selby* was retained mainly for Goole services, particularly on the Ghent–Antwerp run, relieving on other routes from time to time, notably to Copenhagen ; on the important Hull–Rotterdam passenger link, in November 1948 and November 1951, and sometimes between Hull and Hamburg. *Harrogate* on the other hand usually remained at Hull, serving Belgian and Dutch ports. She also appeared twice as relief on the Hull–Rotterdam passenger run in December 1954 and February 1957, and in addition occasionally sailed from Goole mainly on relief to German and Dutch ports. Both ships were withdrawn in mid-1958 (*Selby* in June) and were soon replaced in the fleet by two new

Selby in Associated Humber Line colours in the 1950s

motor vessels bearing the same names. *Selby* was sold for breaking up by H. I. Hansen, Odense, Denmark, and *Harrogate* for breaking up by N. V. Vereenigde Utrecht Ijzerhandel, Rotterdam, arriving there 30 May.

SS DEARNE
SS DON

BUILT	1924 by Vickers Armstrong (Shipbuilders) Ltd, Barrow
GROSS TONS	1,116/1,095
DIMENSIONS	240 ft 4 in x 34 ft 3 in x 15 ft 3 in (depth)
MACHINERY	3-cyl triple-expansion by Vickers
	Coal-fired boilers
SPEED	11½ knots
ROUTE	Goole-Copenhagen

On delivery in September and November 1924 respectively, these ships had black hulls and were placed on general cargo services to the Continent from Goole, with accommodation for passengers. Up to 1933 the

Dearne in the Humber towards the end of her career
242

Copenhagen run was served by *Rother* and *Douglas* (950 tons, built 1907) as regular ships, but in that year it was decided that newer ships were needed. In consequence, *Dearne*, from the beginning of November, underwent alterations at Goole including the installation of refrigeration equipment in the holds. Her hull was painted light grey at the same time. She made her maiden voyage as a 'Beer and Butter Boat' on 2 March 1934, replacing *Douglas*, which was withdrawn soon afterwards for breaking up. *Dearne* then ran with *Rother* until 3 September 1937, when *Don*, having been similarly converted, entered the run, thus relegating *Rother* to third (spare and extra) ship. There were two similar ships to *Dearne* built about the same time; *Rye*, which was sunk by enemy action in the Straits of Dover on 7 March 1941, and *Hebble*, which is described next.

During the war both *Don* and *Dearne* were involved in active service, the latter being given the job of carrying meat after D Day to the British Army, loading at London and discharging at first at Rouen and then at Ostend as the army progressed eastwards. She then was sent to the Mediterranean for similar duties.

Both these ships and *Hebble* were owned by the LMS until the BTC took over in 1948, but were managed by Associated Humber Lines after 1935. *Don* could carry eight passengers, *Dearne* ten, as she had an extra deckhouse on the boat deck containing a two-berth cabin.

By the mid-1950s replacements for the pair were becoming an urgent necessity. In July 1956 *Dearne* was replaced by the new MV *Kirkham Abbey*, and in January 1957 *Don* was replaced by *Byland Abbey*. The old steamers were then sold for breaking up. *Dearne* went to Clayton & Davie Ltd, Dunston, in February 1957; *Don* to N. V. Vereenigde Utrecht Ijzerhandel, Rotterdam, in November 1958.

SS HEBBLE

BUILT	1924 by W. Beardmore & Co Ltd, Glasgow
GROSS TONS	1,078
DIMENSIONS	250 ft x 34 ft 5 in x 14 ft 9 in
MACHINERY	3-cyl triple-expansion by Beardmore
	Coal-fired boilers
SPEED	11½ knots
ROUTE	Goole/Hull-Dutch, German and Belgian ports

Delivered in September 1924, *Hebble* was similar to *Don* and *Dearne* but never served Copenhagen. With a black hull, she remained throughout on near-continental runs mainly from Goole, though occasionally, particularly in postwar years, from Hull. Only once after the war did she serve the Hull–Rotterdam passenger run, as relief ship in December

1951. During the war she served on the Newport–Clyde coal run and on coastal convoys. She re-entered commercial service towards the end of 1946 on the Goole–Holland run, but early in 1947 was switched to the Goole–Bremen/Hamburg service.

It was on this run that she suffered the first of two unusual accidents. While anchored at the mouth of the Elbe she was carried onto the Vogel Sands and severe ice action fractured the stern frame and twisted the rudder post. She was out of action for some time, but before the end of 1947 was back in service, having reverted to the Holland route. Her second adventure came on the night of 30 January 1953 when there was an exceptionally high tide. She was in dry-dock at Immingham at the time when the high water flooded the dock and caused her to capsize to port greatly damaging the superstructure. The method employed to right her was very similar to that used when TSS *Onward* capsized at Folkestone after a fire on board in April 1918. Steel hawsers were attached to two towers welded to her deck, and fixed to two railway engines, which gradually pulled the ship upright while water was let slowly into the dock. To prevent her rolling right over to starboard a local tug, *Deveron*, loaded with gravel, kept the strain on her with hawsers pulling in the opposite direction. A further major overhaul was required, and she did not reappear at Goole until 24 September, taking up the mid-week Antwerp run about a week later.

Hebble in the 1950s
244

She was one of the last passenger-carrying steamers to serve the Humber, and though her accommodation (for eight) was not advertised in 1958, it was available. In her last few months in service she ran as third ship on the Holland run with the new *Darlington* and *Wakefield*. She was withdrawn in May 1959, and subsequently broken up by Simons Metaal Handel, Rotterdam.

SS MELROSE ABBEY

BUILT	1929 by Earle's Shipbuilding & Engineering Co Ltd, Hull
GROSS TONS	1,941
DIMENSIONS	292 ft 6 in x 38 ft 3 in x 15 ft 4¾ in
MACHINERY	3-cyl triple-expansion by Earle's
	Coal-fired boilers
SPEED	13 knots
ROUTE	Hull-Rotterdam

Melrose Abbey, the last and largest ship built for the Hull & Netherlands Steamship Co Ltd, was designed to bolster up the company's reputation on the Hull–Rotterdam passenger service operated, until she appeared, by two smaller ships dating from 1908. Launched on 28 February, she made her maiden voyage on 23 April with an original gross tonnage of 1,908 and passenger accommodation for eighty-four first-class and thirty-six steerage. In 1935, in common with other Humber ships, she came under the management of Associated Humber Lines, but did not change her route, running until April 1936, except for overhaul periods, with the old *Jervaulx Abbey*. From then until the war *Dewsbury* was her running mate during the larger part of the year ie approximately

Melrose Abbey passing up the Humber, about 1958

245

from March to November. She made her last prewar trip from Hull on 29 April 1940, returning home on 6 May.

At the beginning of June she was placed on war service and from then on was used on convoy duties with general cargo, visiting such ports as St Malo, Leith, London, Liverpool, Ipswich and Middlesbrough.

Early in 1946 she was given a refit for commercial service, which increased her tonnage to 1,924, and she took up the Rotterdam civilian run on 14 March 1946, maintaining the passenger service on her own on a weekly schedule for the rest of the year. In January 1947 she was joined by *Bury* and the two ships then ran together until their replacements arrived. Her passenger accommodation after the war consisted of saloon and third-class cabins for 116 including two-berth cabins-de-luxe, two-berth cabins on the bridge deck and four-berth cabins on the main deck. Another refit in early 1948 pushed her tonnage up to its final figure of 1,941. At the end of 1955 her berth accommodation was re-labelled: her cabins-de-luxe, two-berth cabins on the bridge deck and the four-berth cabins on the main deck became first-class, and the four- and six-berth cabins (previously third-class) became second-class. She could then accommodate ninety-two first-class and twenty-four second-class passengers.

To free her name for her successor, the suffix *II* was added to it, and she made her first sailing from Hull bearing this undignified appendage on 12 April 1958. From June she ran alongside the new *Bolton Abbey* until her final voyage from Hull on 10 January 1959, being replaced on the next scheduled sailing by the new MV *Melrose Abbey*. She arrived in Hull on 14 January, having completed very nearly thirty years of service without ever having served another route commercially.

Kriti (ex-*Melrose Abbey*) in Greek ownership—not a particularly good-looking ship

246

A few months of lay up in Humber Dock followed, until she was bought by Typaldos Lines of Piraeus in April for cruising in the Adriatic and the Greek seas. She is still there at the time of writing, ending her days as a 'luxury liner' named *Kriti,* with a reputed speed of 18 knots (and still a coal-burner!) and with a gross tonnage of 2,069. Up to and including 1963 she spent most of her time on weekly sailings from Piraeus taking in places like Istanbul, Patmos and Rhodes, but since then has concentrated mainly on weekly sailings from Brindisi to Piraeus calling at various ports en route. She has been threatened with withdrawal during successive winters since 1964, but is still holding her own. As seen in the picture she is not a particularly good-looking ship.

SS AIRE
SS BLYTH

BUILT	1930 by Cammell Laird & Co (Shipbuilders & Engineers) Ltd, Birkenhead
GROSS TONS	1,116/1,122
DIMENSIONS	249 ft 3 in x 34 ft 3 in x 14 ft 10½ in
MACHINERY	3-cyl triple-expansion by Cammell Laird
	Coal-fired boilers
SPEED	11½ knots
ROUTE	Hull/Goole-Ghent/Antwerp, Rotterdam/Amsterdam Bremen/Hamburg, etc

In 1929 the LMS ordered three cargo-passenger ships specifically for the Goole–Continental trades. *Calder,* launched on 8 October 1930, was the first to appear and made her maiden voyage to Hamburg on 6 December. Unhappily, she was lost on passage from Hamburg about 20 April

Blyth passing up the Humber bound for Goole in June 1957

247

1931, and presumed foundered with all hands 'somewhere off Spurn'.

The second in the series was *Blyth*, launched on 6 November, followed by *Aire* on 9 December. *Blyth*'s delivery was delayed by collision damage during trials, and she had to return to her builders for repairs. She eventually made her maiden voyage, on the Ghent run, on 17 January 1931. *Aire* made hers to Rotterdam on 11 February. The ships served only from Goole until Associated Humber Lines took over management in 1935, but thereafter occasionally sailed from Hull, frequently returning to Hull first from the Continent before proceeding to Goole. During the winters from December 1935 to April 1939 *Aire* was a main relief ship on the Hull–Rotterdam passenger link. *Blyth* served that particular run only once before the war, in September 1939.

During the war *Aire*, after some time in coastal convoys in 1940, was an ammunition ship at Scapa, and *Blyth*, from mid-1940 until the end of the year was engaged in the Newport–Ayr/Troon coal trade, thereafter spending periods both in this trade and in coastal convoys. From May 1941 to March 1946 *Blyth* served for the North of Scotland, Orkney & Shetland Steam Navigation Co Ltd, generally between Leith and Lerwick.

Both ships were back in service by 1946, *Blyth* making one of her extremely rare sailings to Copenhagen on 18 March, *Aire* mainly serving Holland. From then on each ship changed its route fairly frequently, and neither can be specially related to any particular route. The oddities are of most interest. *Aire* made a number of Copenhagen sailings and relieved on the Hull–Rotterdam passenger service several times between November 1954 and February 1956. *Blyth* made odd trips on this service in 1954 only.

Both ships could carry eight passengers in four double-berth cabins amidships. *Blyth*'s accommodation was not advertised in 1959, but she could and did carry passengers when required.

Aire's end came quickly and unexpectedly. Travelling up the Humber to Goole, on passage from Antwerp, she was in collision with the German motor coaster *Helene B. Schupp* on 5 October 1958, and was struck on the starboard side, a rent some 60 ft long being torn in her hull. The engine room flooded and she sank by the stern, but the master succeeded in beaching her on the north bank at Saltmarsh Bight. There were seven passengers and twenty-four crew aboard. One of the latter was killed by being trapped inside the ship, the rest were taken ashore in the ship's lifeboat. Some days later she broke her moorings and slid back into midriver, gradually becoming a difficult salvage operation and a possible hazard to other shipping. Before the end of the month she had been abandoned by her owners to the then Docks Division at Goole who invited tenders for her scrapping. In the event, *Aire* was as far as possible broken up on the spot by Underwater Welders & Repairers Ltd, Cardiff. Those parts of the hull which could not be removed after breaking up were dispersed in the river by explosives. The German ship, carrying some 600 tons of coal at the time, went into dry dock with bow damage above the waterline ; there was no loss of life on her.

Blyth continued to trudge gallantly across the North Sea, serving Antwerp from January 1959 until being withdrawn the following May. She was broken up by Simons Metaal Handel, Rotterdam, in the same year.

PS TATTERSHALL CASTLE
PS WINGFIELD CASTLE

BUILT	1934 by Wm. Grey & Co Ltd, West Hartlepool
GROSS TONS	556
DIMENSIONS	209 ft 7 in x 57 ft x 4 ft 6 in
MACHINERY	3-cyl triple-expansion diagonal by Central Marine Engineering Works, Hartlepool
	Coal-fired boilers
SPEED	13 knots
ROUTE	Hull-New Holland
	Humber excursions

These ships were ordered in May 1934 by the LNER to replace PS *Brocklesby* and *Killingholme* and were both launched on 24 September 1934. One gets the impression that there is something odd about their appearance because of the position of the funnels, and therefore of the

Wingfield Castle, sailing from Hull, 30 April 1966

boilers. Normally a single funnel is placed forward of the paddles but in the case of these two ships it is abaft the paddles, unusual in 'modern' paddlers. About twenty cars can be carried on the after deck, driven on over ramps through doors in the bulwarks which open inwards. The forward part of the vessels, from the wheelhouse forward, is given over to the first-class passengers, of which there are normally very few compared with the numbers travelling second-class. There is a lounge on the main deck, and below it a tearoom which is supplied as a buffet from a central kitchen, which also supplies the second-class cafeteria abaft it on the same deck. Below this is the second-class saloon on the lower deck.

When the ships entered service on 22 December 1934 they were resplendent in grey hulls and white funnel with black tops. About 1937 the hulls were repainted black, but reverted to grey in 1940, when the white on the funnels was also painted over grey. After the war the hulls again became black. Throughout the war they remained in service on the Hull–New Holland ferry run. Radar was fitted in 1958. On 1 January 1959 management was transferred to AHL and this led to the appearance in 1960 of a red band on the funnel between the buff body and black top. Although still managed by AHL they were given the complete new BR livery in 1965.

They carry 10 crew and a maximum of 1,200 passengers on ferry duties, 942 on excursions. In the 1950s excursions took them far afield in the Humber, including Sunday trips from Grimsby to off Spurn Head and trips from Hull to Grimsby, but in recent years they have been restricted to short Sunday afternoon trips to view the docks from Hull. Just how long they will last is anybody's guess, if a river bridge were to be built soon, then clearly they would be withdrawn and not replaced. But if there is no bridge it must be assumed that they will be replaced, although BR has threatened to close the service on a number of occasions recently.

PS LINCOLN CASTLE

BUILT	1940 by A. & J. Inglis Ltd, Glasgow
GROSS TONS	598
DIMENSIONS	208 ft 9 in x 55 ft 6 in x 4 ft 6 in
MACHINERY	3-cyl triple-expansion diagonal by Ailsa Shipbuilding Co Ltd, Troon
	Coal-fired boilers
SPEED	13 knots
ROUTE	Hull-New Holland
	Excursions

Launched on 29 April 1940, *Lincoln Castle* is a conventional paddler, ie she has her boilers, and funnel, forward of the paddles, and she is the only Humber ferry with a mainmast. She ran her trials on the Clyde on 24 July 1940 in LNER colours, but grey paint obliterated her white funnel for the delivery passage, and it remained grey until April 1945. On her delivery voyage in convoy round the North of Scotland she apparently lost contact, and, having compass trouble, put back to the Clyde. She lay at Craigendoran until July 1941, then tried again, successfully this time. She made her first commercial crossing on 4 August 1941. She also remained on station during the war. Her passenger accommodation layout is similar to that of her two running mates, as is her car deck. Of the three, having been the last to get the AHL colours in 1960, she was the first to be given the new BR colour scheme in June 1965. A pleasant touch is the reproduction in colour of the new BR house flag in miniature on the bows; all three have this. Her maximum passenger accommodation for ferry runs is 1,200, like the others, but she can carry more excursion passengers at 1,039. She carries a crew of twelve. She has rarely undertaken cruises from Grimsby, being specially associated with the Sunday afternoon sailings from Hull.

Lincoln Castle in new BR colours, summer 1966

MV FOUNTAINS ABBEY
MV WHITBY ABBEY

BUILT	1954 by Hall, Russell & Co Ltd, Aberdeen
GROSS TONS	1,197
DIMENSIONS	256 ft 2 in x 38 ft 8 in x 13 ft 5 in
MACHINERY	2-stroke single acting 6-cyl Kincaid-Polar diesel by J. G. Kincaid & Co Ltd, Greenock
SPEED	12 knots
ROUTE	Hull/Goole-Continent

In postwar years the Humber was notable in having one of the most ancient fleets afloat, and it is surprising that new tonnage did not appear until 1954. *Whitby Abbey* was the first, making her maiden voyage on the Goole–Amsterdam/Rotterdam service from 15 July. She ran with *Alt* and *Hodder* until *Fountains Abbey* joined her on 9 October. The new ships then ran with *Hebble* alternately to the Dutch ports and Ghent/Antwerp. The latter destination was not advertised but they could and did carry passengers when required. On 16 October 1958 *Whitby Abbey* switched to the Goole–Bremen/Hamburg service, joined by her sister *Fountains Abbey* on 7 December. Until April 1958 they ran with *Hebble* again, but after that time they served alone. It was on this service

Whitby Abbey passing up the Humber 1958

that *Fountains Abbey* was lost. On passage Hamburg–Hull in heavy weather she caught fire and was abandoned on 12 February 1962. There were no passengers aboard, but two crew members lost their lives. When both the storm and the fire had quietened down, her hulk was towed by Dutch tug to Ijmuiden on 15 February, being taken two days later to Bruges for breaking up by Jacques Bakker & Sons.

Whitby Abbey continued to serve German ports alone for passengers until 30 April 1963. From 10 May 1963 she operated between Goole and Amsterdam, and the following September she was switched to a new joint service between Hull and Bremen/Hamburg with the Argo Line of Germany, which already had passenger-carrying ships on the service. *Whitby* made her first sailing from Hull on this service on 21 September and continued to operate thereon until her last arrival at Hull on

West Leyte (ex-*Whitby Abbey*) at Immingham July 1968

253

6 September 1966. After 10 September 1966 she was running between Goole and Antwerp, then switched to the Hull–Antwerp service in January 1968 after spending some eight weeks on the Hull–Rotterdam service as relief.

These ships were sisters in almost every respect. There are three holds (two forward, one aft) each served by two 7-ton derricks, and a 15-ton derrick attached to the foremast serves No 2 hold. Holds are not refrigerated, but fruit and vegetables benefit by a mechanical ventilation system which changes the air six times per hour. There are six double-berth passenger cabins on the boat deck, three on each side, and the lounge-bar runs nearly the full width of the ship at the forward end of the same deck. Beneath the lounge is the dining saloon, shared by passengers and officers. Both ships were transferred from BTC (North Eastern Region) to AHL in 1957 and have occasionally served on routes additional to those already mentioned. *Whitby Abbey* has been in frequent use as relief ship to *Melrose Abbey* or *Bolton Abbey* on the Hull–Rotterdam passenger/cargo service in January and February each year.

After closing the weekly Hull–Antwerp general cargo service on her arrival at Hull on 2 February 1968, she was laid up in Hull awaiting orders. In July 1968 *Whitby Abbey* was sold to the Cebu Bohol Ferry Co Inc (Philippines), and after dry docking at Immingham she left as the *West Leyte* for Antwerp to load cargo for the Far East on 31 July. She will be altered to carry some 400 passengers.

MV KIRKHAM ABBEY
MV BYLAND ABBEY

BUILT	1956/1957 by Austin & Pickersgill Ltd, Sunderland
GROSS TONS	1,372
DIMENSIONS	265 ft 4 in x 40 ft 6 in x 14 ft 5 in
MACHINERY	4-stroke single acting 9-cyl diesel by Ruston & Hornsby Ltd, Lincoln
SPEED	12 knots
ROUTE	Goole-Copenhagen

These ships, built for the BTC (North Eastern Region), are similar in most respects to *Whitby Abbey* (qv). Specially designed for the Copenhagen 'Beer and Butter' trade, they have refrigerated holds with 76,000 cu ft (bale) capacity, and replaced the old steamers *Don* and *Dearne*. For this reason their hulls are painted grey. *Kirkham Abbey* came first, making her maiden voyage from Goole on 14 July 1956 (replacing *Dearne*), and ran with *Don* until the latter was replaced by *Byland Abbey* on her maiden voyage from Goole on 19 January 1957.

Twelve passengers are carried in six double-berth cabins (three on each side of the boat deck). Forward of these, stretching the width of the ship, is the lounge-bar, beneath which is the dining saloon. The holds are served by four 7-ton and two 10-ton derricks. During their winter over-haul of 1960-1 their bow bulwarks were raised by several feet in an effort to stave off some of the worst that the North Sea could throw at them in winter, and painted white.

Both ships were managed by AHL until their sale and subsequent de-livery to Ellerman's Wilson Line Ltd on 16 and 9 September 1965 re-spectively. They were dry-docked at Immingham prior to handover. *Byland Abbey* made her last sailing from Goole for BR on 3 September, was handed over on 9 September and made her first sailing for Eller-man's Wilson Line on 10 September. Respective dates for *Kirkham Abbey* were 10 September, 16 September and 17 September. Since their sale they have continued to serve with regularity and still cater for pas-sengers, though in May 1967 there were changes. On Monday 8 May *Byland Abbey* began operating a weekly service from Goole alone, for unit loads only, and *Kirkham Abbey* took up the company's principal sailings from London to Copenhagen and Aarhus on 12 May. They were renamed *Angelo* (*Byland Abbey*) and *Ariosto* early in March 1968, and from August 1968 both reverted to the Goole general cargo service to Copenhagen for a period.

Kirkham Abbey when new

255

TSMV BOLTON ABBEY
TSMV MELROSE ABBEY

BUILT	1958/1959 by Brooke Marine Ltd, Lowestoft
GROSS TONS	3,268/3,269
DIMENSIONS	302 ft 11 in x 45 ft 5 in x 14 ft before lengthening
	302 ft 6 in x 45 ft 5 in x 14 ft before lengthening
MACHINERY	Two 4-stroke, single acting 8-cyl diesels by Ruston & Hornsby Ltd, Lincoln
SPEED	15 knots
ROUTE	Hull-Rotterdam

These two ships, owned by AHL, were ordered to replace the elderly *Bury* and *Melrose Abbey* (1929) on the Hull–Rotterdam passenger service, and have never served elsewhere. *Bolton Abbey* came first, being launched on 11 December 1957 and entering service on 4 June 1958 replacing *Bury*. *Melrose Abbey* made her maiden voyage on 17 January 1959 replacing *Melrose Abbey II*. During the annual overhaul in January and February each ship was usually replaced by *Whitby Abbey* which carries only twelve passengers. They could carry 960 tons (deadweight) of general cargo, in containers (capacity for 45), or on pallets, in two holds with 'tween decks. Their total capacity was 116,597 cu ft. Passengers' cars are also carried, occasionally on deck.

Originally 80 one-class passengers could be carried in 12 single- and

Bolton Abbey bound for Rotterdam in 1958

256

33 double-berth cabins, inside and outside, and a two-berth cabin-de-luxe with private shower and wc (her publicity material stated private bath but this was incorrect), on A and B decks. However during their 1962 spring overhaul the passenger capacity was increased to 88 by converting eight single cabins into doubles. Both ships actually carry certificates for 96 passengers. All accommodation and machinery is aft. Extra speed of the twin screws reduced the crossing time by 4 hours, and the diesels were at that time the largest ever supplied by Ruston & Hornsby Ltd.

Early in 1967 it was announced that the two ships were to be lengthened by some 50 ft and tenders were invited. Smith's Dock Co Ltd of North Shields were awarded the contract on 17 July, agreeing to lengthen each ship by 52 ft within a period of thirty-five running days each, the work to be carried out during November and December 1967 and January 1968. *Melrose Abbey* was docked on 8 November, cutting started the next day at frame number 70½ (the widest part of the ship) and was completed on 14 November. Temporary bulkheads were then fitted to the two open ends, and the forward section (at the head of the dock) was 'anchored' down. The aft section was suitably weighted so that it

Melrose Abbey in the Humber after lengthening

would remain at the required pre-calculated 'trim' while the water was let in. Water was allowed in on 15 November and tugs moved the aft section out of the dock, then manoeuvred the new 'midships section and the aft section back into the dock in the correct order. When this operation was complete, the aft part was only 14 in from the new part. Water was expelled from the dock, and welding of the three parts was completed on 29 November, while the entire job was finished on 14 December after thirty working days. On the Newbiggin measured mile there was recorded a fractional increase in speed, predicted by some experts. The work on *Bolton Abbey* started on 15 December, followed a similar pattern and was also completed in thirty days. The ships now have three holds instead of two, enabling them to carry between sixty and sixty-five containers. External changes can be seen by comparing the two photographs. Gross tonnage was increased by 528 in each case, bringing *Melrose Abbey* to 3,269 and *Bolton Abbey* to 3,268. Both ships still accommodate eighty-eight passengers.

While the two 'Abbeys' were off the service for this work to be carried out, they were replaced by *Whitby Abbey*.

While the lengthening was being done, a new berth was being developed at 'A' Jetty, Alexandra Dock, for the use of the altered ships, instead of Riverside Quay. The last conventional sailing from Riverside Quay started on 29 January 1968. *Bolton Abbey* inaugurated the new service from Alexandra Dock on 31 January, and thereafter it operated on five days a week in each direction. The Rotterdam terminal was transferred from the Parkhaven to the Beatrixhaven. The Hull (Albert Dock)–Rotterdam unit-load service previously operated by *Leeds* and *Wakefield* was then withdrawn.

MV DARLINGTON
MV LEEDS
MV WAKEFIELD
MV YORK

BUILT	1958/1959/1958/1959 by A. & J. Inglis Ltd, Glasgow *Darlington* James Lamont & Co Ltd, Port Glasgow
GROSS TONS	963/1,113/1,113/1,087
DIMENSIONS	244 ft 4 in x 39 ft 4 in x 13 ft 2 in *Darlington* 232 ft 1 in x 39 ft 5 in x 13 ft 3 in
MACHINERY	4-stroke single acting 7-cyl diesel by Ruston & Hornsby Ltd, Lincoln
SPEED	12½ knots

These ships are four of the series of six general-cargo vessels built for AHL during 1958 and 1959, the others being *Harrogate* and *Selby* (qv).

They have served a variety of routes from the Humber ports of Hull and Goole. All have machinery and accommodation aft, but carry no passengers.

York is the only one of the six to be built with part-refrigerated cargo space, and is thus the only one which could serve the Copenhagen 'Beer and Butter' trade. This she did as third ship fairly consistently from 1961 to 1964. She has also served between Hull and Rotterdam and Antwerp, and between Goole and Dutch ports, on which service she made her maiden voyage on 18 November 1959, remaining thereon until mid-1960. She has also, on occasion, called at Zeebrugge and sometimes returned to Immingham before continuing to Goole or Hull. From late 1964 she served the Goole–Antwerp run fairly consistently as a general-cargo ship until January 1968, her refrigeration plant having been taken out during her overhaul at Immingham in 1965. From February 1968 she was taken on time charter by Ellerman's Wilson Line Ltd for their East Mediterranean cargo service without name change and laid up after three trips.

Darlington made her maiden voyage on the Goole–Amsterdam/Rotterdam service on 19 November 1958. Through most of 1959 she served Amsterdam, and in 1960 mainly Rotterdam, but has also run elsewhere

York arriving at Hull 6 April 1968 from the Mediterranean on
Wilson Line charter

including a few trips to Copenhagen. During most of 1965 she served between Goole and Bremen for the joint AHL/Argo Line trade, but was found to be too large for their requirements and so, being replaced by a German ship, she became spare and was then chartered to BR (Southern Region) for the Folkestone–Boulogne unit-load service from 1 September. While on this run she retained her AHL colours, but had a local master and flew the BR house flag while in port. The charter was expected to terminate at the end of December 1965 but in fact it continued until the end of August 1966. She then returned to the Humber and after one round trip between Goole and Antwerp from 3 September, she took up regular sailings from Hull to Bremen and Hamburg on 13 September, again on the AHL/Argo joint service. When the new roll-on ships took up this service in 1967 she was withdrawn on 20 August, and after some weeks running Goole–Hamburg, was chartered by BR for the Heysham–Belfast service, transferring to the Holyhead–Dublin run from 1 January 1968, and then to the Heysham Station from May 1968 for a time.

Leeds, with 100,969 cu ft cargo space, made her maiden voyage out of Goole on 12 November 1959 and served for some time on the Dutch run before being switched to others, notably between Goole and Antwerp, and Bremen and Hamburg. On 10 June 1965 she inaugurated a new unit-load service between Hull and Rotterdam having been specially converted at Immingham. She continued to run twice weekly between the two ports, until 16 August 1966 when she was joined by *Wakefield*, similarly altered, thus increasing the service to four times per week in each direction.

Wakefield made her maiden voyage on 16 October 1958 and subsequently served on most Continental routes, particularly Goole–Antwerp from early 1965 until her refit at Immingham in February and March 1966 for unit-load carrying, enabling her to relieve *Leeds* during the latter's overhaul. She then reverted to the Antwerp run until permanently taking up the Rotterdam unit-load service as mentioned above.

Leeds and *Wakefield* therefore were the only two Hull-based AHL ships to cater exclusively for unit-loads, until the lengthened *Melrose Abbey* and *Bolton Abbey* appeared on the scene in January 1968. *Leeds* and *Wakefield* were thereupon replaced by the two 'Abbeys', *Wakefield* making the last unit-load sailing to Rotterdam from Albert Dock on 29 January 1968. Both ships then switched to a new thrice-weekly Hull–Antwerp unit-load service, opened by *Wakefield* on 3 February 1968.

The principal alterations carried out on the two ships to enable them to operate the unit-load services consisted of the removal of bipod masts, derrick gear and three winches and the fitting of wooden battens to the tops of upper deck hatches to enable containers to be carried on the hatch covers. From 10 August 1968 *York* took over the weekly Goole–Copenhagen unit-load service on charter to Ellerman's Wilson Line Ltd.

MV ANTARES
MV ARCTURUS

BUILT	1967 by Schlichting-Werft Group, Travemunde
GROSS TONS	499.87
DIMENSIONS	250 ft 8 in x 42 ft 8 in x 13 ft 9 in
MACHINERY	One M.A.N. 4-stroke unidirectional 16-cyl diesel KaMeWa variable pitch propeller
SPEED	14½ knots
ROUTE	Hull-Bremen/Hamburg

Although not owned nor operated by AHL these ships operate on a joint service for Argo Line/AHL under the agency of John Good & Sons Ltd, Hull. They replaced AHL-owned ships on the route, and it is felt that these factors are sufficient reasons for including the vessels in this book.

The ships were designed and built by their builders in close co-operation with the owners specifically for the above services, and were heralded as the 'Shape of things to come'. Singularly unattractive, they none the less meet the requirements of the trade although accommodation for drivers and occasional passengers is, surprisingly, absent. The main struc-

Antares approaching her Hull berth stern first 15 October 1967

261

tural features are a main deck, access being by stern door ramp, and a shelter deck suitable for lighter vehicles and containers, reached by hinged ramp from the main deck near the stern. There is no cargo-handling equipment on the decks, both of which are fitted with hydraulically-operated flush hatch covers. A particularly interesting feature is that there are no stanchions supporting the shelter deck, which posed problems for designers, but makes for a completely unobstructed main deck. Trailers, vehicles, unit-loads and general cargo can all be carried, and there are 'plug-in' facilities for refrigerated containers.

Antares made her first sailing from Hull to Hamburg on 16 August 1967, and *Arcturus* made hers, also to Hamburg, on 23 August 1967. Unloading and loading are carried out at a new terminal at No 23 Shed, Alexandra Dock, Hull, and there are two sailings to Hamburg and one to Bremen weekly. On entering service they replaced AHL's *Darlington* and Argo Lines' *Lumme,* the last ships to operate the conventional service from Albert Dock, Hull. A third ship of similar type is expected to appear early in 1969. The registered owners are Argo-Reederei, Richard Adler & Sohne, Bremen (Argo Line).

SPECIALISED SERVICES

The first part of this book dealt with what are popularly known as 'railway steamers', in fact vessels owned directly by the BTC (later the BRB) or by one of its subsidiaries. These vessels are distinguished from others by one major feature—namely that they tend to operate from port rail-heads. In other words they can be considered purely as continuations of the railway system. When the railways had been built as far as the coast, it was logical for proprietors to wish to extend their services overseas by using their own vessels.

The remainder of the book deals with nationalised shipping concerns which are not so tied to the railway system itself. The position of each company relative to the Railways Board and the Transport Holding Company (and now the National Freight Corporation, etc) is described in the appropriate place. Associated Humber Lines Ltd and its predecessors can be regarded as a 'mixed-bag' in the sense that historically the vessels fall into either category.

Not all state-owned shipping is included in this book, because it is a book primarily dealing with the larger cross-channel vessels. Notable ommissions include the small engines-aft barges which operate for British Road Services between Portsmouth and Cowes (Isle of Wight), and the dozens of small harbour maintenance craft owned by the British Transport Docks Board. It is felt that it is sufficient only to draw readers' attention to these craft in the present edition.

In addition there are the interests held by the THC in David MacBrayne Ltd (about half) and in Anglo-Irish Transport Ltd (minority) now transferred to the Scottish Transport Group and the National Freight Corporation respectively. Due to these not being majority holdings, the vessels of these companies are not included here.

ATLANTIC STEAM NAVIGATION COMPANY LIMITED

This company was originally formed about 1935 for the purpose of operating two Atlantic liners of some 30,000 gross tons. They were to be novel in that meals on board could be paid for 'as taken' thereby making possible a basic fare for the crossing which was apparently much lower than that offered by other lines. War clouds gathering over Europe prevented these plans from reaching fruition. The flag and funnel colours and designs chosen for the intended ships survived, however, and are now in use on the company's present vessels, both owned and chartered.

Nothing further was heard of the company until 1946, when it chartered three tank landing ships from the MOT. These, named *Empire Baltic, Empire Cedric* and *Empire Celtic*, were altered internally and pressed into service in September of that year between Tilbury and Hamburg as military leave ships. One or more of these ships maintained the service until it was closed in 1955.

In the meantime the company's founders, principally members of the Bustard family, one of whom is the present general manager, conceived the idea of operating similar ships as civilian commercial vehicle ferries, and laid the foundations of what was to become a tremendously successful business on 21 May 1948. On that day *Empire Cedric* left Preston for Larne with the first load of vehicles and trailers. This was barely twenty years ago, yet, while other coastal and short-sea operators have gone to the wall since then, ASN has developed with such vigour that its working title 'Transport Ferry Service' has become a by-word in the world of international trade.

There were at first two sailings per week on the Larne route, but trade rapidly expanded so that in 1950 a service to Belfast was opened and within a few years there were commonly seven sailings per week from Preston to Northern Ireland. In 1950 an additional ship, *Empire Gaelic*, joined the fleet.

It was in April 1954 that the company was taken over by the BTC, though there was little apparent change at first.

By the middle of 1956 there were three more ex-tank landing ships in the fleet, *Empire Cymric, Empire Doric* and *Empire Nordic*. All could load vehicles on the drive-on principle through bow doors, and could carry unit-loads on the upper deck. Following the termination of the Hamburg service, one to Antwerp was inaugurated, also from Tilbury, and it was usual to run two or three ships on that route and the rest from Preston.

Late in 1956 the entire fleet was taken over by the government for use in the Mediterranean during the Suez crisis. Until it returned the following January, the company's drive-on services were suspended, but the Preston unit-load services were continued by chartering three British coasters for about a month, and four German vessels for the rest of the time.

From late in 1956 the company was also made responsible for the management of a further twelve ex-tank landing ships with 'Empire-bird' names eg *Empire Guillemot*, and seven with individuals' names eg *Reginald Kerr*. All were given TFS colours and served in a variety of ways in near- and middle-eastern waters. In April and May 1961 management of these was transferred to the British India Steam Navigation Co Ltd, and the ships were given new colours. Little of interest attaches to most of them, though one, *Empire Shearwater*, did appear in civilian service in 1958 and 1959 when she ran between Dover and Calais unsuccessfully for European Ferries Ltd, a subsidiary of Townsend Bros Ferries Ltd.

In 1957 came the first fruits of BTC control and financial backing, when a brand new custom-built stern-loading vehicle ferry *Bardic Ferry* entered service from Preston. In the following year a near-sister *Ionic Ferry* took up the Larne run from Preston. In May 1961 the third new ship *Cerdic Ferry* appeared on the Tilbury station, enabling *Bardic Ferry*, which had been at Tilbury since 1958, to be transferred to Preston. *Cerdic Ferry* mainly served on the Rotterdam route which had been opened in the previous year. In April 1962 a sister to *Cerdic Ferry* named *Doric Ferry* entered service from Tilbury and a 'new' daily service by 'fast, modern ships' was then inaugurated.

The appearance of these new ships led to the gradual withdrawal of the old ex-tank landing ships, so that, by the end of 1962, only *Empire Nordic* was still in service (usually from Preston), while *Empire Cymric* was laid up in reserve at Greenock. She was broken up soon afterwards.

Goodwill Merchant (Dutch) at the 'Containerway' berth in Preston

In the meantime the company was further developing its unit-load business and in January 1960 took over the operation of four container ships previously run by Anglo Continental Container Services Ltd on charter. These were *Prior*, *Clipper*, *Eliza* and *Goodwill*, all Dutch owned, serving in pairs between Preston and Larne, and Ardrossan and Larne. These unit-load services have since then been run in close co-operation with British Road Services Ltd, and its successor in the ferry business, British Road Ferry Services Ltd. The latter was formed early in 1964 out of BRS to concentrate on the over-water section of general and specialised haulage. The distinction between the parts played by TFS and BRFS respectively in the business is not always clear cut, but basically it is the latter which organises the collection, carriage by road and delivery of goods in the form of unit-loads, while the former charters or owns and operates the ships and is responsible for all nautical aspects of the trade including the drawing-up of manifestos. Thus BRFS ('Roadferry') and ACCS ('Containerway') and associates have prior claim to space aboard the TFS ships, though the units of other companies are not by any means precluded. 'We carry anything!'

The chartering by TFS of unit-load ships expanded quite considerably after 1960 to meet the demand for space on Irish Sea routes. In addition to the Preston–Ardrossan route, a twice-weekly run between Preston and Drogheda was opened on 18 December 1961 by the Dutch coaster *Noach* and by *Stream Fisher*, owned by J. Fisher & Sons Ltd. A daily service between Preston and Dublin was inaugurated early in March 1963 using *Eliza* and, again, *Stream Fisher*. Trade has grown so much that at any one time there can be up to nine or ten unit-load ships in

J. Fisher & Sons unit-load vessel *Derwent Fisher* (1,000 tons, built 1966) leaving Preston for Dublin in July 1966

service on these routes. Dutch vessels seem to be favoured for most routes, while those chartered from J. Fisher & Sons Ltd tend to be used mainly between Preston and Dublin and Larne. There is, however, fairly frequent interchange of ships on the various routes.

The following disposal of vessels was typical and is taken at random from records (September 1965):

Preston–Larne (drive-on)	*Bardic Ferry*, *Ionic Ferry*
Preston–Belfast (drive-on)	¹*Empire Nordic*
Ardrossan–Larne (unit-load)	*Goodwill* (288 tons), *Trinitas* (147 tons). Both Dutch.
Preston–Larne (unit-load)	*Clipper* (315 tons), *Eliza* (319 tons), *Goodwill Trader* (227 tons) and *Goodwill Merchant* (281 tons). All Dutch.
Preston–Dublin (unit-load)	¹*Eden Fisher* (684 tons), ¹*Race Fisher* (446 tons) and ¹*River Fisher* (451 tons). All Fishers' vessels.
Preston–Drogheda	²*Noach* (326 tons). Dutch.

¹These vessels have now been replaced by modern container ships.
²*Noach* operated in Link Line colours, being on charter to Coast Lines Ltd. The Drogheda service is jointly-run by Coast Lines Ltd and TFS (ACCS).

Reverting to the drive-on services, we find *Bardic Ferry* and *Ionic Ferry* based at Preston and *Cerdic Ferry* and *Doric Ferry* at Tilbury late in 1962. From the beginning of 1963 the ASN and British Road Services Ltd became subsidiaries of the Transport Holding Company, as did AHL (see under 'Humber Ports') and plans were made for further expansion of the drive-on services.

In April 1964 it was possible to increase the frequency of sailings to Antwerp and Rotterdam from six to eight per week, following the appearance early in the year of the new *Gaelic Ferry* and the completion of the regular ships' overhauls. On 12 July 1965 *Gaelic Ferry* opened the new link between Felixstowe and Rotterdam, and in January 1966 that between Felixstowe and Antwerp. Felixstowe was developed because it is nearer to Rotterdam giving a journey of eight hours compared with one of nearly sixteen hours from Tilbury, and because constant labour troubles at the latter terminal have caused great inconvenience. Improvements to berth accommodation at the various ports have been carried out, and in fact the new better-equipped 11-acre terminal at Antwerp officially opened on 10 December 1964 is the first continental terminal specially designed to handle and accommodate this kind of traffic.

Pending delivery of a new drive-on ship, similar to *Gaelic Ferry*, ordered in April 1966 from Associated Shipbuilders Ltd (Swan Hunter yard) and due in August 1967, the company bought two 'stop-gaps', an ex-tank landing craft renamed *Baltic Ferry*, and a converted landing ship dock renamed *Celtic Ferry*. The former has served mostly from Preston,

267

and her arrival on that station ultimately led to the withdrawal of *Empire Nordic*, the last of her type and the last reciprocating steamer in regular service in the area, in January 1967.

When the vehicle ferries have been taken off for overhaul in recent years they have been replaced by one of Thoresen's passenger/car ferries taken on charter. This usually takes place between January and March. In 1965 *Viking II* was used ; in 1966 and 1967 *Viking I*. In all cases they operated from Tilbury until January 1967, when *Viking I* served between Preston and Belfast until the end of February. She cannot use the ramp at Larne. Each can carry up to forty trailers/vehicles on the car deck, but has no upper deck suitable for the carriage of unit-loads. They are, therefore, not very efficient. Normally capable of bow and stern loading, only the stern is used during charter to TFS.

All the drive-on ships now owned and operated by TFS, with the exception of *Baltic Ferry,* can and do carry passengers and private cars, as well as commercial vehicles and their drivers, and offer superb accommodation on all routes. All cabins are 'outside' and the ships are fitted with stabilisers.

A new drive-on terminal being built at the Herdman Channel, Belfast, was completed in August 1967. Since the Felixstowe–Europort service opened, the link between Tilbury and Rotterdam has been withdrawn.

From 13 September 1968 the company is withdrawing all services from Tilbury.

'EMPIRE' CLASS TRANSPORT FERRIES
(converted bow-loading tank landing ships)

GROSS TONS	4,157 to 4,295
DIMENSIONS	347 ft 6 in x 54 ft 2 in x 10 ft 6½ in
MACHINERY	8-cyl triple-expansion, twin screw
	Oil-fired boilers
SPEED	10 knots
ROUTE	Tilbury-Hamburg (to 1955), Antwerp, Rotterdam
	Preston-Larne, Belfast

Seven of these ships were taken on charter by the ASN from the Admiralty and used on the above routes after suitable conversion to bring them up to civilian peacetime standards. Latterly only one remained in service, named *Empire Nordic*, which frequently though not regularly, served Belfast, and also made occasional trips to Larne. She was typical of the class, and a description of her will suffice for all.

Built by Blyth Dry Docks & Shipbuilding Co Ltd and engined by Walker Bros Ltd of Wigan, she was converted for ASN use by Harland & Wolff Ltd, on the Mersey. The main alterations involved the fitting

268

out of twelve berths in outside cabins in the superstructure for first-class passengers, the building of a wooden wheelhouse above the existing bridge, and the alteration of the original wheelhouse/bridge to accommodate the master's suite. The ship could carry sixty or more vehicles or trailers, and great use was made of the two 15-ton sampsons immediately forward of the bridge in loading and unloading, though the maximum generally lifted was 12 tons. Her maximum speed, in fact, was a little in excess of 13 knots, but the service speed was kept down to 10 knots for reasons of economy.

She made her maiden voyage from Preston on 17 May 1956 and has also operated from Tilbury, mainly on relief runs. On 17 August 1964 she sailed for Dublin, her only visit there, and another interesting trip came on 14 August 1961, when she sailed from Ardrossan for Antwerp with military stores. Her passenger certificate was surrendered in January 1964, and the ship's engineer officers moved into the cabins previously used by first-class passengers. There was, incidentally, also dormitory accommodation for some eighteen lorry drivers. The whole fleet was sent to Malta to assemble for the Suez operation in October and November 1956, and served there throughout in ASN colours.

As the years passed the ships were gradually withdrawn and replaced by new twin-screw motor vessels. Given below is a list of the seven ferries, with the names of their builders, years of service with the company, and ultimate fate. The 'Empire' names were operative only during the time they were chartered by the ASN and the choice of suffix (*Celtic*,

Empire Nordic passing down the Ribble bound for Belfast
19 September 1966

Baltic, etc) reflects the connection previously held with the White Star Line by Lt-Col Frank Bustard, founder of ASN.

Empire Baltic	Canadian Vickers Ltd, Montreal	1946–62	broken-up	Spezia
Empire Cedric	Yarrows Ltd, Esquimault	1946–59	,,	Ghent 1960
Empire Celtic	Davie Shipbuilding & Repairing Co Ltd, Lauzon	1946–61	,,	Spezia 1962
Empire Cymric	Harland & Wolff Ltd, Belfast	1955–62	,,	Faslane 1963–4
Empire Doric	Harland & Wolff Ltd, Govan	1948–60	,,	Port Glasgow
Empire Gaelic	Davie Shipbuilding & Repairing Co Ltd, Lauzon	1948–60	,,	Belgium
Empire Nordic	Blyth Dry Dock & Shipbuilding Co Ltd	1955–66		

Notes—*Empire Baltic* was the first operated by the company and opened the Tilbury–Hamburg route in September 1946. *Empire Cedric* opened the Preston–Larne service on 20 May 1948. *Empire Cymric* was laid up at Greenock from August 1962 until going to breakers on 1 October 1963.

Empire Nordic made her last sailings in December 1966, and then went to Liverpool (Langton Graving Dock) for overhaul. Here the decision was taken not to go to the expense of bringing her up to Lloyds specifications, and she arrived at Barrow to lay up on 10 January 1967. In January 1968 she was reported as having been sold for further trading to Greek buyers, but was still at Barrow at the end of August.

TSMV BARDIC FERRY
TSMV IONIC FERRY

BUILT	1957/1958 by Wm. Denny & Bros Ltd, Dumbarton
GROSS TONS	2,550/2,548
DIMENSIONS	339 ft 4 in x 54 ft 11 in x 12 ft 6 in/12 ft 8 in
MACHINERY	Two 2-stroke single acting 10-cyl Sulzer diesels by Denny
SPEED	14 knots
ROUTE	*Bardic Ferry* Tilbury-Antwerp, Rotterdam (1958-61) Preston-Larne, Belfast (1957-58; from 1961) *Ionic Ferry* Preston-Larne, Belfast

Bardic Ferry was the first of a series of new drive-on vehicle ferries built for the ASN. Specially designed for the carriage of commercial vehicles, trailers, etc, she also carries passengers and their cars. Launched on 5 March 1957 and delivered the following August, she left Preston for Larne on her maiden voyage on 2 September 1957 and from October 1958 served Antwerp only until 1960 when she began sailing also to Rotterdam. *Ionic Ferry*, launched in May 1958, entered service on 10 October from Preston and has remained attached to that station ever since. The arrival of another new ship *Cerdic Ferry* at Tilbury in May 1961 freed *Bardic Ferry* which was then transferred to Preston. Although they can, and do, serve Belfast occasionally, it is general practice for them to provide a nightly service to Larne, departures from and arrivals at Preston being dependent on the tides.

Each ship can carry up to seventy vehicles or trailers on the car deck, reached by stern ramp, the headroom of which is just sufficient near the stern to allow high loads (eg double-decker buses) to be carried. About twenty containers or flats can be accommodated on the upper deck, loaded by either dock-side crane or the ship's own. There is berth accommodation for fifty-five passengers in two classes all in outside cabins. First-class (17 berths) consists of a cabin-de-luxe with bath and wc on the sun deck and double- and single-berth cabins, dining room and lounge-bar on the upper deck, while for second-class there are two- and four-berth cabins, dining room and lounge-bar distributed on promenade and upper decks. The ships are fitted with Denny-Brown stabilisers, twin rudders aft controlled by electro-hydraulic steering gear and a bow rudder

Ionic Ferry leaving Preston for Larne 12 May 1966

271

similarly controlled. *Bardic Ferry* has, on occasion, run between Stranraer and Larne for special purposes, eg on 8 October 1961 she transported Bertram Mills' Circus from Larne to Stranraer on charter to the Caledonian Steam Packet Co (Irish Services) Ltd.

TSMV CERDIC FERRY
TSMV DORIC FERRY

BUILT	1961/1962 by Ailsa Shipbuilding Co Ltd, Troon
GROSS TONS	2,563/2,573
DIMENSIONS	361 ft 5 in/361 ft 6 in x 55 ft x 12 ft 8 in/12 ft 9 in
MACHINERY	Two 4-stroke single acting 16-cyl Vee diesels by Davey Paxman & Co Ltd, Colchester
SPEED	14 knots
ROUTE	Tilbury-Antwerp, Rotterdam
	Doric Ferry Preston-Belfast (from November 1967)

Both ships were built for the ASN roll-on commercial vehicle services. Slightly larger than the prototype, *Bardic Ferry*, they are generally similar, but incorporate certain improvements. About 100 vehicles and trailers (maximum height 14 ft 6 in) can be carried on the main vehicle deck driven on over a stern ramp, and there is space on the upper deck for some 30 unit-loads, handled by a 20-ton electric deck crane. There is accommodation for 35 one-class passengers in two-berth cabins-de-luxe on the promenade deck, and two-, three- and four-berth cabins on the upper deck. There is also a dining room and lounge bar, and a separate club room for lorry drivers.

Cerdic Ferry entered service early in November 1961 and from then on usually made one trip per week to Rotterdam and two to Antwerp.

Doric Ferry showing extensive container space on deck

272

When *Doric Ferry* joined her near the end of April 1962 a daily service to the continent became possible with new ships. Each has, in different years, appeared on the Preston station as relief ship early in the year, about February to March, and occasionally served the continent from Felixstowe. *Doric Ferry* actually made her maiden voyage on the Preston–Larne run on 19 February 1962, in a relief capacity, and in November 1967 inaugurated a new regular thrice-weekly service between Preston and Belfast.

Cerdic Ferry now operates solely between Tilbury and Antwerp.

Gaelic Ferry summer 1964

TSMV GAELIC FERRY

BUILT	1963 by Swan Hunter & Wigham Richardson Ltd, Tyneside
GROSS TONS	2,760
DIMENSIONS	365 ft x 56 ft 1 in x 13 ft 6 in
MACHINERY	Two 2-stroke single acting 10-cyl diesels by Sulzer Bros Ltd
SPEED	16 knots
ROUTE	Felixstowe-Antwerp/Rotterdam
	Tilbury-Antwerp/Rotterdam

Launched on 3 October 1963 and delivered the following January this stern-loading commercial-vehicle ferry is the fourth of a series of similar ships being built over a number of years for the ASN. She is similar to her predecessors in design but differs in detail. She can carry over 100 vehicles and trailers on the main deck and a number of unit-loads. Individual loads of up to 18 tons can be handled using Boden semi-trailers. Twenty-eight passengers are carried, accommodation consisting of a special cabin with bath, and three- and four-berth cabins. Dining room and lounge are shared by lorry drivers and independent passengers, hence she is truly one-class. She is fitted with the usual modern navigational aids and Denny-Brown stabilisers.

She entered service on the Tilbury station, but, when the new terminal at Felixstowe was opened, she was chosen to operate from there, inaugurating the new service to Rotterdam on 12 July 1965. She is, so far, the only one of the series of five new ships which has not served from Preston. Currently, her regular service is that between Felixstowe and Antwerp.

MV BALTIC FERRY

BUILT	1943 by American Bridge Co, Ambridge
GROSS TONS	1,909
DIMENSIONS	327 ft 9 in x 50 ft 2 in x 10 ft 8 in
MACHINERY	Two 12-cyl 2-stroke single acting oil engines by General Motors, Cleveland
SPEED	About 12 knots
ROUTE	Continental and Northern Ireland services

Pursuing its policy of providing more drive-on ships as quickly as possible, the ASN bought this US tank landing ship in 1965. Previous names held by the ship were *LST 1080* and *Pima County*. After purchase, she was towed from Philadelphia across the Atlantic to the Tyne yard of

Baltic Ferry leaving Preston for Larne 20 September 1966

Smith's Dock Co Ltd for alterations to bring her up to more modern standards in her accommodation. A number of changes came about, including modification of the bridge structure and the fitting of twin exhaust funnels abreast. Previously exhaust fumes had been expelled through the stern of the ship. She has no passenger accommodation and is not fitted with any deck cranes, so until the new terminal at Belfast was ready she could not use that port to unload unit-loads from her deck. In 1966 she served from both Tilbury and Felixstowe until being sent to Preston in July. She made her first voyage between Preston and Larne on 6 July 1966. She is bow-loading only, and can carry about forty-five vehicles/trailers on her main deck. During much of 1967 and in 1968 she has been laid up at Barrow.

TSS CELTIC FERRY

BUILT	1943 by Newport News Shipbuilding & Dry Dock Co, Virginia
NET TONS	2,226
DIMENSIONS	457 ft 9 in x 72 ft 2 in x 18 ft
MACHINERY	Geared turbines
	Oil-fired boilers
SPEED	15 knots
ROUTE	UK-Continental ports

Bought by the ASN on 20 April 1966 at an auction at Kiel, this ship has quite a history. She was built for the US Navy as a floating mobile dock for landing craft, with a US standard tonnage of 4,790. She was launched on 18 November 1943 and prior to completion on 15 February 1944 she seems to have had three names, *BAPM 3*, *LSD 11* and *Cutlass*. After completion, under 'Lease-Lend', she was transferred to the UK and served as HMS *Northway*. On her return to the US in January 1947 she was laid up for a time until being either bought or chartered by The Suwanee Train Ferry Lines Inc who had railway lines fitted on the main deck and used her as a train ferry. In 1955 she was taken over by the West Indian Fruit and Steamship Co of Miami, refitted to carry pas-

Celtic Ferry on the Tyne immediately after conversion

sengers and cars, and put into service in the general Caribbean area named *City of Havana*. For this duty she was registered under the Liberian flag on 18 November 1955, a prudent political move, as most of her crew at this time were Cubans. In April 1962 she was bought by the West German government and towed to Hamburg where she was pressed into service as an accommodation ship for the Navy, known at *WSI*. At some later date she was taken to Kiel and at some time was named *LSD I*.

After purchase by the ASN, she was towed to Palmers' Hebburn-on-Tyne yard, arriving there 1 August 1966, for further alterations, including the fitting of new accommodation and a new vehicle deck, capable of carrying vehicle loads up to 22 tons. A new watertight door was fitted at the stern, navigation equipment was modernised, new lifeboats fitted and ventilation introduced to the vehicle decks. She carries a crew of sixty and twelve passengers. She was completed in 1967, ran trials on 14 February and soon afterwards took up regular service from Felixstowe, though she generally operates relief and extra sailings where required. During most of 1968 she has been laid up at Barrow.

TSMV EUROPIC FERRY

BUILT   1967 by Swan Hunter (Shipbuilders) Ltd, Wallsend
GROSS TONS   4,190
DIMENSIONS   450 ft x 66 ft 6 in x 15 ft
MACHINERY   Two S.E.M.T.-Pielstick 4-stroke, single acting diesels by
                 A/B Lindholmen-Varv, Gothenburg
SPEED   19 knots
ROUTE   Felixstowe-Europort

Launched on Tuesday 3 October, and delivered on 29 December 1967, *Europic Ferry* is the latest of the specialised drive-on vehicle ferries designed for ASN. She is also the largest and fastest, and provides the quickest UK–Netherlands crossing with a time of only six hours port-to-port. A new terminal has been built at Europort.

The vessel has two continuous decks, vehicle and upper, accommodating nearly 100 road vehicles and a large number of unit-loads. Maximum use is made of space in the ship by placing the machinery and accommodation as far forward as possible. There is a lower vehicle deck suitable for small vehicles (eg export cars) abaft the engine-room reached by an hydraulic ramp from the (main) vehicle deck. The stern ramp is also hydraulically operated. Denny-Brown stabilisers and a bow thrust unit are fitted. The main propulsion machinery can be controlled from the bridge. There is accommodation for forty-four drivers and passengers in two- and four-berth cabins, and there is a crew of fifty-two.

She left Felixstowe on her maiden voyage on the late afternoon of Wednesday 17 January 1968, after visiting Tilbury.

Europic Ferry at Felixstowe immediately before her maiden voyage
17 January 1968

BRITISH RAIL HOVERCRAFT LIMITED

This company, a wholly-owned subsidiary of the British Railways Board, was set up in 1966 following ministerial approval in March of that year. One object of the exercise was to purchase and operate at least one Westland SR.N6 during 1966 and to negotiate for the purchase of a SR.N4 for operation in 1968. The title 'Seaspeed' was coined for the new venture.

The new company acted swiftly, and on 6 July a Westland SR.N6 opened the service between Southampton and Cowes. It was now possible to travel from London to Cowes *via* Southampton or Portsmouth in little more than 2½ hours. The venture was a success. Before the end of the season the decision was taken to continue the run during the winter months, on a reduced frequency. The second SR.N6 was bought at about the same time for relief and training duties.

When the SR.N4 appeared in 1968 for BRH (only four are being built) it is intended that she may, in time, replace the existing smaller craft on the Isle of Wight service, but will certainly be introduced to cross-channel work. The SR.N4 is a very much larger craft than the SR.N6 and will be able to carry about 700 passengers on short hauls, or 250 passengers and 30 cars on cross-channel routes. It will be possible to drive on at bow or stern.

Great credit is due to the railway authorities for pressing ahead with these plans in an effort to stave off overseas intervention on the channel, though already one Swedish firm operates thereon. It is perhaps inevit-

Seaspeed arriving on shore 10 June 1966

able that in time these 'Horror-craft' will replace the conventional cross-channel packet, but we must not regret the passing of the 'steamer' too much.

In this book we have rarely proffered any opinion on this or that, but a comment here is, we feel, not out of place. 'Business is Business' it is said, but we submit that BRH has been a little unfair in operating its air cushion vehicle services from Southampton in competition with Red Funnel Steamers, who are already hard put to it to gain custom, when the BRB already has a complete monopoly of all other regular passenger/car-ferry services to the Isle of Wight.

---

¹ACV 'WINCHESTER' CLASS SR.N6

BUILT	1966 by British Hovercraft Corporation Ltd, Cowes
TYPE	Westland SR.N6
TONS	10.3 tons (maximum weight)
DIMENSIONS	48 ft 5 in x 23 ft x 15 ft (overall height)
MACHINERY	Marine Gnome gas turbine by Bristol Siddeley Engines Ltd
SPEED	59 knots (max)
ROUTE	Portsmouth/Southampton-West Cowes

Entering service on Tuesday 6 July 1966 this is the first air-cushioned vehicle owned and operated by BRH. The craft, now in standard production at Cowes, can carry thirty-eight passengers, or, with the seats removed, three tons of cargo. Her normal cruising speed is around the 40 knot mark, and she can travel easily over shingle beaches, thus rendering complicated terminals unnecessary. A second similar craft was bought by BRH towards the end of the 1966 season to be used for training purposes and to relieve the first one (No 011) for overhaul. When she entered the service, No 011 was overhauled and refitted to enable her to operate at night.

The service operates all the year round, and offers a through time London–Cowes of only two hours, the sea passage taking about twenty minutes. The terminal at Southampton is in Cross-house Road, on the town side of the River Itchen, and that at Cowes is by Medina Road. The Portsmouth–Cowes service was opened in March 1967, and also operates in winter months, 'flights' being from a terminal within the boundaries of Portsmouth Harbour station.

¹Air-cushioned vehicle.

HOVERMARINE HM2

BUILT	1967 by Hovermarine Ltd, Southampton
TONS	16.4 (maximum weight)
DIMENSIONS	51 ft x 20 ft x 12 ft (above waterline)
MACHINERY	Two Cummins diesels for propulsion, one similar smaller one for lift
SPEED	35 knots (service)
ROUTE	Portsmouth Harbour-Ryde, Isle of Wight

This craft is slightly different from the conventional hovercraft, in that she is fitted with rigid immersed sidewalls making her more economical in operation because of less loss of air. She is basically designed for use in sheltered waters. In appearance and conception she is similar to the Denny prototype which appeared on the Thames some years ago. Her two propulsion diesels are connected to twin propellers which are situated about 18 ft below the waterline. Some sixty to sixty-five passengers can be carried, or five tons of cargo.

BRH ordered two of these craft, and were due to begin operations with the first in spring 1968. A regular service was envisaged giving between twelve and forty-eight trips daily, on a crossing time of twelve minutes.

Demonstration runs by this non-amphibious craft were run successfully in the Solent on 7 February 1968. The service was started on 1 April 1968, but soon suspended due to operational difficulties.

HM2 on trials

281

ACV PRINCESS MARGARET
ACV 'MOUNTBATTEN' CLASS SR.N4

BUILT	1967 by British Hovercraft Corporation Ltd, Cowes
TONS	185 (maximum weight)
DIMENSIONS	130 ft 2 in x 76 ft 10 in x 42 ft 5 in (overall height)
MACHINERY	4 Marine Proteus gas turbines by Bristol Siddeley
SPEED	77 knots (max)
ROUTE	Dover-Le Portel (Boulogne)

The British Hovercraft Corporation's first SR.N4, the largest hovercraft in the world, first appeared in public early in October 1967. During the following few months interior equipment and 7-ft flexible skirts were fitted, and she took to the water on Sunday 4 February 1968.

The craft ordered by BRH was due to be available for service by 1 August 1968. She is expected to be able to operate over waves up to 10 ft in height. There is accommodation for about 254 passengers and 30 cars, but this can be altered to a total of 500 persons on shorter runs, or between 700 and 800 commuters. Her trials in the Solent were successful, and she was delivered to the company in May 1968. The total cost of the craft was about £1¾m.

The service as planned allows a crossing time of about thirty-five

SR.N4 *Princess Margaret* near Dover on trials, May 1968

282

minutes in calm weather, with departures from each terminal at peak periods at about two-hourly intervals giving seven trips in each direction daily. The *Princess Margaret* made her first flight on the route on 30 July 1968, carried Her Royal Highness the next day, and entered public service on 1 August. At the end of August 1968 she was withdrawn and returned to builders for skirt alterations.

TUGS AND OTHER VESSELS

Besides possessing a large fleet of passenger and cargo ships in 1948, the BTC also had a large number of tugs, dredgers, hopper barges and the like based in widely scattered ports. With certain exceptions (notably those in South Wales ports) vessels with funnels were given the new BTC livery of buff funnel and black top; though many of them had this already. Most of the craft were of considerable age and were withdrawn gradually over the years, some being replaced by new tonnage, others not.

Of particular interest was the iron paddle-tug *Petrel*, built in 1897 for the North British Steam Packet Co. She was taken over in turn by the North British Railway Co, the LNER and finally the Railway Executive, and was based at Silloth throughout. Whether she actually worked after January 1948 is not known, but she was sold to the Caledonia Canal Company, leaving Silloth on 5 May 1949. She worked for her new owners for a short time before being broken up.

When the BTC was dissolved at the end of 1962 and the various boards were set up in its place, all craft, with the exception of those at railway packet ports, were transferred to the British Transport Docks Board and given deep blue funnels with black tops.

At least one of the tugs formerly owned by the BTC and then by the British Transport Docks Board, eventually found its way into private hands. This is the Lowestoft based *Lound*, which was sold to Messrs R. Edwards & Sons of Lowestoft in 1963. In the same year the other Lowestoft tug, *Ness Point*, was sold for breaking up, and towage operations in that port then ceased.

Only a handful of these craft is now owned by the BRB, based on ports from which its ships operate. One is the only tug TSMV *Meeching*, based on Newhaven. Of 160 gross tons and built in 1960, she replaced *Fore-*

Tug *Petrel* at Silloth

284

most *22* (211 tons, built 1924), which had been based at Newhaven since she was built for the SR. Another is *Tidworth* (54 tons, built 1944), a wartime harbour tug of prefabricated construction bought by the railway after the war. (Both were subsequently sold.)

The modern tug *Meeching* at Newhaven 12 November 1965

CHARTERING

Throughout the years of railway-operated shipping services the chartering of outside tonnage has been fairly common, and has increased considerably in recent years. There are several reasons for this, including the fact that when old cargo ships have been withdrawn they have not always been replaced by a similar number of new ships. Another factor is the almost unprecedented growth of unit-load traffic which existing railway-owned ships were not always suitably designed to handle.

For example, in the early 1950s there were no fewer than eight cargo steamers (all dating from the 1920s) and one motor vessel serving French and Channel Island ports from Folkestone, Southampton and Weymouth. By early 1965 the steamers had been disposed of and yet have been replaced by only two new railway-owned cargo ships. It is true that some services have been curtailed and others terminated altogether, and that much of the cargo traffic is now carried by drive-on vessel or lost to the airlines or to competitors, but none the less the three existing ships are unable to cope with the traffic offered at certain parts of the year (particularly the Channel Islands tomato and flower trade). Consequently, in the Western Channel, short-term chartering is the general rule.

The charter of passenger ships is comparatively rare, and is usually done only in times of acute crisis due eg, to engine failure on an important mail route. To date only one station (TFS Tilbury) has chartered passenger ships for any length of time, and this has been to cover its own ships' annual overhaul periods.

Below is given an outline of the charter situation in each port during the period of nationalisation from 1948 to 1968. As much detail as possible has been included for passenger ship charters, but not for cargo ships. In many instances, although accurate dates are often available for the periods of charter of cargo ships, they would make monotonous reading, take up too much space, and would not be very helpful to the reader.

It has not been possible to obtain extensive details of chartered ships serving from three of the ports, Harwich, Southampton and Fishguard, but from what has come to light it does seem that, in fact, there has been very little.

DOVER

Charters of any kind here have been extremely rare. Cargo ships were never needed to the extent they were in other ports, because the establishment of the train-ferry service to Dunkirk in 1936 on which vehicles could also be accommodated has meant that initially the whole system had been geared to meet the requirements of the service. In addition, the development and growth of drive-on services, particularly in recent years has ensured that whatever cargo was offering from Dover found its way to France without requiring the provision of special cargo-only ships. Passenger ships have not generally been chartered either, because Dover since the early 1930s has had prior claim over available shipping, and if an extra or relief was needed it was borrowed from Folkestone or elsewhere.

Just occasionally it has been necessary to charter, eg in the height of the season when a service ship has had to undergo repairs and all other shipping has been occupied. The SNCF train ferry *Saint Germain* has been technically chartered by BR on occasion for the Dover-Boulogne car-ferry service, notably for a short period in July 1965 and July 1966.

The charter of BR Dover ships to outside bodies is also rare, but one example is worth recording. *Dover* was chartered by the 'Action of the Crippled Child' group from 24 to 25 September 1966 to sail from Dover to Boulogne, from whence a midnight fishing trip to the Varne Ridge was made, returning the following day to Folkestone via Boulogne.

FOLKESTONE

A general cargo service has been operated to Boulogne for decades with the railways' own steamers, but the last of these, *Deal*, was withdrawn in 1963, having operated on her own since 1958. Up to 1960 there were no cargo ship charters, but from 1960 to 1962 the authorities chose to charter outside tonnage for relief work rather than bring round a Southampton or Weymouth ship.

Only ships owned by J. Fisher & Sons Ltd were used, as follows:

March–April 1960	*Firth Fisher*	979 tons	Built	1950
*April 1960	*Seatern*	604 ,,	,,	1939
February–June 1961	*River Fisher*	733 ,,	,,	1941
July–August 1962	*Race Fisher*	739 ,,	,,	1942

*Actually owned by the Fisher subsidiary, Seaway Coasters Ltd

Dorset Coast at the Harbour (tidal) berth at Folkestone 10 June 1963. When the service became daily at set hours, the old No 2 passenger-berth on the pier had to be used

When *Deal* was withdrawn *Dorset Coast* (1,125 tons, built 1959, owned by Coast Lines Ltd) was taken on long-term charter which lasted from 3 March 1963 to 1 September 1965. She was relieved during overhaul by further chartered ships: *Brest* February–March 1964 and J. Fisher & Sons' *Lune Fisher* in March 1965. *Dorset Coast* was replaced by the AHL vessel *Darlington*, also chartered, until August 1966, after which she was replaced by the railways' own *Winchester* and then the chartered *Brest*.

The only passenger ship charter of any importance at Folkestone took place in 1949, when there was a general shortage of ships and, as we have seen, Dover had prior claim over what there was. The TSS *London-Istanbul*, owned by the Belgian Marine Administration, was taken on for the Calais service from mid-July to early September.

NEWHAVEN

The Dieppe joint service, supplied with passenger ships by BR and French Railways, and with cargo ships by the latter, has had no need of charters. In August and September 1965 the tug *Meeching* was out of commission, and the locally-owned tug of Metrec Engineering Co Ltd (a Sussex salvage firm) named *MNS 52* was chartered during that period.

WEYMOUTH

There have been no charters of passenger ships at Weymouth, with the exception of the technical charter of the F & R *St Patrick* each summer from 1948 to 1959. In the latter year she was transferred to the BTC and given a yellow funnel with black top. As the BTC and now the BRB have a

Sea Fisher—one of the few reciprocating steamers chartered by BR

large holding in the F & R it would give a truer picture of the situation if the move were described simply as borrowing rather than chartering.

Over the years, as the number of railway-owned vessels has decreased and the specialised trade with the Channel Islands has increased, the chartering of cargo ships has also increased. In 1948 and 1949 only two vessels were taken on, and from 1950 to 1958 only one in each year. In 1959 there was an increase to three while in the following year there were four. The busiest year to date has been 1962, when there were six. Currently four or five a year is normal. Most of these charters are seasonal only, lasting mainly from February to May, but some ships are taken on much longer terms.

Rather more than half the total number of ships chartered are British owned. Favoured companies include J. Fisher & Sons Ltd, whose ships *Stream Fisher* and *Lune Fisher* were chartered in 1960 and from 1962 to 1965 respectively; Comben Longstaff & Co Ltd, whose *Winchesterbrook* served in 1960 and whose *Worcesterbrook* served in 1961; and Tyne-Tees Steamship Co Ltd, whose *Frisian Coast* was chartered in 1961 and 1962. It has also been the practice to take over one of the French flag Newhaven cargo ships from time to time, *Brest*, for example, served for short periods early in the year every year 1959-65, and was again on this station in 1967, but *Rennes* served only in 1965.

In terms of length of service for BR at Weymouth, *Lune Fisher* probably holds the record, having served for most of the year each year and not just seasonally. One interesting point in connection with this ship is that on 23 May 1964 she was pressed into carrying twelve passengers from Guernsey to Weymouth because the mail boat was full and many intending passengers were left behind when she sailed.

IRISH SEA PORTS

The postwar increase in the use of containers has been mainly responsible for most of the charters from these ports. Charters have usually

Stena Nordica turning at Larne in May 1966. She now carries BR funnel colours

been of short duration either to relieve the regular railway-owned ships or to provide extra sailings. With but few exceptions the ships of J. Fisher & Sons have been used since 1948 to undertake sailings from Fishguard, Holyhead, Heysham, Fleetwood, Barrow and Stranraer. The Barrow–Belfast sailings operated from 1951 to 1954 on a fairly regular basis, but have not been revived since. Sailings from Stranraer and Fleetwood were occasional up to about 1961. The charter of a ship to serve from Fishguard has been a rare occurrence, though at present J. Fisher & Sons' *Eden Fisher* (1,200 tons, built 1965) is maintaining the Waterford link, on which she has been occupied since the beginning of January 1967, three times per week. Both Heysham and Holyhead have had this company's ships virtually throughout. In 1948 and 1949 only one ship was taken on, namely their *Sea Fisher* (2,991 tons, built 1940). It is probable that she can go on record as the first ship to be chartered by the BTC and, passenger ships apart, she was certainly the largest. In recent years there have often been as many as four or five on charter in the same year, though not necessarily at the same time. Among these may be named the motor vessels *River Fisher* (733 tons, built 1941), *Stream Fisher* (745 tons, built 1943), *Firth Fisher* (979 tons, built 1950) and *Seatern* (604 tons, built 1939).

In many instances a vessel is chartered for a single trip only, on one occasion early in 1967 a Fisher ship on passage from Barrow to the Mediterranean called at Holyhead to take a load to Dublin and then proceeded on its original voyage. It is also fairly common for one ship to serve more than one route in a year. In 1964, for example, *Bay Fisher* (1,240 tons, built 1958) spent some time in June and July running between Heysham and Belfast, while in September, and again in December, she appeared on the Holyhead-Dublin route. It has been known for one ship to serve more than one route within a single week. It is thus extremely difficult to keep track of Irish Sea cargo ship charters.

To date no foreign ship has been chartered by the railway authorities for Irish Sea cargo services, but one non-Fisher ship deserves special mention, namely *Mowbray Road* (3,595 tons, built 1943 in USA) owned by Seafreeze Industries Ltd, Glasgow and chartered in 1949 and 1950. Originally a tank landing ship, *LST 665*, she was refitted in 1948. She served between Barrow and Belfast from 1 November 1949 to 31 October 1950. She eventually found her way to Indonesia but cannot be traced after 1961.

Since 1948 only one passenger ship has been taken on charter to serve any present London Midland port (see also Stranraer). This was on 6 August 1959 when the Isle of Man Steam Packet Co's *Snaefell* made a single sailing from Dun Laoghaire to Holyhead, and then returned to Douglas. She was needed because the regular ship *Hibernia* had engine trouble.

Darlington of AHL served the Heysham-Belfast route for the last few weeks of 1967, and Holyhead–Dublin from 1 January, 1968.

STRANRAER

As already mentioned, J. Fisher's vessels have occasionally been chartered to run between Stranraer and Belfast.

The charter of passenger ships and car carriers was quite rare until after the 'new' company CSP (Irish) became responsible for the Larne service after December 1960. For the whole of the next year *Princess Margaret* was technically chartered by that company from BR, as was *Hampton Ferry* during the peak season. From time to time a TFS stern-loader has been taken, eg in October 1961, when *Bardic Ferry* made a special sailing to carry Bertram Mills' Circus.

After the 'new' company's new ship *Caledonian Princess* appeared it was necessary to charter tonnage from BR to replace her during overhauls. In order to provide extra sailings to cope with increased traffic in the summer of 1964 *Slieve Donard* was taken on to run on the route from 4 July to 24 August. She was not a success, so in 1965 a German car carrier named MV *Lohengrin* was chartered to operate the service from 7 June to 25 September. On neither of these ships could passengers be accommodated, and in 1966 yet another foreign ship was chartered. This was the Stena Line's *Stena Nordica,* better known as 'The Londoner' which had operated between Tilbury and Calais in the previous year. She was taken on a long-term basis, starting in February 1966 and was due to finish in October 1967 when the station's new ship was expected to enter service, but in 1968 she is still there.

THE CLYDE

Few ships seem to have been taken on charter by The CSP and those which have are usually short-term. For example, the locally-owned *Maid of Bute* was chartered in the summer of 1965 for a Friday evening Rothesay–Tighnabruaich connection, returning the following morning.

The charter of Clyde ferry and excursion vessels to outside bodies is, however, quite another matter. Not only are such charters frequent, but they are an essential part of the company's business. They are basically of two types, those to factory and works parties on the one hand, and those to shipping or railway enthusiasts' societies on the other. The former tend to be operated on existing Clyde routes and are generally not open to the public, while the latter type is usually open to all comers and an unusual route is often chosen. Hence we find *Maid of Argyll* visiting Paisley in September 1966, *Caledonia* calling at Stranraer in May 1965 and *Countess of Breadalbane* calling at Strone also in May 1965.

THE HUMBER (Associated Humber Lines)

Chartering of cargo-only ships has been common almost throughout the period under review. No passenger ships have been chartered. Chartered vessels have been used on most routes from time to time, but the Hull–Rotterdam route, being the most important, has used them most. Until the late 1950s British ships were used with but few exceptions, those of the Kyle Shipping Co Ltd and the Holderness SS Co Ltd being particularly favoured. For example, on the Rotterdam service four of the latter's ships were used in 1951 and one or two in subsequent years until 1956 when there were three which served during January and February, namely *Holdernoll* (1911), *Holdernaze* (1925) and *Holdervine* (1920) in that order for about two weeks each. The oldest recorded Holderness Co vessel chartered was the *Holdernidd* (1902), which also served Rotterdam in January and February 1951. All these were reciprocating steamers with engines aft.

During the late 1950s and the early 1960s Dutch coasters of the 500 gross-ton type gradually replaced British ships on AHL services, but chartering steadily declined as the company's services were curtailed or withdrawn, with the result that in recent years very few ships of any type have been chartered, and then only for short periods.

The Dutch coaster *Vedette* (500 gross tons) leaving Humber Dock, Hull for Rotterdam on charter to Associated Humber Lines Ltd, March 1959. On the left is *Melrose Abbey* laid up pending sale

INDEX

Italicised page numbers indicate illustrations

293

ADDENDA / CORRIGENDA

Page 11
and
page 170

The Stranraer–Larne service is to be operated by a company separate from the Scottish Transport Group and the National Freight Corporation from 1 January 1969.

Page 16 para 2

Vibration troubles in the *St George* delayed the opening of the new Harwich–Hook service until 8 November 1968.

Page 25

Arnhem last voyage arrived Harwich 28 April 1968; *Amsterdam* still available December 1968.

Page 31

Colchester was running between Weymouth and the Channel Islands from 18 November 1968.

Page 34

Avalon was chartered to run to Bantry Bay 26–31 October 1968; and Fishguard–Cork round trip 23–28 December 1968.

Page 67

Normannia ran Harwich–Hook 25–26 October 1968.

Page 71

Dover is to run Holyhead–Dun Laoghaire summer 1969.

Page 80

La Duchesse de Bretagne to serve from Southampton exclusively summer 1969.

Page 95

Ryde is now expected to serve again in 1969 and possibly longer.

Page 116

That *St David* would be transferred to Weymouth in summer 1969 was officially denied December 1968.

Page 133 para 1

New winter timetable operative from 2 January 1968. Tuesdays, Thursdays and Saturdays only, in both directions, during daylight ex-Fishguard.

Page 149

Hibernia ran Harwich–Hook 27–31 October 1968.

Page 173 para 1

The CSP requested permission from BRB to order a new ship for the Stranraer station, December 1968.

Page 177

Caledonian Princess to run Fishguard–Rosslare summer 1969.

303